Policy Innovation in the Saskatchewan Public Sector, 1971–82

Edited by

Eleanor D. Glor

Captus Press

Policy Innovation in the Saskatchewan Public Sector, 1971–82

Canadian Cataloguing in Publication Data

Main entry under title:

Policy innovation in the Saskatchewan public sector, 1971–82

Includes bibliographical references and index.
ISBN 1–895712–94–7

1. Political planning – Saskatchewan.   2. Saskatchewan –
Politics and government – 1971–1982. I. Glor, Eleanor D.,
1946–   .

JL310.P65 1996   320.6'097124   C96–930695–4

0 9 8 7 6 5 4 3 2 1
Printed in Canada

Table of Contents

iii

iv

Preface

This book highlights two crucial contemporary issues — whether and how the public sector can be innovative — by presenting a case study of what we argue was an innovative government. The innovations described flow out of the left-wing perspective of a government attempting to achieve greater control over the economic development of a province and greater justice and equality in its society.

There are two unique aspects to this book. First, the public servant's voice is one rarely heard. I am aware of only two other books written about innovation by civil servants; they are concerned with only one program each (Vantour, 1991; Hale, 1989). Second, a literature is beginning to accumulate on innovative programs and administration; however, a book has never been written before about an innovative government as a whole.

This book will be of interest to those challenged by the need to redefine and reorient government, by those interested in public policy, public administration, provincial politics, provincial history, and the New Democratic Party in Canada. It will be of special interest to public servants trying to bring about innovations, employees of research and development sections of large private sector corporations, and those working with bureaucracies to bring about change.

Enormous change is occurring in our society. Innovation may be the only response which will allow governments to accommodate, control and direct these changes. It is therefore of special interest, if possible, to discover conditions under which the public sector can be innovative.

The Saskatchewan government of 1971–82 was one of the last in a world-wide cycle of post-war social democratic governments which sought their objectives through expansion of the public sector. It is therefore a marker of how much such governments had achieved in Canada during this period. Many leftists advocated these changes, few achieved them; only Saskatchewan achieved so many. The record of this Saskatchewan government in implementing its innovations is examined here. The period which followed the government's defeat in the 1980s involved a more right-wing search for public sector reform. Its innovative push was to serve other goals, such as structural adjustments to achieve better economic performance

v

in a changing global environment, deficit reduction, a reduction in the size and scope of the public sector, and improved efficiency and effectiveness of the public sector (PUMA, 1990).

From 1944 to 1982, however, the Saskatchewan government had a reputation throughout Canada among students of politics, public administrators, journalists and the public for innovative programming. What were these innovative policies and programs that Cooperative Commonwealth Federation (CCF) and New Democratic Party (NDP) governments in Saskatchewan introduced? What was the total picture of new programming created? Why were these governments able to create successfully so many innovative programs at the same time? The province's history explains a good deal, for it has compelled its people to display pragmatic creativity and resourcefulness in solving basic problems of survival. The party's politics — moderately leftist, interventionist and possessed of a missionary zeal dating back to the ideology of the social gospel movement — explains more.

The Party's extensive, innovative platform as it came to power explains even more. *The New Deal for People*[1] was the most comprehensive election platform which had ever been introduced by any political party in Canada, outlining 149 reforms the NDP would implement, if elected to office.

Given this extensive change platform, and a change mandate, was the government successful in implementing its agenda? If it was, can we conclude that the Saskatchewan government was an innovative government? What is an "innovative government?" Does widespread innovation equate to fundamental social change? Can we learn about innovation in the public sector more generally from this Saskatchewan case study?

This book explores comprehensively the innovations of the Saskatchewan government of 1971–82 and scrutinizes the policies, structures and, to some extent, the impacts of this inventive government. It looks at the decisions to implement innovations, the content of policies and programs, the management strategies used to achieve them and the outcomes of these efforts. It draws conclusions about the elements which came together to make an innovative government possible, the successes and failures of the innovations, and the implications for innovation as a whole.

Here we present the insights and experiences of the civil servants who were responsible for implementing imaginative and often experimental policies, but also the perceptions of some of the politicians who were members of that government. This approach provides interesting contrasts. Civil servants responsible for setting up a program understand the detailed nature of that program. They may not, however, have the politicians' sense of whom they were trying to help, what they were trying to accomplish, why

---

[1] The *New Deal for People* was released by Allan Blakeney, as party leader, one day after the Liberal Government Throne Speech, in the Winter of 1971. The daily newspapers printed the full text of the program.

they were trying to do it, and what they accomplished. It is therefore revealing to see, in this book, two former Cabinet Ministers' perspectives and the former Premier's wrap-up, in relation to the more specific explanations of the bureaucrats.

But for the most part, we offer here the voice of the silent partner in government. This is phroneisis in action, Aristotle's combination of knowledge and experience that make judgment possible. Let me give you an example of phroneisis. In 1975 in the sweltering heat, Mohammed Ali fought Joe Fraser in the "Thrilla in Manila." Ali spent the first 11 rounds of the fight on the ropes, under constant attack from Foreman. After every round, Ali's coaches, the best in the world, urged him, "Stay off the ropes, stay in the middle of the ring!" In the twelfth round Ali knocked Foreman out.

After the fight Ali explained that he knew something that the coaches, commentators, officials and Foreman did not; namely, whether Foreman was hurting him. He said the ropes had been improperly installed and were softer than usual; as a result, he had used the ropes to absorb the impact of Foreman's punches, without much harm. By the twelfth round an exhausted Foreman let down his hands, and Ali let him have it.

Like the boxer, the bureaucrat has not just a front row seat, but is in the ring. Academics and journalists may not fully agree with or even appreciate this perspective, but it has its own validity. The civil servant's perspective has, moreover, never been offered before on the Blakeney government.

The participant observer approach is not that of the journalist nor again that of the academic, and, of course, precludes pristine objectivity. Yet the elusive goal of dispassionate analysis, much less of scrupulous scientific rigour also escapes journalists and academics, whose conceptual frameworks, offered in the aloof voice of the journalist or the opaque lexicon of higher scholarship, rarely ring true to the experience of the participants. This book for the most part takes a phenomenological approach, although where possible authors also offer experimental evidence.

Participant observation has gained its credibility through the philosophy of phenomenology, not of science, particularly the work of Edmund Husserl and Martin Heidegger, and is now seen as a more legitimate approach than in the past (e.g. Garfinkel, 1967). Some authors even see a phenomenological approach as the solution to the rigid and uncreative states in which rationally and scientifically based bureaucracies now find themselves (e.g. Hummel, 1987).

The comments and critiques offered in this book are based on the authors' understanding of the issues being played out at the time. In hindsight an academic can develop critiques based on other dimensions, but we were not academics and do not for the most part see these issues differently today than we did then. Our book gives public servants — elected and appointed alike — an opportunity to tell our stories our way.

While this record is primarily about successful innovation, these stories are not always ones of full attainment. Cases of opportunities foregone, approaches and results which were less innovative and less successful than they might have been, are also examined. It is likewise the account of an administration which was more innovative initially than finally.

The experience of the Saskatchewan government remains relevant today for those trying to implement change and innovation. During the last ten years the Government of Canada introduced an income subsidy for poor working families and is now discussing the possibility of a diversion program for non-violent offenders who would otherwise go to jail. Ontario is considering a work for welfare program and reducing the costs of community colleges. Most governments are implementing a variety of partnerships, including alternate service delivery by new agents such as Crown corporations. All of these, and many other approaches, have already been tested in Saskatchewan, but often without the knowledge of other governments and delivery agents. Reinventing programs, without knowledge of what others have learned, is wasteful. This book offers public and private sector planners and change leaders the opportunity to learn from the experience of others.

In addition, many of the conditions outlined in the Conclusion which made innovation possible in Saskatchewan are replicable by other bureaucrats: be ready with good ideas, develop commitment within the service, create excellent management and administration, and retain a results-oriented outlook. Other aspects of the Saskatchewan government's approach are also relevant: pay attention to the major economic and social issues, be willing to make fundamental changes of benefit to those who need the help the most, balance the budget, introduce most of the innovations immediately after taking office and keep the public involved.

Because policies and approaches were tried in the past does not necessarily render them irrelevant — quite the contrary — it offers those introducing changes now the opportunity to examine similar approaches, and to learn from them. This book offers such an opportunity to those who are not aware of the Saskatchewan experience with innovation and the many new policies and programs introduced during the 1970s and early 1980s.

REFERENCES

Garfinkel, H. 1967. *Studies in Ethnomethodology.* Englewood Cliffs, N.J.: Prentice-Hall.

Hale, S. and M. Williams, eds. 1989. *Managing Change: A Guide to Producing Innovation from Within.* Washington, D.C.: The Urban Institute Press.

Hummel, R.P. 1987. *The Bureaucratic Experience.* New York: St. Martin's Press.

PUMA. 1990. *Public Management Developments. Survey 1990.* Paris: Organization for Economic Cooperation and Development.

Vantour, J., ed. 1991. *Our Story: Organizational Renewal in Federal Corrections.* Ottawa: Canadian Centre for Management Development, Government of Canada.

Acknowledgements

Editing this book has been an interesting and challenging experience. We are primarily a group of bureaucrats, who are non-professional, mostly unpublished writers. As the editor, I asked us to recapture activities and ideas from between 15 and 25 years ago, often having painful associations. The authors are those who had enough nerve or who felt safe enough to write about a government which was out of power, in a province with a highly polarized political environment. Those who are now academics will benefit somewhat from publishing a chapter; others took the opportunity to tell things as they saw them: everyone felt we had a story to tell.

Those who saw it through to the end have participated in a task of the heart. The authors gave a great deal of their own time, tracking down information which was for the most part no longer easily available in government records.

I attempted to find former civil servants of the Saskatchewan government to write all of the chapters. When I was unable to do so, I turned to some of the former ministers. They turned out to be an articulate and enthusiastic group of authors, with a somewhat different perspective on the government. I hope readers will also find their perspective interesting.

The role of editor has been one of conceiving an idea and then trying to find people who could share it enough to devote a great deal of their personal time and some of their finances to making it come about. An editor is also a critic, and above all persistent. I confess to this, and hope that those who participated and those who considered it, but were unable to, remain friends.

I would like to thank all the people who have contributed to this book, by giving of their ideas, contacts, friends, time and long distance phone bills. Above all, I would like to thank the authors, who hung in there, and laboured until they gave birth to a publishable chapter. Without your knowledge and encouragement I could not have completed my part of the project. We shared a special experience: I hope I have been true to it. We hope that you, the reader, will find it as interesting to read as we did to live and reflect upon.

I would also like to thank the many people I consulted regarding content, approach, and publishing, particularly Dwayne Adams, David Anderson, Allan Blakeney, Garry Beatty, Frank Bogdasavich, Wes Bolstad, Lois Bordon, Sandy Borins, Ted Bowerman, John Dingwall, Bruce Doern, David Dombowski, Philip Dore, Craig Dotson,, Virgil Duff, George Ford, Ken Fyke, Alex Guy, Phil Halkett, Jim Harding, Dave Hawkes, Brian Hill, Wendy Hollinger, Bill Howard, Ken Huffman, Dave Innes, Al Johnson, Jake Katarna, Dave Kelly, Bill Knight, Archie Laroque, Ernie Lawton, Howard Leeson, Paulette Legeihn, Michael Lewis, Roy Lloyd, Albert and Wendy Macdonald, Judith Martin, Doug McArthur, Tommy McLeod, Jack McPhee, Jim Miller, Bob Mitchell, Steven O'Connor, Doug Patriquin, Lynne Pearson, David Penman, Steve Petz, Ian Potter, Merran Alexander-Proctor, Ray Purdy, Lou Readerer, Stan Rice, John Richards, John Ronson, Donald Savoie, Adel Shalaby, Richard Simeon, John Sinclair, Mel Skinner, Walter Smishek, Doug Stevens, Dave Stuewe, Ron Sully, Ken Svenson, Hugh Walker, Murray Wallace, Bob Weese, Kurt Wetzel, Flo Wilkie, Cynthia Williams, and Elaine Wood. Thank you as well to the Boag Foundation, Douglas-Coldwell Foundation and Crown Life Insurance Company for their financial support; and to our publisher, Randy Hoffman and Captus Press for seeing us into print.

Above all, I would like to express my appreciation to Howard Doughty, my husband Ron Bell, and my children Jessie, Chris and Elizabeth, who gave their ongoing support for this project.

Section I

About Innovation in Government

Introduction | ## What Makes Innovation Possible?
by Eleanor D. Glor

In the midst, as we are, of major changes in the scope of the public sector, and as we ask ourselves what the appropriate mandate for the public sector is, we realize that innovation is a possible approach and solution to many of our emerging problems. Until recently innovation has not been much encouraged in the public sector; it also has not been studied much in government. I begin with some questions. What is an appropriate definition of innovation in the public sector? What are the factors which other authors think make innovation possible? What are the necessary distinctions which will permit us to discuss innovation in government effectively? What is involved in trying to innovate in a bureaucracy? What innovations did the Saskatchewan government introduce? If it introduced many innovations, does that make Saskatchewan an "innovative government"?

DEFINITION OF INNOVATION

The literature contains a number of definitions of innovation, each revealing important aspects of it. Several authors emphasize newness, including anything perceived to be new by the people doing it (Rogers and Kim, 1985). Others define it as something different for each organization into which it is introduced (Downs and Mohr, 1976), or as the generation, acceptance, and implementation of new ideas, processes, products or services (Thompson, 1965) in an applied setting (Mohr, 1969). Some see it as early adoption of a new idea (Rogers and Kim, 1985), others as synonymous with creativity (Jacques and Ryan, 1978), still others as the same thing as improvements (Ellwein, 1985), and a final group as substantive but not revolutionary changes (Merritt, 1985; Deutsch, 1985).

The problem with many of these definitions is that they, especially Rogers and Kim's definition, allow for a completely subjective definition of innovation. If it is new to the doer, then it is innovative, regardless of how many others have already done it. Thus everyone and every organization that perceives itself as doing something new is considered to be innovative.

3

As I see it, the concept of innovation is more objective than that. "Innovation" should be reserved for attempting something objectively new in an environment in which, even with a reasonable amount of research, much is unknown. It is therefore incumbent on innovators to have informed themselves about what others have done and learned before they can claim a change as innovative.

We bring several of the key concepts of other authors, with modification, to our definition of innovation. Innovation includes the notion of creativity: the conception, adoption and implementation of new services or ideas. "New" is something which has never been done before in this way in North America, or something which may have been pilot tested but has not been introduced before as government policy. Innovation also includes risk. Something is an innovation only if there are unknowns which must be understood, implemented, supported and evaluated. Moreover, something is an innovation only if it is an improvement: whether a change is recognized as an innovation will therefore depend to some extent on the point of view of the observer. We agree with Merritt and Deutsch that innovation is substantive but not revolutionary change. Finally, our definition acknowledges the concept of "early adopters," that is, being among the first governments to introduce a new policy, program, or approach, as opposed to the very first, the innovator. The concept of early adoption is particularly useful when looking, as we do, at innovation in a whole government, and not just a single policy innovation.

Innovation as used in this book, then, is the conception and implementation of significant new services, ideas or ways of doing things as government policy in order to improve or reform them, and involves taking risks. An innovative government is an innovator or early adopter of many innovations within a short period of time.

INNOVATION IN ORGANIZATIONS

Over the last thirty years, a number of authors have attempted to identify the factors that made innovation possible, more likely, and more successful. The literature on innovation in organizations has had two phases relevant to public sector innovation. The traditional approach to studying innovation in organizations focused on organizational innovativeness, in a manner parallel to the way earlier authors had focused on individual creativity. Authors attempted to identify key correlates of innovativeness.

According to Rogers and Kim, for example, the four main correlates of innovativeness were the innovation, communication channels, time, and the members of a social system (Rogers and Kim, 1985, pp. 85–94). Jacques and Ryan also suggested there were four characteristics of innovative organizations: uncommitted resources were available for innovative ventures, uncertainty was diffused throughout a structurally-loose organization, personal and organizational objectives were closely related, and organizational

4

conflict was used to stimulate creativity (Jacques and Ryan, 1978). Mohr, in turn, identified the key factors in innovation as the interaction among the motivation to innovate, the strength of obstacles against innovation, and the availability of resources for overcoming such obstacles (Mohr, 1969).

Merritt suggested six factors affected a government's capacity to innovate: the resources it could reallocate for this purpose, including the absolute quantity available to the government, their diversity across social sectors, replaceability and liquidity; the government's information-processing system, including indicators of effectiveness, multiplicity and diversity of sources, rapidity, and "noise" levels; its procedures for encouraging nonroutine thinking about public policy; the intensity, limits and rigidity of support for governmental flexibility on the part of relevant publics; procedures for evaluating and choosing proposals for tentative adoption; and the ability to develop behavioral patterns to institutionalize innovative policies (Merritt, 1985, p. 12).

Walker, who examined 88 innovations in U.S.A. states, found that the states most likely to adopt new programs were those which were "bigger, richer, more urban, more industrial, have more fluidity and turnover in their political systems, and have legislatures which more adequately represent their cities." (Walker, 1969, p. 887). Gray (1973) found a similar result. Mohr (1969) also found that big organizations were the ones that innovated most, because of the resources available to them. These findings about size of innovators would not lead one to expect Saskatchewan to be an innovative government.

A major criticism of these and other studies of innovation was that the findings were inconsistent (Downs and Mohr, 1976; Rogers and Shoemaker, 1971; Downs, 1978). Of 38 generalizations cited by Rogers and Shoemaker (1971), almost 90% were found to be unstable. Downs (1978) suggested that contradictory findings were the result of nonsimple interaction.

During a second stage, beginning in the mid-1970s, some new approaches to the study of the diffusion of innovation were developed. The focus shifted from the organization of the innovation to the innovation application process or the organization in relation to an innovation (Rogers and Kim, 1985, pp. 86–87). The new approach emphasized the process of innovation, instead of organizational innovativeness; implementation, not just the decision to adopt an innovation; the active role of adopters; the fact that there are both negative and positive consequences to the adoption of innovations; and in-depth case studies instead of cross-sectional surveys (Rogers and Kim, 1985, pp. 96–97). This approach was characterized as a process model, as compared to the earlier variance model (Mohr, 1978), which dealt with variables and their associations (Rogers and Kim, 1985, p. 97).

Moving beyond correlates, a Rand Corporation study (Yin, Heald and Vogel, 1977) of technological innovations in state and local services focussed on the success of innovations and the importance of the way in which the innovations were introduced in determining success. Some factors studied

5

included time pressures, number of decision points, degree of professional organization, the reward structure among service practitioners, amount of client contact and influence, and the traditions and other inherent organizational differences among the different types of local services (p. 14). In reviewing 140 case studies, this study revealed the importance of the characteristics of the innovation, background factors (characteristics of the community and the stable state of the organization), and implementation factors (pp. 16, 123). It identified two components of success: service improvement and evidence of incorporation into the daily activities of the organization, the former as a result of improved production efficiency, the latter as a result of bureaucratic self-interest. Innovations which presented opportunities for bureaucratic growth, status and power were the most likely to be adopted. Federal policies were not found to be important for state innovation (pp. 124–5).

Bureaucracy and Innovation

Some say that the term "public sector innovation" is a *non sequitur*, that bureaucracies by their nature are antithetical to innovation. Max Weber and later Warren Bennis described the nature of bureaucracy as structured, hierarchical, specialized, impersonal, an excellent organizational form for accomplishing tasks (Weber, 1958, pp. 196–244; Bennis, 1968, p. 55).

Thompson (1976) examined the impact of Weberian monocratic bureaucracies on innovation. He found bureaucracies have great inequality among their members and are unable to legitimize conflict; the inability to legitimize conflict depresses creativity. Even if a bureaucratic organization allows new ideas to be generated, it will probably veto them. It is conservative and politically minded, with a focus on internal politics. If it tries to meet its innovation needs through a segregated research and development unit, it will have trouble getting the unit to be innovative, and will experience its ideas as divisive and upsetting.

The generation of new ideas is not likely to be a hierarchical phenomenon, unless unusually risk-taking persons have found their way into some of the hierarchical roles (p. 27). Innovative behaviour from the standpoint of a production ideology is unreliability, since as many as 80% of research and development projects are never profitable. Yet successful organizations are more innovative than unsuccessful ones (p. 29). Control in a bureaucracy is facilitated by defining jobs narrowly; characteristically the job is cut smaller than the person filling it. Bureaucracy, formed around the notion that "like activities should be in the same place," lacks the stimulation of different skills, views, and perspectives. The desk classes, including managers, are generally conservative and resistant to new ideas. The theory of responsibility also militates against innovation: errors are punished. And innovation is full of errors. Moreover, failure for bureaucrats also means loss of part of their identity, so innovation is far more risky for a bureaucrat than for an entrepreneur. As a result, security is more important to a bureaucrat than to other people.

6

A monocratic organization's characteristics are in conflict with innovation, and make innovation not just unlikely in a bureaucracy, but its enemy. Thompson indicated public administration was not only resistant to innovation, but was becoming increasingly so, due to its reaction back to economy, efficiency, and even Taylorism (p. 48).

Recently, some authors have been even more critical of bureaucracies (Barzelay, 1992), seeing them not only as stifling innovation, but as being at the root of major modern problems. Ralph Hummel and John Ralston Saul have been vitriolic in their criticisms of the effect of bureaucracy. Hummel (1987) saw bureaucracy as contradicting basic human values, treating people as cases rather than individuals, as a new and destructive culture, lacking rationality, with great power but no legitimacy. Saul (1992) went even further, seeing bureaucracy as being rational without guidance from values, and thence responsible for some of the most heinous of modern crimes, including the Inquisition and the Nazi Holocaust. These authors called for new forms of organization to replace bureaucracy, rather than trying to innovate within bureaucracy.

Despite the conclusions of these authors, this book argues that the Saskatchewan government of 1971–82 was innovative. Although it was small and rural, contrary to predictions, it introduced many innovations, and may even have been an innovative government. This book is dedicated to the notion that the public sector can be innovative, although it rarely is, and that it will need to be more innovative in the future than it has been in the past.

ADDITIONAL KEY INNOVATION ISSUES

This section will look briefly at six other important issues in the study of innovation: the role of ideology, which political ideologies are more likely to lead to innovation, the optimism of the concept, the risk involved, the role of success and failure, and the significance of innovations.

"Innovation" is a concept which is presented in the literature without regard to the ideology motivating it. It is described in a way which attempts to cross over ideologies, or more accurately, which ignores ideologies. But does the concept of innovation successfully cross over ideologies? Although he is the only author to examine the issue, Gow (1991, 1994) notably found that politics as ideology was present in almost all of the cases of administrative innovation he studied. It is realistic and important to recognize that ideologies motivate innovation.

Given this, is one ideology more likely to generate innovation than another? My conclusion is that reform or progressive governments are more likely to attempt new approaches. This does not mean, however, that conservative governments are never innovative and in fact experience during the 1980s and 1990s indicates that neo-conservative governments can introduce many changes. They have not always been innovative changes, however,

7

and when they have been innovative, they have usually been focused in public administration rather than public policy. While ideology is present in innovation and public sector innovativeness is more likely from progressive or reform governments, progressive governments — like other governments — can be more or less innovative.

While the ideology driving innovations must be understood, we should also examine the way in which the innovation literature treats change as beneficial. In this sense it is an optimistic concept. But is innovation always positive? It is not. Change and innovation are for the most part approaches used when a society, organization or individual is under sufficient duress, and perceives the present situation as bad enough that it is worth risking losing in order to create a (presumably) better solution. In fewer cases, change is accepted because of the positive opportunity it presents. In either situation, innovation requires risk taking.

Because of the high risk involved, many innovations fail in the public sector; some Saskatchewan innovations failed too (see Conclusion). Whether an innovation succeeds or fails, it provides an opportunity for learning. As a result, examination of innovation must move beyond looking only at the conception and implementation of innovations to consider their outcomes. This I also do in the Conclusion.

Having acknowledged the role of ideology and the possibility of poor outcomes, it is also important to make clear distinctions about the significance of innovations. Minor changes in public administration or policy by themselves are not of special interest here, but major changes, which make meaningful differences for the civil service or the public, are. I recognize that there are value judgments involved in making a distinction based on the significance of changes, but this book addresses what we consider to have been major innovations.

In contrast to the current dominant attitude emphasizing administrative and management change, in the Saskatchewan government what mattered most were policy innovations; good management of the innovations was essential but not the central concern. Our approach in this book is that policies (what government should and does do) rather than public administration (how government does it) is of primary importance. Some literature seems to support our conclusion. As we do, Osborne and Gaebler (1992, pp. 108–160), for example, conclude that government should be mission driven, focusing on results rather than rules. To explain innovative governments, Jacques and Ryan (1978) suggested a broader scope was required than for other organizations. Gow discovered a sense of mission in all the cases of innovation he examined (Gow, 1991).

During the course of this book we will examine these issues — the role of ideology in the Saskatchewan government, what motivated the willingness to change, strategies used for reducing risk, innovations that failed, and the significance and impact of the innovations introduced.

POLICY INNOVATIONS IN
THE SASKATCHEWAN PUBLIC SECTOR

The NDP platform for the 1971 election in Saskatchewan outlined the majority of the major policy innovations implemented during the life of the eleven-year Blakeney administration (1971–82). Policy changes in many areas were identified including provincial, federal, agriculture, values of rural life, labour, employment, resource and economic development, small business, taxation, education, health, social security and welfare, senior citizens, pollution, housing, consumer affairs, Indian and Metis issues, human rights, and electoral reform. The policy innovations which the government actually implemented are presented in Table 1. This was a large and comprehensive agenda for change.

Economic Policy Innovations

During the Blakeney years the Saskatchewan economy was primarily dependent on agriculture, crude oil, potash, uranium, and food and beverages, in that order. The government's principal economic objective was to stabilize the economy by maximizing the benefits of the resource boom of the 1970s and supporting rural life. Chapter 1 analyzes the effectiveness and impact of the government's structure, the Crown Investments Corporation, for intervening in the economy through the Crown corporation sector. The province became an active partner in every new major hard rock mining project; partnership eventually became official policy for all northern mining projects, through the Saskatchewan Mining Development Corporation (SMDC), a Crown corporation created for this purpose in 1974. The Potash Corporation of Saskatchewan was created in 1974 and expanded in 1976 to manage and extend the provincial investment in potash and assure provincial control of the industry. Four potash mines and interest in a fifth, representing forty per cent of the Saskatchewan potash industry, were purchased between 1976 and the early 1980s.

Saskatchewan was not alone in relying on Crown corporations to carry out its economic development strategy: Canada and other provinces also were investing, especially in the energy industry, during this decade. The federal government created Petro Canada in July 1975, to explore for, develop and retail oil and gas. Alberta made major investments in the Athabasca tar sands and Ontario in Sunoco during the 1970s. In Saskatchewan, SaskOil was initiated in 1973 to establish a Saskatchewan presence in the oil industry.

Amok, a French consortium, proposed development of uranium deposits in northern Saskatchewan during the 1970s. In response, in February 1977 the government appointed The Cluff Lake Board of Inquiry, under Judge Ed Bayda of the Saskatchewan Court of Appeal, to conduct a comprehensive and controversial environmental, socio-economic and ethical review of the development proposal and of the industry. Development of the very rich deposit was recommended and approved, over the opposition of a sizable

9

TABLE 1

Innovations and Early Adoptions Introduced by the Government of Saskatchewan, 1971–82

Innovation	First	Second	Third
PART 1: ECONOMIC INNOVATIONS			
Crown Corporation Innovations:			
*1. Establish head office activity in own jurisdiction for all major primary industries (through Crown corporations)	Sask		
*2. Monitor economic development of province through Crown corporations	Sask		
3. Government as "manager" of the economy	Japan	Sask	
*4. Establish different expectations of different kinds of Crown corporations	Sask		
*5. Create Crown corporation to explore for and develop oil and gas	Sask Sask Oil May 1973	Canada Petro Canada July 1975	Alberta Alberta Energy
6. Establish Crown corporation to run and manage computer facilities for the government (and Crowns and universities)	Sask Jan. 1973	BC 1980s	
7. Create a lateral relations model for managing Crown corporations	Sask Feb. 1977		
8. Create holding company for all commercial Crown corporations and most provincial investment in private sector.	Sask		
9. Crown Corporation advertising campaign	Sask		
Resource and Industrial Development Innovations:			
*10. Legislation giving province right to purchase up to 50% of all new hard rock mining claims	Sask		
*11. Purchase controlling interest in a major industry (40% of potash industry)	Sask		
*12. Establish a profit-sensitive royalty system	Sask March 1981		
13. One-stop entry into government for approval of development projects (interdepartmental coordinating committee)	Sask late 1970s	Ont early 1990s	
*14. Secure a larger percentage of the gross value of resources	Sask		
15. Establish Heritage Fund to receive portion of resource revenues	Alberta	Sask	

16. Crown corporation to actively buy and sell local products into international markets (Sask Trading Co.)	Sask 1975		
17. Fibre optics production	Sask		
18. Fibre optics network	Sask		
Agricultural Innovations:			
*19. Introduce a program to permit intergenerational transfer of land (Land Bank)	Sask May 1972		
20. Agency to facilitate start-up of new farms by young farmers (Farmstart)	Sask May 1974		Alberta
21. Restriction of foreign ownership of farmland	PEI + Sask (1974)	Manitoba	
22. Crop insurance program	Sask and Canada (joint)		
*23. Farm income stabilization program designed around the insurance principle (SHARP)	Sask April 1975	Alberta	Manitoba
*24. Hog price enhancement program (Commission to do central desk selling with no supply management)	Sask	Alberta/Manitoba	
*25. Hog price stabilization program (SHARP)	Sask	Alberta	Manitoba; BC was 4th; followed by remaining provinces with significant hog production
*26. Program to enhance applied farm research, based on farmer involvement and self-help principles (Farm Lab) (also listed under *Part III: Innovations with Cost-Control Elements,* below)	Sask		
Environmental Innovations:			
*27. Compulsory environmental assessment policy	Sask 1979–80	Alberta 1981	New Brunswick 1983
*28. Environmental protection legislation — air	Sask		
*29. Ban the sale of carbonated beverages in non-returnable containers (pop and beer cans)	Sask 1974		
*30. Open, honest environmental public involvement & consultation process. Financial & other assistance made available to interest groups.	Canada 1974	Sask	

TABLE 1 (continued)

Innovation	First	Second	Third
PART I: ECONOMIC INNOVATIONS (continued)			
*31. Environmental impacts include economic and social implications	Sask		
*32. Public opinion and recommendations solicited not only for projects, but for subjects and policies of major importance to the province (uranium and land use)	Sask		
*33. Establish a comprehensive environmental assessment of a project	Canada MacKenzie Valley Pipeline Inquiry 1974	Sask Cluff Lake Board of Inquiry 1977	
34. Review an entire policy area and industry through public inquiry	Sask Cluff Lake Board of Inquiry 1977		
35. Ecological reserves	Sask June 1980		
36. Large parks established by statute and with a statutory land and financial base.	Sask		
37. Environment and heritage protection by Department of Highways	Sask		
PART II: SOCIAL JUSTICE INNOVATIONS			
Public Participation Innovations:			
38. Actively develop processes for public consultation and participation	Sask		
39. Cultivate community activism	Sask	Canada	
*40. Require all day cares to be run by a parent board	Sask		
41. Educational institutions create and actively use employer and community advisory committees	Sask		

Innovations to Improve Working Conditions:

	British Columbia	Sask 1972	
42. Workplace joint employer-employee safety committees			
*43. Joint employee-employer occupational health and safety committees, which were pivotal to the program.		Sask 1972	
44. Occupational Health and Safety Branch acknowledged, recorded and made public the reports of the joint committees.		Sask 1972	
45. Three rights as an integral part of workplace health and safety reforms: the right to know, to participate and to refuse work believed (not known) to be dangerous.		Sask 1972	Quebec White Paper 1978 · Newfoundland 1979
46. No limitations on Worker's right to know		Sask 1977	
47. Jail sentences for individuals convicted of offences under the Occupational Health and Safety Act (two years)		Sask 1977	
48. Employers required to consult and co-operate with the Committee in the resolution of problems of health and safety.		Sask 1977	
49. Liability of directors and officials of corporations who knowingly participated in offences committed by corporations.		Sask 1977	
*50. Universal 40 hour week, with time and one-half for overtime		Sask	
*51. Change basis for workers' compensation from injury-type-and-severity to injury compensation and income replacement		Sask	
*52. Workers' advocates: advocates for injured workers making claims against the Workers' Compensation Board		Sask	
*53. Employers required to give notice and negotiate technological change		Sask May 1972	
*54. Right of an employee to obtain a leave of absence to run as a candidate and serve a term in any public office		Sask	
*55. Equal pay for similar work		Sask 1973	
*56. Four weeks' annual vacation after 20 years of service and three weeks' annual vacation after one year of service		Sask	

TABLE 1 (continued)

Innovation	First	Second	Third
PART II: SOCIAL JUSTICE INNOVATIONS (continued)			
*57. Paternity leave	Sask		
58. Bereavement leave	Sask		
*59. Two consecutive days off, subject to a more mutually acceptable arrangement to be agreed to by the employee and employer	Sask		
60. Worker could not be discharged for activities or involvement as a member of an Occupational Health and Safety Committee	Sask		
61. Legislated locking-in of pension benefits	Sask June 1980		
62. Pensions fully funded for new employees coming into the public service and teacher's pension funds	Sask		
*63. Workers' right to participate in work environment matters	Sask		
*64. Workers on Board of Crown Corporation — Potash Corporation (step in the direction of Industrial Democracy)	Sask		
*65. Right to refuse to perform what the worker believed to be "unusually dangerous" work	Sask		
66. Industry-wide labour negotiations (construction)	Sask		
*67. Women's Division with teeth (responsibility for investigating violations of the "equal pay," maternity, paternity and adoption leave legislation)	Sask		
68. Government can only end a strike through an act of the Legislature	Sask	none	
Innovations to Strengthen the Social Fabric:			
69. Secure federal cost-sharing for day care, enabling expansion of program	Sask		
*70. Family income support program for the working poor (FIP)	Sask 1974	Canada 1992	

	Canada		
71. Seniors income support program (SIP)		Sask 1975–6	Alberta
*72. Developmental support program to help those on welfare to work (ESP)	Sask		
73. Workers' Compensation converted to income replacement program	Sask 1979		all other provinces
Disabled:			
74. Comprehensive province-wide home care program (also listed under **Health Innovations,** below)	Manitoba	Sask 1980	
75. Free prostheses, orthotics, wheelchairs, canes, crutches, walkers	Sask		
76. Free hearing tests and hearing aids at cost	Sask		
77. Free telecommunication aids to disabled	Sask		
78. Lifetime payment to people disabled in auto accidents without proof or fault (AAIA)	Sask		
Health Innovations:			
*79. Implement Lalonde Report (demonstration programs of preventive health initiatives)	Sask		
80. Provide global funding to community health centres†	Sask		
81. Establish health and social centres‡	Sask 1973	Quebec CLSCs	Ontario
Establish comprehensive province-wide home care program (also listed as #74 under **Disabled,** above)	Manitoba	Sask 1980	
82. Establish Health Research Fund	Alberta	Sask April 1979	Ontario
*83. Universal prescription drug plan	Sask May 1974		
*84. Universal children's dental program (SDP), staffed by dental paraprofessionals (also listed under *Part III: Innovations with Cost-Control Elements,* below)	PEI and Sask 1974	Manitoba 1976	
85. Capitation fee for provincial dental program administered by the College of Dental Surgeons (to fund care for adolescents transferred from the SDP to dentists in private practice)	Sask Sept. 1981		

TABLE 1 (continued)

PART II: SOCIAL JUSTICE INNOVATIONS (continued)

Innovation	First	Second	Third
86. Regular quality assurance monitoring for care provided to children in the SDP	Sask 1974	Manitoba 1976	
*87. Compulsory seat belt legislation	U.S. county	Ontario	Sask
Educational Innovations:			
88. A compulsory one-province library system	Sask		
89. Reciprocal borrowing agreement for all libraries in the province	Sask		
90. Community College system	Ontario	Sask April 1973	
91. Arms-length agency to recommend funding levels and manage funding to universities	Sask May 1974		
92. Media-based educational program	Ont	Alta	Sask (SaskMedia) May 1974
Aboriginal Empowerment Innovations:			
93. Agency with comprehensive mandate to address inequality of disadvantaged (aboriginal and disabled) people.	Sask HRDA 1972		
*94. Comprehensive social development program for Indian and Metis people (based on their participation and general consultation)	Sask		
*95. Indian groups take the lead in determining programs which should be created and financed by province for them	Sask		
*96. Non-government employment equity program for Indian and native people (Cluff Lake)	Sask		
97. Active processes for public consultation and participation	Sask		
*98. Northerners participate in both developing policy and making local resource use decisions	Sask**		

*99. Provincial response to Indian land claim includes an offer to settle by providing Provincial Crown land as part of the entitlement	Sask 1976		British Columbia 1995
100. Program to enhance involvement of aboriginal parents in their children's schooling (community schools program)	Manitoba	Sask 1980	
101. Indian professional program	Sask (law)	Manitoba	Canada
*102. Creation of provincially-funded, Indian-controlled cultural college	Sask		
*103. Creation of provincially-funded, Indian-controlled community college	Sask		
*104. Introduction of provincially-funded, university-affiliated, Indian-controlled degree granting institution	Sask (SIFC)		
*105. Special program for Indian teacher education (Saskatchewan Indian Teacher Education Program—ITEP)	Sask		
*106. Special program for Indian social work education (Saskatchewan Indian Social Work Education Program—ISWEP)	Sask		
*107. Introduction of provincially-funded, Metis-controlled, post-secondary educational institution (Gabriel Dumont Institute***)	Sask 1975–78		
*108. Special program for teacher education for Aboriginal residents of urban centres (SUNTEP)	Sask		
109. Special program for distance teacher education for Northern Aboriginal people (NORTEP)	Sask		
110. Indian special constable program	Sask		
111. Indian court workers program	Sask		
112. Community built its own social housing to foster local economic development and build community capacity (DNS/Rural and Native Housing of CMHC)	Sask 1977	Canada 1992	
113. Use of local materials to build social housing	Sask		
114. Urban Native Housing	Sask		

Justice Innovations:

115. Human Rights Code	Canada 1977	Sask May 1979	
116. Human Rights Commission	Ontario April 1972	Sask April 1972	

TABLE 1 (continued)

Innovation	First	Second	Third
PART II: SOCIAL JUSTICE INNOVATIONS (continued)			
117. Unified Family Court	Sask Jan 1978		
118. Lower age of majority from 19 to 18	Sask 1972		
119. Legal aid	Sask May 1974		
120. Option of working off fines through community service (fine option program)	Sask May 1974		
121. Equal sharing of family property between husband and wife	Sask May 1979		
PART III: INNOVATIONS WITH COST-CONTROL ELEMENTS			
*122. "Brokerage" community college system without permanent facilities, staff or programs	Sask		
* Universal children's dental program, staffed by dental paraprofessionals (SDP) (also listed as #84 under **Health Innovations**, above)	PEI and Sask 1974	Man 1976	
*123. Strategy for reducing drug prices	Canada	Sask	
* Program to enhance applied farm research, based on farmer involvement and self-help principles (Farm Lab) (also listed as #26 under **Agricultural Innovations**, above)	Sask		
Other Innovations:			
124. Comprehensive heritage program	Sask 1980		

	Canada	Sask
125. Science Council		
126. Elite bus service	Sask	

* Innovations discussed in this book.

** Announced

*** Although Jerry Hammersmith, in his article, indicates that creation of an aboriginally-controlled educational institution was no longer innovative, this was the first creation of a Metis-controlled one, and therefore deserves to be identified as an innovation, in my opinion.

† Community health centres (community clinics) were first established in Canada in 1962 with union funding in Sault Ste. Marie (first) and with provincial government funding in Saskatchewan (second).

‡ To replace closed hospitals in areas where there was no hospital which could have physician services. Linked to the nurse practitioner program which was announced and nurses were trained, but the program was cancelled just before implementation, due to opposition from the medical profession.

These innovations were identified from:

Poel, D. 1976. "The Diffusion of Legislation among the Canadian Provinces: A Statistical Analysis," *Canadian Journal of Political Science* IX, no. 4 (December): 605–26; and

Harding, J., ed. 1995. *Social Policy and Social Justice.* Waterloo, ON: Wilfrid Laurier University Press;

and the cumulative knowledge of the authors of this book. It is difficult to identify innovations in other jurisdictions and to be sure of the judgments made. If readers have any information with which to augment or correct this table, please contact: Eleanor Glor, 1238 Castlehill Cres., Ottawa K2C 2B3.

minority within the New Democratic Party and Saskatchewan society. Based on the Cluff Lake study and a second, smaller inquiry, development of a second uranium mine by SMDC and private partners was also approved at Key Lake. Of special note here is the innovative affirmative action program developed on the basis of the inquiries' recommendations and of the NDP platform for the northern part of the province. Both developments were required to meet a hiring quota of 50% northerners, the vast majority of whom were aboriginal people.

These comprehensive assessments overlapped somewhat with the first major public Canadian environmental evaluation of a development, the Mackenzie Valley Pipeline Inquiry, which was established in May 1974 with Justice T.R. (Tom) Berger of the Supreme Court of British Columbia as the Commissioner.[1] Like the Mackenzie Valley Pipeline Inquiry, the Bayda Inquiry funded opponents to make their case, but its mandate moved beyond the Pipeline Inquiry's approach of limiting the study to specific development proposals to examining an entire policy area. The first compulsory environmental assessment policy in Canada, examined in chapter 2, was also introduced by the Blakeney government through legislation in 1980.

The Saskatchewan government further demonstrated its quest for a comprehensive approach to economic development and fiscal policy when it made a major change in the philosophy of taxing primary industries. It introduced a two-tier royalty system, composed of a base royalty (the minimum acceptable public benefit to make development worthwhile) plus a profit sensitive royalty. This two-tier system was used in taxing oil, uranium, forestry and potash. In chapter 3, John Burton shows how this approach prevented windfall profits, but supported industry by lowering taxes during economic down-turns.

A second major economic priority was to support rural Saskatchewan. The government introduced supply management systems, low interest loans, and the transfer of land between generations. Two new marketing boards, one for hogs and a partial one for beef were created. The controversial Land Bank Program permitted farmers to sell land at market prices to the provincial government, then farmers to buy it at a later date, with preference given to the former owner's family members. The program took on a very political character, with the Opposition accusing the government of introducing socialist collectivism. In reality the program did not work well. Land prices were increasing and family members remained unable to purchase the land, creating a situation with many losers and only one winner (the purchaser), an unenviable position for any government. In small towns the government provided funding for many activities, such as the building of recreation facilities and seniors' housing; backing for small businesses to

---

[1] It reviewed two proposals for rights-of-way for gas pipelines from the Yukon and Northwest Territories to southern Canadian and American markets.

20

beautify main streets; and ongoing funding for small, over-built hospitals in medium-sized towns. Rural people also were supported by a provincial network of agricultural representatives and decentralized governing structures for programs. In chapter 4, Gerry Gartner describes the government's agriculture innovations. The land was also a key environmental problem: degradation of the prairie soil was a major concern, which Hugo Maliepaard discusses.

Social Justice Innovations

The government introduced many social policy[2] innovations, whose major themes were public participation and empowerment, strengthening the social fabric, and access to health.

Community and public participation was built upon Saskatchewan prairie populist traditions. Community development was stressed by the Blakeney government in supporting community infrastructure and improving recreation facilities, roads, town main streets, hospitals, schools, and community colleges.

Public participation was encouraged through community and citizen boards for local, regional and provincial programs. All day care centres had to be run by parent boards. The new home care program created 45 new community-run boards throughout the province. Community colleges and libraries sought public input and were managed by community boards; Al Walker and Keith Turnbull discuss them, respectively, in chapters 10 and 6. Community participation was high: it was said that one in ten persons in Saskatchewan sat on a program board.

Public empowerment took the form of enhancement of government control over the economy, as described above, and support of the public when dealing with the government. Workers' advocates in the Workers' Compensation Board and Native Court Workers in the provincial court system, for example, assisted disempowered people to deal more effectively with government systems. In the Human Resources Development Agency (HRDA), in the Employment Support Program reviewed in chapter 11, and among aboriginal people, analyzed in chapter 5 the government initially cultivated and later, in some cases, tolerated activism within the government.

The second social theme, improving the social fabric, was pursued through income security programs and support of key disadvantaged groups. Progress was made in creating an income safety net for working people by introducing the family income plan (FIP) for the working poor and by making changes to the Workers' Compensation Act to create an income

---

[2] In this book the term "social policies" refer to policies whose focus is people, and includes income security programs (transfers to individuals or families) such as workers' compensation, pensions, welfare, and services provided to individuals and families free or at prices well below cost such as education, health care and housing. Source: OECD.

21

replacement system of compensation. A province-wide, universal pension plan and a sickness and accident insurance plan were proposed. By comparison, the federal government announced its first family supplement for the working poor with the earned income supplement portion of its Child Tax Benefit in 1992 (Government of Canada, 1992). Seniors' incomes were supplemented through the new Saskatchewan Income Plan, introduced in 1975–6, and increased several times during the government.

Also in the name of social improvement, the administration supported several advocacy groups and social issues, including labour and aboriginal people. Labour was an important client group for the NDP. Although Saskatchewan was a highly agricultural province, it still had a substantial wage sector; in fact, non-agricultural paid workers represented 64% of total employment in 1972 and grew to 74% in 1981[3]. Because of this and the Saskatchewan NDP's historical links with labour, labour issues were prominent, as depicted by Gordon Snyder in chapter 8. The worker's right to participate in assuring the safety of the workplace was recognized through a well-known program of joint workplace occupational health and safety committees. Worker participation in decision-making in the workplace was explored through an experimental Work Environment Board. Bob Sass evaluates these innovations in chapter 9.

Of course, special needs were apparent among aboriginal people. During the 1970s the aboriginal population of Saskatchewan was the fastest growing population sector: fifty percent of the native population was under 15 years old, and one report, prepared for several federal government departments, predicted that nearly 50% of school age children and 26% of work force entrants in Regina would be of Indian ancestry by 2001 (Swenson, 1978). Aboriginal populations have indeed grown greatly, and this was the era when the importance of that growth began to be realized and acknowledged.

Aboriginal people generally had very little opportunity in Saskatchewan. Aboriginal initiatives over the course of the government, including the creation of DNS in the early 1970s and the urban native initiative in the late 1970s, attempted to redress some of the imbalances. They are evaluated in chapter 5.[4]

---

[3] In 1972 there were 209,000 non-agricultural paid workers while total employment (including agricultural and unpaid family workers) was 327,000. In 1981 there were 314,000 non-agricultural paid workers, a growth of 50%, out of total employment of 425,000 (Statistics Canada, 1972, 1989).

[4] The urban native program included: a Native Affairs Branch and Native Career Development Program (Continuing Education); community schools (Saskatchewan Education); a fine option program, to allow fines to be worked off through community service rather than jail sentences, Native court workers to assist aboriginal people involved with the court system (Department of the Solicitor General); and increased core funding and program grants to the aboriginal organizations to strengthen them to deal with their own problems (this was the early years of land claims negotiations with the federal government). Funding was provided for the Gabriel

In order to provide equal access to health care, a third social theme, Saskatchewan undertook to reform its health system during the 1970s. The Hall Commission, established by Prime Minister Diefenbaker's Progressive Conservative government in 1960, recommended in 1964 that a truly comprehensive medical insurance program should include, in addition to hospital and medical coverage, fully insured dental and drug programs. Saskatchewan, which already had pioneered universal hospital and medical care, introduced both a comprehensive children's dental program and a universal drug program during the Blakeney years. In chapter 7, Steve Wolfson describes the children's dental plan, piloted in Saskatchewan and implemented almost simultaneously in Prince Edward Island, which in a cost-effective manner systematically added additional ages each year. The program emphasized preventive approaches to dental care. In chapter 12 Dr. John Bury assesses the cost-effectiveness of the drug plan.

Saskatchewan introduced new programs in four other health areas. Saskatchewan Aids to Independent Living (SAIL) and the Saskatchewan Hearing Aid Plan (SHAP) were the first provincial programs in Canada to provide disabled people with free prostheses, orthotics, wheelchairs, canes, crutches, walkers, and hearing tests, plus hearing aids at cost. In addition, Saskatchewan established the second province-wide home care system in Canada, providing services to the elderly and the disabled. It was uniquely organized as a self-standing agency, outside the long term care stream. Initially located in the Department of Social Services, not the Department of Health, it was highly decentralized into 45 autonomous administrative districts. Finally, the province also took action on prevention and promotion, an area of emphasis in the federal government in the 1980s, and in other provinces during the early 1990s, by being the only province to develop a series of demonstrations of preventive initiatives based on the principles presented in the Lalonde Report, *A New Perspective on the Health of Canadians* (Lalonde, 1974; Glor, 1987, 1989, 1991).

While economic policy was the primary interest of the Blakeney government after 1975, social policy was the emphasis before that time, and a very considerable number of innovative social programs and policies were introduced.

Innovations with Cost-Containment Strategies

One of the distinct characteristics of the NDP innovations was the attempt to create them at as low a cost as possible. Use of paraprofessionals

---

Dumont Institute of Native Studies and Applied Research. The first Metis self-governing institution in Canada, it developed the Saskatchewan Native Teacher Education Program which has graduated over 100 aboriginal teachers with bachelor's degrees in education. Despite a comprehensive attempt to support and empower aboriginal people, this initiative did not show short-term discernable benefits for the broad section of aboriginal people.

in the drug plan (chapter 7) and joint worker-employer health and safety committees (chapter 9) saved the government considerable resources. The Farm Lab research program used farmers to conduct research, thus reducing costs. While the drug program covered the whole population from the beginning, as outlined by John Bury in chapter 12, it also effected a strategy for reducing drug prices. The Employment Support Program, which focused on helping long-term unemployed persons move back into the workforce, also moved them off welfare onto the federal Unemployment Insurance Program, thus reducing provincial expenditures.

The Saskatchewan government's policy agenda included many innovations. But was it an innovative government?

IS AN INNOVATIVE GOVERNMENT POSSIBLE?

There is great interest today in what makes innovation possible, but no agreement yet on what those factors are. Observers are also asking: what is an innovative government? Is there such a thing, given that bureaucracies resist innovation? Because the Saskatchewan government introduced so many (126) policy innovations, this case study presents an opportunity to consider these fundamental questions. This book asks whether and why the Blakeney government in Saskatchewan was innovative, that is, a first or early adopter of many significant policy innovations. Dale Poel has already demonstrated that the very early years of the Blakeney government were innovative in the introduction of legislation (Poel, 1976). This book will holistically describe the many policy innovations introduced by the small Blakeney government and assess whether it was innovative.

WHAT PROMOTES AND
DISCOURAGES INNOVATIONS?

With so many cases of innovation, it is also possible to attempt a description of the conditions that made innovation possible in Saskatchewan, and to speculate about what discouraged it. This will be taken up again in the Conclusion, but in broad terms, the major strengths which enhanced the capacity of the Blakeney government to produce and implement innovative policies were public support, a highly innovative political platform, commitment to innovation, excellent management, a results-oriented outlook, and its ongoing capacity to identify and test new ideas. Its weaknesses were its commitment to speedy implementation (although this was also a strength); its inability to maintain the innovative thrust; its incapacity to support and implement the innovations of its own left wing, which was promoting more fundamental, community-based, community participation approaches to major problems (although the wisdom of this in political terms is questionable); and its inability to maintain an active public participation program.

This chapter discussed definitions of innovation, reviewed the public sector innovation literature, examined some concepts important when talking about public sector innovation and an innovative government, and outlined the government's policy innovations overall. Subsequent chapters of this book will look at the decisions to implement innovations, the content of policies and programs, and the management strategies used to implement them. The Conclusion will outline the ingredients that came together to permit the Blakeney government to introduce so many innovations, assess the innovations and discuss the implications of the Saskatchewan case study for the understanding of innovation.

REFERENCES

Barzelay, M. 1992. *Breaking Through Bureaucracy*. Berkeley: University of California Press.

Bennis, W. 1968. "Beyond Bureaucracy." In *The Temporary Society*, by Bennis W. and P. Slater, 53–76. New York: Harper and Row.

Deutsch, K.W. 1985. "On Theory and Research in Innovation." In *Innovation in the Public Sector*, edited by Richard L. Merritt and Anna J. Merritt, 17–35. Beverley Hills: Sage Publications.

Downs, G.W. and L.B. Mohr. 1976. "Conceptual Issues in the Study of Innovation." *Administrative Science Quarterly* 21 (December): 700–14.

Downs, G.W., Jr. 1978. "Complexity and Innovation Research." In *The Diffusion of Innovations: An Assessment*, edited by M. Radnor et al., 1–21. Evanston: Northwestern University, Center for the Interdisciplinary Study of Science and Technology.

Ellwein, T. 1985. "Innovation in West Germany's Public Sector." In *op. cit.*, edited by Merritt and Merritt, 111–42. Beverley Hills: Sage Publications.

Glor, E. 1987. "Impacts of a Prenatal Program for Native Indian Women." *Canadian Journal of Public Health* 78:4 (July/Aug.): 249–54.

———. 1989. "Comprehensive Accident and Injury Experience of High School Students in Saskatchewan." *Canadian Journal of Public Health* 80:6 (Nov./Dec.): 435–40.

———. 1991. "A Successful Evaluation of a Small Scale Senior's Health Promotion Centre." *Canadian Journal on Aging* 10:1: 64–73.

Government of Canada. 1992. News Release: Child Tax Benefit Legislation Introduced in House, 1992–44, May 13. Ottawa: Department of Finance.

Gow, J.I. 1991. *Innovation in the Public Service*. Ottawa: Canadian Centre for Management Development, Government of Canada, March.

———. 1994. *Learning from Others: Administrative Innovations Among Canadian Governments*. Toronto and Ottawa: The Institute of Public Administration of Canada and the Canadian Centre for Management Development, Government of Canada.

Gray, V. 1973. "Innovations in the States: A Diffusion Study." *American Political Science Review* LXVII (Dec.): 1174–85.

Jacques, J. and E.J. Ryan. 1978. "Does management by objectives stifle organizational innovation in the public sector?" *Canadian Public Administration* 21 (Spring): 17–25.

Lalonde, M. 1974. *A New Perspective on the Health of Canadians: A Working Document.* Ottawa: Health and Welfare Canada, Government of Canada.

Merritt, R.L. 1985. "Innovation in the Public Sector: An Introduction." In *op. cit.*, edited by Merritt and Merritt, 9–16. Beverley Hills: Sage Publications.

Mohr, L.B. 1969. "Determinants of Innovation in Organizations." *The American Political Review* 63: 111–26.

Osborne, D. and Gaebler, T. 1992. *Reinventing Government: How the Entrepreneurial Spirit Is Transforming the Public Sector.* Reading: A William Patrick Book, Addison-Wesley Publishing.

Poel, D. 1976. "The Diffusion of Legislation among the Canadian Provinces: A Statistical Analysis." *Canadian Journal of Political Science* IX, no. 4 (December): 605–26.

Rogers, E.M. and J.I. Kim. 1985. "Diffusion of Innovations in Public Organizations." In *op. cit.*, edited by Merritt and Merritt, pp. 85–108. Beverley Hills: Sage Publications.

Rogers, E.M. and F.F. Shoemaker. 1971. *Communication of Innovations: A Cross-Cultural Approach.* New York: Free Press.

Saul, J.R. 1992. *Voltaire's Bastards: The Dictatorship of Reason in the West.* New York: Viking, The Penguin Group.

Statistics Canada. 1972. *The Labour Force.* Catalogue 71-001. December. Ottawa: Government of Canada.

———. 1989. *Labour Force Annual Averages, 1981–88.* Catalogue 71529. March. Ottawa: Government of Canada.

Swenson, K. 1978. "Indian and Metis Issues in Saskatchewan to 2001." December. Unpublished.

Thompson, V. 1965. "Bureaucracy and Innovation." *Administrative Science Quarterly* 10:1 (June): 1–20.

———. 1976. *Bureaucracy and Innovation.* University, Alabama: University of Alabama Press.

Walker, Jack L. 1969. "The Diffusion of Innovations Among the American States," *American Political Science Review*, LXIII (September): 880–99.

Weber, M. 1958. *From Max Weber: Essays in Sociology.* Translated, edited and with an introduction by H.H. Gerth and C. Wright Mills. New York: Oxford University Press.

Yin, R., K. Heald and M. Vogel. 1977. *Tinkering with the System: Technological Innovations in State and Local Services.* Toronto: Lexington Books.

Section II

Innovations with Impacts on Economic Development

1

Framework for Economic Development: The Role of Crown Corporations and the Crown Investments Corporation of Saskatchewan

by Tom Waller

Introduction

Public enterprises functioning through Crown corporations were a significant part of the Saskatchewan economy during the 1970s. By 1982 Crown corporations represented the largest employer in the Province. The assets exhibited in the financial statement of the Crown Investments Corporation of Saskatchewan (CIC), reflecting the activities of all of the Province's commercial Crown corporations, placed CIC fourteenth on the *Financial Post*'s 1982 list of top 500 companies in Canada.[1]

The operation of public enterprise through Crown corporations became a key element of the Douglas government with the establishment in the late 1940s of North America's first public auto insurance scheme, a public bus company and several corporations operating in the resource area producing timber products, sodium sulphate and clay. While the results achieved by the corporations was mixed, at least measured on a narrow basis of profit and loss, the use of the Crown corporation as a vehicle was well established during the years of the first CCF-NDP administrations under Premier Douglas and his successor, Premier Lloyd.

When the CCF-NDP government was defeated in 1964, a number of Crown corporations established by the previous government were disposed

---

[1] These statistics and those found elsewhere is the chapter are found in the August 12, 1982 edition of *The Regina Leader-Post* and in the annual reports of CIC and other Crown corporations for the 1982 fiscal year and for other years as noted in the text of the chapter.

of by the Liberals. However, other Crown corporations, several of which continue to exist to the present day, were created during the years when the Liberal Party was in power. Crown utilities providing telephone, power and insurance services were continued under the Ross Thatcher administration and one new utility, the Saskatchewan Water Supply Board, to provide water to municipal and industrial users, particularly to potash producers, was established in 1966.

Under the NDP adminstration elected in 1971, Crown corporations were to play a significant role in the economic affairs of the province. In order to understand the initiatives which were taken, it is important to appreciate the framework within which Crown corporations functioned and the views of Premier Allan Blakeney.

When Premier Blakeney took office, the provincial economy had been through a period of recession with the agricultural sector having suffered particularly difficult times. Like a number of Premiers before him (and those that would follow), the Premier's stated objective was to broaden the base of the provincial economy so that provincial fortunes would not be as closely tied to the fortunes of the agricultural sector as previously. Unlike others however, Premier Blakeney's view was that success in achieving this objective could come only from a combination of four sources: the private sector, the co-operative sector (which, in the Province of Saskatchewan has developed to a far greater extent than in other Canadian jurisdictions), the public sector, and, finally, through joint ventures involving two or more of these sectors.

The Premier believed that the private sector, if left alone, had never and would never develop a broadly based provincial economy.[2] This view was not a function of pure ideology but represented a pragmatic approach which recognized both geography and demography. Saskatchewan has a relatively low population base and is, in the case of most manufactured products, located far from major markets. Where opportunities existed in the private sector, those opportunities have generally yielded a higher rate of return when located closer to markets, with the result that the province has not fared well as a site for private-sector development.

It did however appear that Saskatchewan had one potential advantage — an abundance of natural resources such as oil, potash and uranium. International think-tanks such as the Club of Rome in 1971 were predicting a scarcity of natural resources in the future. The Premier believed that public enterprise could be used to encourage growth in the resource sector.

A former civil servant, the new Premier was interested in the structures and the management processes of government. He had joined the Saskatch-

---

[2] The views which are attributed to the former Premier are the writer's distillation of discussions with him and with others who were present at relevant times, particularly Garry Beatty.

ewan civil service in the late 1940s as Secretary and Legal Advisor to the Government Finance Office (GFO), a position which he occupied until 1955. In the early 1960s, he had served as a Cabinet Minister in the Douglas and Lloyd governments. Familiar with both the practical operations of Crown corporations and with their political and philosophical underpinnings, he was keenly aware of the roles of various components of public enterprise including Cabinet, individual Cabinet Ministers, Ministers responsible for Crown corporations, the boards of directors of Crown corporations, their management and what he had described in 1953 as "the Crown Corporation holding corporation." In a speech to the Institute of Public Administration of Canada in 1953 Mr. Blakeney succinctly summarized his views at that time:

> The Government Finance Office and the Cabinet are the bodies who make top policy decisions on Crown corporations and who control these policies. I propose to dwell at some length on the procedure for making policy decisions and for exercising policy control. I do not wish to imply that most or even many decisions must be referred by boards of operating corporations to the Government Finance Office or to Cabinet for approval. Such is not the case. But the chief problem of operating public enterprise is to ensure administrative efficiency up to the best business standards within policies determined and controlled by representatives of the people. Surely the representatives of the people must control policy or the Crown corporations become "bureaucratic" in the worst sense of the word. Surely also this policy control must be exercised through the Cabinet to be consistent with the absolute responsibility of the Cabinet for all governmental activities, which is the cornerstone of Cabinet government. Accordingly, if the chief problem is to reconcile administrative efficiency with ultimate Cabinet control of policy, then the chief purpose of an administrative structure must be to provide a means whereby policy questions can be referred to the people's representatives without appreciably reducing the operating efficiency of the enterprises. This, to me, requires that an operating corporation have available to it a clearly defined procedure for raising policy questions and getting authoritative decisions and the assurance that those who make the policy decisions will have before them information upon which an intelligent decision can be made. It is because of the prime importance of these matters to successful operation of government enterprise that I believe that an account of our efforts here in Saskatchewan to meet the problem might be of interest to you.
>
> In the Saskatchewan structure policy making and policy control are exercised chiefly through financial control. Operating corporations are financed by advances from the Government Finance Office. (Blakeney, 1953)

There is no evidence to suggest that his views had changed when he became Premier.

The concept that Cabinet should ultimately be responsible for the operation of Crown corporations was fundamental to the approach taken by the government. Unlike governments in other jurisdictions, this government and Premier did not attempt to distance themselves from the decisions of Crown corporations for which they accepted ultimate responsibility. Upon his election Mr. Blakeney assumed not only the position of Premier but also acted as Provincial Treasurer and the Minister responsible for GFO. In the budget speech delivered March 10, 1972 he indicated:

> At the outset let me make it clear that this government will encourage the continued operation and expansion of Crown corporations. We will develop our resources for the benefit of Saskatchewan people. Where appropriate, this will be done through Crown corporations.

His words would prove to be prophetic.

Recognizing that Crown corporations would play a key role in the development of the provincial economy, it was then necessary, in the minds of the Premier and his Cabinet, that an instrument of direction and control over what would become a multifarious collection of provincial assets was required. A provincial holding company, CIC, incorporating functions not unlike the Government Finance Office of the 1950s, was ultimately chosen as that instrument. In this context, the writer is hesitant to use the words "direction and control" although the words were used at the time of the restructuring of GFO to become CIC. What is key to an understanding of the concept is the level of "direction and control" which was appropriate. It was not to involve day-to-day operational matters but matters of public policy affecting the size, shape and direction of the corporations. In some respects this view is, in itself, not unlike the private-sector model where shareholders of corporations are required to approve major decisions affecting such matters as the structure of the corporation in which they hold shares. Cabinet, in that sense, functions as the "shareholders" of the corporation.

While the framework of operating public enterprise through the vehicle of Crown corporations had been developed previously, a number of initiatives were begun after the election of the Blakeney government. This chapter will attempt to identify several of the initiatives and innovations related to the role of the CIC, the successor to GFO.

Growth of Crown Corporations in the Early 1970s

The early part of the 1970s represented a period of significant growth in the Province's Crown corporations both in terms of the creation of new corporations and the expansion of the operations of existing corporations. In 1973 and 1974 a total of 10 Crown corporations were created.

A number of them were small in terms of assets and revenue generated, and were created to fill specific needs. For example, Saskatchewan Computer Utility Corporation (Sask Comp) was established initially by Order-in-Council in January, 1973 for the purpose of ensuring the availability of computing services and equipment at reasonable cost to government departments, Crown corporations and the province's two university campuses. The corporation was structured as a utility on the recommendation of a committee involving representatives from university and government users. The committee had been created after it became apparent that significant funds would have to be budgeted for computer hardware and services in the early part of the decade. It was later continued under a specific Act. During the same period the government established the Saskatchewan Trading Corporation (later renamed Agricultural Development Corporation of Saskatchewan) pursuant to an Order-in-Council under Part I of *The Crown Corporations Act* and the Saskatchewan Development Fund Corporation pursuant to an act of the Legislature. Both of these corporations were service oriented. Sask Trading's activities were directed towards sales and service functions in exporting agricultural and other products produced within the province. Its activities were later confined to agricultural products through an amendment to its constating Order-in-Council in 1978. The Development Fund was designed as an investment vehicle which would allow the citizens of the province to participate in a pooled fund of investments. Its objectives were to maximize returns for its investors while giving preference to Saskatchewan-based investments. All three corporations were included within the mandate of GFO.

Several other Crown corporations were established to administer departmental programs including Saskatchewan Housing Corporation (whose objectives were primarily to promote the construction and improvement of housing for low-income groups and to improve the overall quality of housing stock in the Province), Farm Start (created to administer agricultural loan programs), the Crop Insurance Corporation (created to administer the federally and provincially-funded crop insurance program), and the Saskatchewan Educational Communication Corporation (Sask Media) providing audio-visual materials for education institutions.

An eleventh corporation, the Saskatchewan Land Bank Commission, was created to acquire, lease and dispose of farm land in 1972. It was never regarded as a Crown corporation and was not reviewed by the Select Standing Committee on Crown Corporations, a committee of the Legislature which annually reviewed the operations of Crown corporations.

As might have been predicted, the new NDP government emphasized development in the resource area, with its first initiative being the creation of Saskatchewan Oil and Gas Corporation in August 1973 pursuant to *The Saskatchewan Oil and Gas Corporation Act, 1973*.[3] Sask Oil was given broad general powers to explore for and produce petroleum and natural gas. Initially its activities were directed towards the acquisition of both proven and unproven reserves through acquisitions from other corporations operating

---

[3] *The Saskatchewan Oil and Gas Corporation Act, 1973*, Statutes of Saskatchewan, 1973, c. 96.

in the oil and gas area. An acquisition of the Saskatchewan reserves of Atlantic Richfield Canada Ltd. during 1976 would, in subsequent years, form the basis of the corporation's growth and financial success. As it developed, the corporation became an active participant in the oil and gas industry in Saskatchewan and incorporated a subsidiary, Kywan Petroleum Ltd., to acquire properties and carry on business outside of the Province's boundaries. As the decade drew to a close, the corporation devoted significant energies to heavy oil projects although it was recognized that this was an investment which would not provide immediate returns. For its March 31, 1979 year-end, the corporation reported assets of $65.0 million, earnings of $5.7 million.

In 1974, an Order-in-Council was passed under Part I of *The Crown Corporations Act* creating Saskatchewan Mining Development Corporation (SMDC)[4] with its objective being to participate in the development of the Province's hardrock mineral resources. In its formative years, the corporation concentrated primarily on developments in the uranium industry. Under amendments made to mineral resource regulations, the corporation was given a statutory right to become an equal participant in all developments in the northern part of the province. This right was continued until the regulations were further amended after the election of the Conservative government under Grant Devine in 1982. The corporation became a significant player in uranium development in northern Saskatchewan after its formation, acquiring a 50% interest in the Key Lake Uranium Mine. By 1979 the corporation had assets in excess of $272.0 million and a deficit to that point of approximately $4.0 million.

As well, 1974 saw the creation of the Potash Corporation of Saskatchewan (PCS), initially again by Order-in-Council under Part I of *The Crown Corporations Act*. The corporation was later continued pursuant to *The Potash Corporation of Saskatchewan Act, 1976.*[5] By the early 1980s PCS had acquired four potash mines with an interest in a fifth mine. It had assets approaching $1 billion and had reported a profit of $242.0 million in 1981. PCS controlled, at that point, more than 40% of the province's productive capacity in the industry.

The potash industry in Saskatchewan is unique in that the province contains vast deposits of high-grade reserves. It is an industry where the province's producers can effectively dominate the fixing of world prices for potash. It was also an industry where the provincial government and producers had been engaged in a series of legal battles over the Province's right to control production levels and impose royalties or taxes. In practical terms, the establishment of PCS was a direct result of this battle.

---

[4] The corporation was later continued under a special Act, *The Saskatchewan Mining Development Corporations Act, 1977*, Statutes of Saskatchewan, 1976–77, c. 74.

[5] *The Potash Corporation of Saskatchewan Act, 1976*, Statutes of Saskatchewan, 1976–77, c. 2.

In addition to the corporations which were created in the 1970s, significant expansion occurred in the province's two major utilities. Between 1972 and 1981, consolidated revenues for SPC (including both gas and electrical divisions) increased from $126.0 million to $525.0 million. Assets had increased from $630.0 million to $1.723 billion. Major increases had taken place in the corporation's electrical generating capacity with the completion of the first phase of the Poplar River electric generation facility near Estevan. Construction of a hydro electric dam near Nipawan was about to begin in 1981. SPC was, at the time, a fully integrated power utility producing, distributing and delivering both electrical and natural gas energy to customers within the province. It was, in that respect, unique in Canada.

The other major utility, SaskTel, experienced sustained growth throughout the 1970s with assets of $584.7 million as at December 31, 1979. In the late 1970s, construction on a fibre optic network linking major portions of the province was under way.

By the beginning of the 1980s, the Crown corporation sector played a significant role in the province's economy with assets of $4.363 billion in 1980 ($5.065 in 1981), earnings of $182.6 million ($119.1 in 1981), and retained earnings ("reinvested earnings") of $589.5 million ($708.6 in 1981). Employment within the sector accounted for more than 15,000 jobs.

The Regina Leader-Post, in its August 12, 1982 edition described the Crown corporation sector as "the largest employer in the Province. With more than 13,700 full-time workers, it has even more employees than the provincial civil service...."

In spite of the size of the sector and the rapid growth of both the utility and resource sectors throughout the 1970s, it was nonetheless recognized that the corporations were in developmental stages. The utilities were engaged in significant expansion, while the major resource corporations established in the 1970s were involved in long-term projects to develop mines and reserves.

It is perhaps appropriate to mention one other development undertaken by the Blakeney government during the 1970s. With the major price increases in oil in the early part of the decade, it became apparent that the Province would receive significant revenues through the collection of what was considered to be the Crown's share of production — royalties. As time went on, it also appeared that the production of potash and uranium would make additional contributions of a significant nature to provincial coffers. Recognizing that there will always be competing demands to spend revenues collected by government, a decision was made to create the Saskatchewan Heritage Fund. The fund was established pursuant to an act of the Legislature passed in May, 1978.[6] While bearing a name similar to that of the Alberta Heritage Fund, funds paid into the Saskatchewan Heritage Fund represented

---

[6] *The Heritage Fund (Saskatchewan) Act*, R.S.S. 1978, c. H-2.1.

only a small fraction of those which had been and were being placed into the fund in Alberta. There was one other significant difference between the Alberta Heritage Fund and that created for Saskatchewan. A portion of the Heritage Fund in Saskatchewan was utilized to fund the operations of developing resource corporations. By 1982, approximately $418.5 million had been advanced to the Potash Corporation, $218.7 million to Saskatchewan Mining and Development Corporation, $91.5 million to Saskatchewan Gas Corporation and approximately $110 Million to CIC. These were non-interest bearing advances and were, for all intents and purposes, treated as the equivalent of equity injections to private-sector, resource corporations.

The Crown Investments Corporation of Saskatchewan

Saskatchewan has a long history of having a Crown corporation holding company. GFO was initially created by special act of the Legislature and began operations in April, 1947. In the paper given to the Institute of Public Administration, Mr. Blakeney had described GFO as both a holding company and as "in effect, a Cabinet committee on Crown corporations."

GFO had a staff consisting of an Executive head, two personnel administrators, two lawyers and an accountant. The Secretary of GFO was secretary to the boards of individual Crown corporations and industrial relations advice was provided to the boards. Policy making and policy control were exercised chiefly through financial control by having GFO provide advances for operating purposes to individual Crown corporations. Advances were regarded as equity advances in the sense that there was no interest due on them and the operating Crown corporations paid their annual profits to GFO.

Under the Thatcher government, this basic structure was retained although it does not appear that the other element of the holding company concept (the provision of advice) was continued. While the practice under the CCF had been to return surpluses to GFO, under the Thatcher government Crown corporations were allowed to retain some surpluses to cover future capital expenditures. By 1970, staff functions of GFO had been minimized and were, in fact, performed by Treasury Board staff with an administrative fee charged to the corporation.

With the election of the Blakeney government the former Secretary of GFO (Blakeney) returned as Minister Responsible for the corporation. At the time, staff functions of the corporation were still provided by Treasury Board staff but the 1971 Annual Report notes that the practice of allowing Crown corporations to retain surpluses generated from their operations was discontinued in that year.

Two conclusions can be drawn from the 1971 GFO Annual Report. First, the report attempts to consolidate the financial results of the six corporations coming under the scope of the Government Finance Office. It is not, however, a true consolidated financial statement since it does not contain a consolidated statement of assets and liabilities nor does it contain an overall statement of the operations of the corporations. Second, the scope of GFO's operations was confined to a small number of Crown corporations (6) which had historically related to it. Corporations such as the Saskatchewan Economic Development Corporation (SEDCO) established in 1963, the Saskatchewan Water Supply Board established in 1966, and the Municipal Financing Corporation established in 1970 were excluded from the scope of GFO's operations. In addition, the Province's two major utilities, the Power Corporation and SaskTel had not been included within the scope of GFO's operations since the early 1950s. Some of the corporations created by the Blakeney administration in the early 1970s had similar statutory provisions which excluded these corporations from GFO's jurisdiction as, for example, Section 18 of *The Saskatchewan Oil and Gas Corporation Act, 1973* and Section 24 of *The Educational Communications Corporation Act* establishing Sask Media.[7] While some of the corporations were excluded from GFO's responsibility, others such as the Saskatchewan Computer Utility Corporation, the Potash Corporation and Saskatchewan Mining Development Corporation were subsequently included.

The Premier had discussions with the then Deputy Minister of Finance, Garry Beatty, as early as January 1972 on the subject of how the government could best relate to its Crown corporations. The Premier's previous association with GFO suggested that some form of holding company model would be a logical approach. He also believed that Crown corporations would be more willing to accept policy direction from a Crown corporation than from the Department of Finance. As a result of these discussions some early changes were made.

As noted previously, during the early months of the Blakeney administration, staff functions of GFO continued to be provided by the Department of Finance. Effective November 1, 1972, however, GFO resumed responsibility for its own staffing functions and for the provision of administrative and other services to Crown corporations. The staff of the office remained small, providing largely financial or administrative services.

Significant changes to GFO's operations were not finalized until 1976. In July, Garry Beatty, who had left the Department of Finance earlier in the year, was added as the only non-ministerial member of GFO's board of directors. On September 29 and 30, a special Cabinet Planning Session involving Cabinet Ministers on the GFO board, others who acted as chairpersons on Crown corporation boards and senior bureaucrats was held. A consensus on the expansion of GFO's operations appears to have been reached at that meeting. In October, Beatty was appointed Managing Director of GFO with instructions to review proposals with Crown corporation boards

---

[7] *The Educational Communications Corporation Act, 1974*, Statutes of Saskatchewan, 1973–74, c. 35.

and to prepare a summary paper of the September discussions for Cabinet review and approval. Final Cabinet approval for the proposal was given in February, 1977.

The specific events leading the Cabinet Committee to focus its attention on the matter do not appear to have been recorded. Some involved suggest that the matter was simply the outcome of an evolutionary process involving the Premier, and senior Cabinet Ministers and officials. This is likely the case.

However, there was a need for more effective administration and control of the Crown corporations. A mechanism was required for review of requests to Cabinet from Crown corporations. Under the system then in effect, Cabinet ultimately approved rates to be charged by the Province's two major utilities. As energy prices soared in the early to mid 1970s, there were significant increases in the rates levied by utilities. A concern developed at the highest level of Cabinet that when recommendations on rates were provided to the Cabinet they came forward with only two alternatives; to approve a proposed rate increase developed largely by management of the utility or, alternatively, to have the corporation making the request face what amounted to economic disaster. That form of submission was not, in the minds of the Blakeney Cabinet, satisfactory. Cabinet needed more effective policy analysis of utility prices.

Secondly, there was growing recognition by the mid-1970s that significant capital would be required by a number of Crown corporations to carry out their programs. The need to ration capital among competing Crown corporations was clearly identified. If capital plans were independently developed by the various Crown corporations, with Cabinet having the responsibility to decide on matters as they came forward on an individual basis, the government could lose control over financial planning as a whole. As well, when a Cabinet Minister brought matters to Cabinet in his capacity as Minister Responsible, there was a natural tendency for the Minister to defend it as "his own." A rejection of the proposal by Cabinet could be viewed by the Minister as a personal rejection and could lead to disharmony among the members of Cabinet. The difficulty inherent in a Minister discharging both his collective responsibility as a member of Cabinet and his individual duty as Minister responsible for a Crown corporation or department was recognized. It was thought that access to independent third-party analysis and advice through the holding company, whose duty was to Cabinet as a whole, would assist in resolving some of the inherent difficulties by removing the Minister versus Cabinet colleagues' perception.

For these and other reasons, Cabinet perceived the need for access to an independent source to review and provide advice on major, primarily financial, issues before the issues arrived at Cabinet for a decision. This body would also allow Cabinet to maintain a greater appreciation of future capital requirements.

Cabinet's decision was to expand the operations of GFO to fill this role. A number of actions flowed from the decision of the Cabinet Committee. First, Beatty was charged with the responsibility of staffing the expanded organization. Second, a review was done of the operations of all of the Crown corporations in the province to determine which should be brought within the expanded purview of GFO. Finally, work was undertaken on new legislation for both GFO and Crown corporations incorporated by Order-in-Council.

In the area of recruiting, Beatty had added a number of individuals to the GFO offices by the beginning of 1977, relying heavily upon his contacts at the Department of Finance, but also recruiting from outside of the civil service proper. Virtually all divisions of GFO, by then renamed the Crown Investments Corporation of Saskatchewan, were staffed and operational by the end of 1978.

The analysis of Crown Corporations found there were twenty-two corporations carrying on what might, in some fashion, be categorized as "commercial activity" in the Province at the end of 1976. Of these, ten[8] had already been included within the scope of GFO's operations. To the list of those to be dealt with by GFO were added three utilities, Saskatchewan Power Corporation, Saskatchewan Telecommunications, and Saskatchewan Water Supply Board; one resource corporation, Saskatchewan Oil and Gas Corporation; and three other corporations, Saskatchewan Economic Development Corporation, Saskatchewan Development Fund Corporation and the Municipal Financing Corporation.

A decision was made to exclude five other possible corporations from the list of those to be brought under the scope of GFO's operations. The decision to exclude corporations was made on one of two bases. First, several Crown corporations were funded directly by appropriations through government departments. Farmstart Corporation, the Saskatchewan Crop Insurance Corporation and the Land Bank were funded through appropriations from the Department of Agriculture. The Saskatchewan Housing Corporation received appropriations through the budget for the Department of Urban Affairs and Sask Media from the Department of Education. In each case, the corporation was charged with responsibility for delivering specific government programs. A decision was made to exclude these corporations. One corporation subsequently established in the early 1980s, the Saskatchewan Grain Car Corporation, was also excluded for a similar reason.

The Liquor Board was excluded for a second reason. It operated a monopoly in the sale of liquor within the province. The corporation consistently

---

[8] The ten were Saskatchewan Forest Products Corporation, Saskatchewan Minerals, Saskatchewan Government Printing, Saskatchewan Transportation Company, Saskatchewan Fur Marketing Service, Saskatchewan Mining and Development Corporation, Saskatchewan Trading Corporation (later called the Agricultural Development Corporation of Saskatchewan), the Potash Corporation of Saskatchewan, Saskatchewan Government Insurance Office and Saskatchewan Computer Utility Corporation.

generated revenue which was transferred to the province's consolidated revenue fund. However, it was recognized that the Liquor Board (and its profits) were operated not as a commercial Crown corporation but as part of the fiscal policy of the government. For that reason it was excluded from the group coming within the scope of GFO's operations. A different decision was reached by the Government of Manitoba when it subsequently adopted a Crown corporation model. Had Saskatchewan made a similar decision on the issue, it would have improved the financial results of the Crown corporation sector by at least $20 Million per annum in 1977 dollars. However, given the true nature of the Board's operation, such an "improvement" was not thought to be appropriate.

The group of seventeen Crown corporations were formally brought under the jurisdiction of CIC by adoption of an Order-in-Council designating that all activities of the corporations were subject to Part II of *The Crown Corporations Act* (meaning CIC's authority) in 1978 and as O/C 1267/78 were maintained until the defeat of the Blakeney government in 1982. A significant group of assets consisting of equity in share-capital corporations owned by the Province or by SEDCO was also added to CIC's responsibility at a later date.

A new Crown Corporations Act was introduced into the Legislature during the spring session of 1978.[9] The legislation followed a format similar to the then existing legislation, *The Crown Corporations Act*.[10] Like its predecessor, it was divided into two parts; Part I dealing with Crown corporations established by Order-in-Council; Part II dealing with CIC. These provisions established a clear legal relationship between CIC and the other Crown corporations. In fact, the legal authority given to CIC under the legislation extended beyond that which might exist between a parent and a subsidiary in the private sector. Although the individual Crown corporations did not have share capital and therefore were not "subsidiaries" in the same way as found in the private sector, the ability of CIC to advance funds to those corporations and to treat such advances as equity advances coupled with the extraordinary powers vested in CIC to withdraw funds from the individual Crowns clearly established, in a practical manner, the holding company relationship.

In 1981 a further amendment was made to *The Crown Corporations Act*. Under this amendment, the ability of CIC to pay dividends to the Saskatchewan Heritage Fund was made clear. For reporting purposes, advances made by the Heritage Fund to resource Crown corporations were treated as having flowed through CIC to those corporations. Dividends from the resource corporations also flowed to the Heritage Fund through CIC.

---

[9] *The Crown Corporations Act, 1978*, R.S.S 1978, c. 50.1.

[10] *The Crown Corporations Act*, R.S.S. 1978, c. 50

CIC Responsibilities

The expanded role which CIC would ultimately play fulfilled essentially two primary functions which, while overlapping in some respects, were also significantly different. First, and perhaps not understood by many beyond Cabinet and senior levels of bureaucracy, CIC was assigned a significant responsibility in the area of economic development. Second, as an instrument of direction and control, CIC was to assist Cabinet and Cabinet's Committee on Crown corporations, the CIC Board of Directors. This was to be accomplished through use of the holding company model.

With its access to information assembled through Crown corporations and later through corporations in which the Province held equity, CIC was uniquely placed to serve as the government's "eyes and ears" on the economy in general. While admittedly this function had not been fully developed by 1982, it was intended that CIC become a centre where investment opportunities could be identified and, in appropriate cases, nurtured. With a government that was pragmatic in its approach and which recognized that four forms of enterprise were necessary to develop the provincial economy, CIC was not expected to develop all of the potential which it identified. Its role was to identify the potential and then take steps to encourage the development.

Operationally this role in economic activity was accomplished in part with the incorporation of CIC Industrial Interests Inc., a share-capital corporation incorporated under the Saskatchewan *Business Corporations Act*. Virtually all of the Province's investments in major projects were transferred to CIC Industrial Interests Inc. in 1980. The inclusion of these assets within CIC expanded the corporation's ability to function as the government's "eyes and ears" on the economy. The transfer also allowed for a rationalization of the Province's investments in private-sector corporations. These investments, which had previously been carried as debt on the statements of some Crown corporations, were all converted to equity.

Beginning in the fall of 1976, CIC began to fulfil the second role assigned to it in respect to the Province's Crown corporations, functioning both as a holding company overseeing the operations of individual Crown corporations included within its jurisdiction and providing advice to Cabinet and Cabinet's Committee on Crown Corporations. Although clearly the paper presented by Mr. Blakeney in 1953, in his capacity as Secretary to GFO, contained the concept of CIC in the 1970s, the scope of the corporation's activities were broadened to reflect the increased number of Crown corporations and the increased size and complexity of their operations.

In carrying out its duties, CIC's operations were divided into a number of divisions. These divisions are more fully described in the succeeding part of this chapter. However several key elements of CIC's activities and the manner in which they were carried out should be noted here.

As a holding company, CIC had, under *The Crown Corporations Act*, the legal authority to control the disposition of income and surpluses from Crown corporations. However, income generated by corporations did not automatically flow to CIC as had previously been the case. Decisions were made, on an annual basis, after discussions between individual Crown corporations and CIC on amounts to be retained by the individual Crown corporations. As had been previously stated by Mr. Blakeney, control was effectively exercised through review of capital budgets. Final approval over capital budgets remained with the CIC Board of Directors or, depending upon the corporation involved, with Cabinet. CIC staff was involved in reviewing capital budgets at an early stage and had access to financial information from individual Crown corporations so as to be in a position to evaluate those plans at different levels. CIC explained its approach to capital budgets in a 1981 publication, *Public Enterprise in Saskatchewan*:

> Today, final approval of capital spending is given by the CIC Board and, ultimately, by Cabinet. However, earlier steps in the process leading to those final decisions are primarily the responsibility of the individual corporations and their boards. CIC Management works closely with corporation officials to make sure that capital budget proposals are fully supported with the necessary technical analysis; this enables the corporation board to make an informed decision on the merits of a proposal from the point of view of the corporation. The subsequent review by the CIC Board is concerned primarily with the magnitude of total capital expenditures and with questions of broad policy.

CIC did not approve, nor generally review, operating budgets. The preparation of operating budgets was the responsibility of individual Crown corporations and approval of such budgets was handled at the board level in those corporations. The difference in treatment between the operating and capital budgets reflected what was considered to be an appropriate level of involvement by a holding company. It also reflected the reality that an organization such as CIC lacked either the technical expertise or the human and other resources to, in effect, act as a shadow manager of the individual Crown corporations.

Assuring that Cabinet received independent advice on proposals affecting Crown corporations was a second important activity within CIC. Through various divisions, CIC obtained information which allowed for the assessment of plans and for informed decisions to be made at the CIC Board and Cabinet level. Information was obtained from CIC corporate officers who were members of the boards of directors of individual corporations, the secretaries for individual Crown corporation boards who were staff members of CIC, and the process of reviewing capital budgets.

A third responsibility assigned to CIC was to monitor issues of general application to Crown corporations or government as a whole. One of the early functions served by GFO was to ensure some consistency in labour relations matters. This function was continued by CIC. Senior compensation and benefit packages and some legal issues were also of common interest.

A fourth activity of CIC has not generally been commented upon: attempting to improve the operation of boards of directors of individual Crown corporations. Several methods were employed to achieve this objective. One of CIC's corporate officers served as a director on each of the Crown corporation boards. This individual was assigned the responsibility not only of providing information to CIC on major items coming to the attention of the board of directors but also of assisting in improving the manner in which boards functioned. For example, the corporate officers spent considerable time with boards of directors encouraging them to work on long-term planning, corporate mission statements and similar matters. Boards were encouraged to question and consider proposals brought by management. On the corporate level, CIC conducted seminars for board members, covering the legal and practical roles of directors, financial statements and planning models. Finally, CIC was charged with the responsibility of actively recruiting prospective board members with particular expertise.

The Internal Structure of CIC

In the period from 1977 until 1982, CIC continued to add staff to fill out various divisions within the corporation. It is important to recognize that the corporation was always intended to have a relatively small staff compliment. At no time during this period did the total number of professional and support staff exceed 50. This is a characteristic of the holding company model as opposed to a government department or treasury board model where the level of review or involvement is extended to not only review of capital budgets but also to operating budgets.

One of the key elements of the structure of CIC was its Board of Directors. Throughout the Blakeney years the Board consisted of Cabinet Ministers with two exceptions: Garry Beatty who was Managing Director (later President) of the corporation and, for a brief period, Eiling Kramer, a retired member of the Legislative Assembly who had held various Cabinet positions for a number of years. With the exception of the years when the Premier was Chairman and Minister Responsible, Elwood Cowley served as Chairman of the Board and Minister Responsible. Mr. Cowley was recognized as one of the brightest of the NDP Cabinet Ministers. His portfolios included responsibility for a number of major Crown corporations during their formative years including PCS and Sask Oil.

In addition to Mr. Cowley, CIC's Board contained the Ministers responsible for most of the major Crown corporations or those significantly involved in economic development. With these Ministers on the Board of CIC, and with the analysis provided by CIC's staff, major issues tended to be dealt with at this level.

The strength of virtually any organization is not its corporate form or structure but the people who serve in it. The staff at CIC was an interesting mixture of youth and experience drawn from a varied background.

Specific Innovations Flowing from CIC

As a model, CIC of the late 1970s was not totally "new." Its operations represented a continuation of the original concept of GFO updated to take into account the increased complexity of both the legislative and business environments. However, the scope of the operation and the complexities of the Crown corporation sector as a whole might well be considered, in the late 1970s, a first example of innovation. Never before in the province and nowhere else in Canada had an all-inclusive holding company been created with responsibility over all commercial Crown corporations and most of the Province's investment in major private sector corporations. The inclusion of the major utilities made CIC a significantly different organization than that of GFO in the 1950s.

A second innovation was the economic development functions assigned to CIC. While Crown corporations in Saskatchewan (including GFO at times) and elsewhere have had economic development responsibilities, none appear to have been positioned as was CIC. With its various sources of information at the board level of Crown corporations, through the corporate offices and corporate sectors, through other contacts with Crown corporations in the Finance division, through administration of the Province's major equities, through the Special Projects functions of CIC itself, and through contacts with the Department of Finance, there was little economic activity in the Province which could not be monitored.

Third, the government established different expectations of different kinds of Crown corporations. When the commercial Crown corporations were brought under CIC's jurisdiction in 1978, they were divided into utility, resource and financial and service sectors as outlined in Table 1. For the first time, virtually all of the Province's commercial Crown corporations came under one umbrella. Consideration turned to the expectation of the government for each of utilities, financial, service and resource sectors. It was recognized that the expectations or measurements of performance applicable to the three sectors might be significantly different.

The primary objective of utilities was to provide assured services at a reasonable cost. To guarantee that services could continue to be provided, each of the utilities would have to be on a financially sound footing. The primary objective of the corporations was not, however, to generate large profits.

The corporations involved in the financial and service sectors similarly did not have, as their primary objective, the generation of profit. While each corporation was expected to show a profit or at least break even, the primary objective of these corporations was not the maximization of profits but the delivery of services. (One exception to this might have been the

TABLE 1
Crown Investments Corporation of Saskatchewan

Utilities	*Resources*	*Financial and Service*
Saskatchewan Power Corporation (SPC)	Potash Corporation of Saskatchewan (PCS)	Saskatchewan Economic Development Corporation (SEDCO)
Saskatchewan Telecommunications (Sask Tel)	Saskatchewan Mining Development Corporation (SMDC)	Municipal Financing Corporation of Saskatchewan
Saskatchewan Computer Utility Corporation (Sask Comp)	Saskatchewan Oil and Gas Corporation (Sask Oil)	Saskatchewan Government Insurance (SGI)
Saskatchewan Water Supply Board	Saskatchewan Forest Products Corporation	Saskatchewan Development Fund Corporation
	Saskatchewan Minerals	Agricultural Development Corporation of Saskatchewan
		Saskatchewan Transportation Company (STC)
		The Saskatchewan Government Printing Company
		Saskatchewan Fur Marketing Service

general insurance operations of SGI.) This part of SGI's operations were conducted in competition with private insurers.

The resource sector was, however, subject to different expectations. Participation by the government in the resource sector was philosophically designed to allow the people of the province to share in the returns generated by those resources. The definition of "profit" may well have been broader than that applied to a private sector corporation in the sense that the creation of employment in general and more highly paid "head office" jobs was an important consideration for a Crown corporation. At an appropriate time, the corporations were nonetheless expected to generate a return on the investment placed in them.

The resource corporations were, in the late 1970s, in their formative stage. PCS, SMDC and, to a lesser extent, Sask Oil, were in a phase emphasizing the accumulation of capital and assets. As such, the payment of significant dividends from their operations was not expected at that time. The Province's investment in these corporations was viewed as a long-term investment, a situation not unlike that encountered in the private sector particularly in connection with the development of resource corporations. The relationship between Great Lakes Forest Products Ltd. and Canadian Pacific Ltd. during the formative years of Great Lakes might well be referred to as a close parallel to that in Saskatchewan. In spite of this however, significant dividends were paid with the payment in 1980 of $50 million in dividends to the Province.

The fourth and perhaps most innovative aspect of CIC's operations was the preparation, beginning with the 1978 fiscal year ending December 31, 1978, of a consolidated financial statement reflecting all of the operations of the Province's commercial Crown corporations. CIC and its predecessor, GFO, had previously prepared a financial statement which consolidated the results of the operations of those corporations relating to the holding company. However, beginning with the 1978 Annual Report of CIC, a consolidated statement of financial positions showing assets totalling almost $3.0 billion, equity of $817.0 million, retained earnings of $327.0 million and net earnings of $61.4 million provided the population of the province and others including its investment bankers with a precise view of the **overall situation** in the Crown corporation sector.

This represented the first such statement prepared in Canada. For the first time, a single statement could be referenced to show the size of the corporations and their consolidated results. Prior to this, a party attempting to assess the overall position of the Province vis-à-vis its Crown corporations would have had to review statements relating to the Province's Consolidated Revenue and Heritage Funds and each of the individual corporations' financial statements. An attempt would have then had to be made to estimate the effect of transactions between the various corporations. Such an analysis would be both time consuming and imprecise in its result.

The preparation of the statement was particularly well received by the investment banking community at a time when, in contrast, there was some question as to the number of Crown corporations that the federal government had. Individuals familiar with the operation of Crown corporations in Saskatchewan since 1981, including the writer, believe that the primary reason why the Devine government did not wind down the operations of CIC is the preparation of the Consolidated Statement and its reception in the investment community.

In order to facilitate the consolidation, over succeeding years the fiscal year-ends for each of the Province's commercial Crown corporations were changed to December 31 with the result that Saskatchewan is also one of the few jurisdictions where fiscal periods in the Crown corporation sector have been standardized.

Post 1982 and Approaches in Other Jurisdictions

The defeat of the Blakeney government in the April 1982 Saskatchewan general election brought to power the Progressive Conservative Party under the leadership of Grant Devine. Premier Devine's views on economic development and those of his administration varied significantly from their predecessors.

Whereas the NDP government had accepted, as a key element in the administration of Crown corporations, Cabinet's collective responsibility for their operation, contact with the government was de-emphasized under the Devine administration. The previous approach was not one favoured by the new government which appeared more comfortable to distance itself from the operation of the Crown corporations. Shortly after taking office, the Devine government commissioned an inquiry headed by a chartered accountant, Wolfgang Wolff, under the name of the "Crown Investments Review Commission." Their report contained a number of recommendations which they summarized to be "a general reordering of corporate mandates, restructuring the roles of Ministers and directors, and, specifically, a redefinition of the central purpose of CIC." In the area of CIC, it was recommended that "CIC be given, as its central objective, the maximization of dividend payments for the Province."

Fundamental changes to the operation of CIC were suggested. While the committee ostensibly advised that CIC continue to function as a "holding company," changes flowing out of the report clearly called for a reduced role for the corporation and for the elimination of a number of the avenues by which CIC had been able to obtain information. In due course, the corporate officer and corporate secretarial functions performed by CIC were eliminated.

Among the chief recommendations of the Wolff Commission was a diminution of the involvement of Cabinet Ministers in Crown corporations and on the CIC board of directors. These recommendations were consistent with the philosophy of the new government and were, in due course, implemented.

Part of the justification for the changing role of CIC was ostensibly based upon views held by Crown corporation executives that CIC had been overly involved. It is perhaps inherent in the holding company model or in any other model involving review by a control agency, that those whose activities are reviewed could prefer not to be participants. Similar arguments had been advanced by the utilities in the 1950s which led to their removal from the operations of the old GFO. The real issue to be addressed by any government is not, however, the relative comfort level of those executives in the Crown corporations but the level of information which Cabinet feels it requires to operate government and to set policy.

After the defeat of the Devine government in the 1991 Saskatchewan general election, another NDP government was elected under the leadership of Premier Roy Romanow. A public inquiry was called by the new government shortly after its election. The report of the Financial Management Review Commission was released in February, 1992. The Commission was called to review the financial position of the Province, to review significant transactions occurring after January 1, 1983 involving Crown assets and to offer advice on improving the financial management and public accountability of government. Many of the Commission's conclusions and recommendations appear to be a direct reversal of the views expressed in the Wolff Report.

CIC remains today as one of the Province's Crown corporations although its responsibilities have remained much reduced from those of the Blakeney era. It remains to be seen, however, whether some of the innovations of that administration will be re-introduced.

It is interesting to note that in 1987, the NDP government under Premier Howard Pawley in Manitoba reviewed the operations of its various Crown corporations. At the time, the Pawley government had a Department of Crown corporations which fulfilled some of the aspects of "control and direction" that was a part of CIC's operations in Saskatchewan. After considering various models including the Saskatchewan model and the federal Treasury Board model, the Pawley government introduced legislation which created the Public Investments Corporation of Manitoba. This corporation modelled closely the corporate structure of CIC in Saskatchewan.

Shortly after the legislation was adopted by the Legislature of Manitoba, the Pawley government was defeated by the Conservative Party lead by Garry Filman. Among the first acts taken by the new government was the elimination of the holding company concept set out in the legislation.

A review of events which have occurred in Saskatchewan and Manitoba might lead to the conclusion that the Crown corporation holding company model is one closely aligned to political philosophy. This is, however, somewhat difficult to support, given that the structure and operation of these holding companies more closely parallel the operation of holding companies in the private sector such as those found in the operation of the Canadian Pacific group of companies or with the Edpar-Bronfman group.

At this point in time, there do not appear to be any other holding company models being utilized by governments in Canada outside of the form found in Saskatchewan.

REFERENCES

Blakeney, A. 1953. "Saskatchewan Crown Corporations, A Case Study." In *The Proceedings of the Fifth Annual Conference of the Institute of Public Administration of Canada, Saskatoon, Sept 9–12, 1953*, edited by P. Clark. Toronto: The Institute of Public Administration of Canada.

Crown Investments Review Commission. 1982. *Report of the Crown Investments Review Commission* (Chairman W. Wolff). Regina: Government of Saskatchewan.

Government of Saskatchewan. 1971–82. *Saskatchewan Crown Corporations Annual Reports*. Regina: Government of Saskatchewan.

Government of Saskatchewan. 1977–78. *Minutes of Meetings of the Board of Directors of GFO* (Board Secretary, J. Little).

Maclean, G. 1981. *Public Enterprise in Saskatchewan*. Regina: Crown Investments Corporation of Saskatchewan.

Saskatchewan Management Review Commission. 1992. *Report of the Saskatchewan Financial Management Review Commission* (Chairman D. Gass), February. Regina: Government of Saskatchewan.

CHAPTER 2   Environmental Policy

by Hugo Maliepaard

Background

During the late 1950s and early 1960s, the industrial world began to recognize that our improved living standards incurred an environmental cost. This growing environmental awareness triggered the emergence of an "environmental conscience." While many events can be identified which contributed to this development, there can be little argument that Rachel Carson's book *Silent Spring*, published in 1962 (Carson, 1964), was greatly responsible for alerting the world that something was seriously wrong with the environment. The first environmental interest groups sprouted in central Canada and started to make "noises" for which governments were quite unprepared.

Concerns were raised with such issues as the development and use of nuclear power, air emissions (particularly oxides of carbon and nitrogen), heavy metals, effluents of the pulp and paper industry and mining, and water pollution of the Great Lakes. The initial government response of ignoring or paying lip service only, did not have any "quieting" results.

The interest and actions of the mass media kept the fires burning. Public affairs programs, such as "This Hour Has Seven Days," rapidly accumulated an alarming inventory of environmental sins which were very effectively aired. The public outcry became louder and more persistent: "Something must be done!" Subsequent reactions of governments were also predictable; reorganize! In the beginning these moves were mostly cosmetic and tentative. However, they did buy some valuable time to gauge if the outcry would persist and to determine how the matter could best be handled. The subject matter was entirely foreign to governments, but some politicians started to recognize some of the frightening aspects of this new issue and pressed for a much more thorough examination of the entire problem. The term "environment," which in the 1950s was restricted to textbooks, became a household word in the 1960s, and by the end of the decade most Canadian governments had an environmental agency in their administrative structure.

Saskatchewan, lacking large population centres and heavy industries, did not exhibit the environmental degradation usually associated with these

49

developments elsewhere in the country. In addition, Saskatchewan's extensive agriculture and forestry activities did not require the massive use of chemicals, unlike the market gardening and fruit growing industries in other provinces. Hence, interest groups were slower to develop in our province and the range of environmental issues and concerns was more limited.

The first group to emerge was in the mid-1960s on the campus of the University of Saskatchewan in Saskatoon. The "Resources Study Group," which consisted mainly of students and some university staff, concentrated their early efforts on the fledgling pulp and paper industry. One important target was insufficient treatment of the effluent released in the North Saskatchewan River. Other concerns were large areas of clear-cutting (one half square mile or more) and completely inadequate reforestation practices. It was rather surprising that the well publicised mercury pollution of the South Saskatchewan River, caused by a chloro-alkali plant in Saskatoon, was not more of an issue and did not trigger other chemical-related concerns.

The Liberal government of the time did not show much appreciation for these new developments and was reluctant to come to grips with the situation. Questions about the Prince Albert pulp mill and its associated wood activities were seen as particularly unwelcome interference. One can appreciate this better realizing that the establishment of a second pulp mill in the Meadow Lake area was high on the political agenda of the late sixties.

Another environmentally sensitive issue was the announcement by the uranium industry that substantial, high grade ore deposits had been discovered in the Rabbit Lake and Cluff Lake areas. The Eldorado mine in Uranium City, which had been in operation for years, was never a point of contention in the province. However, the possible expansion of this industry in other northern locations alarmed a growing number of people.

The government's initial reaction to these environmental concerns was to establish an Interdepartmental Pollution Control Committee comprised of senior staff from such departments as Natural Resources, Health, Agriculture, Labour, and the Water Resources Commission. This group was mainly responsible for the coordination of environmental activities and reported to the Minister in Charge of the Water Resources Commission. Its main areas of activity centred around the high mercury levels in the South Saskatchewan River, the proposed Meadow Lake pulp mill, and the potential growth of the uranium industry.

Election Time

When Premier Thatcher announced the election in early 1971, the government's position on environmental matters consisted of the establishment of an environmental protection agency, structured similarly to the existing Water Resources Commission. Some steps to achieve this objective had already been taken, but otherwise no major initiatives were identified.

In contrast, the NDP's *New Deal for People* outlined in considerable detail its electoral platform. Highlights of the NDP's environmental position were the establishment of a full-fledged environment department, environmental assessment requirements, a ban on the use of non-returnable bottles and cans, and the establishment of an independent environmental advisory council to the Minister. Other initiatives dealt with air and water quality controls. What, if any, contribution the NDP environmental platform made to its election victory is difficult to assess. The proposed Athabasca Pulp Mill near Meadow Lake was very much in the limelight, possibly more so for the resource sell-out it represented than for the dismal environmental implications which were anticipated.

Implementation Strategy

After the NDP government took office, its first environmental priority was to establish the environment department. Some Cabinet members were leaning toward a modest agency, possibly attached to an existing department. This option was difficult to sell, because of their election commitments. The real choices were to create a department with considerable legislative clout over the major constituents of the natural environment, or a modest agency with a strong coordination role. Clive Dennis of the provincial Health Department and John Richards, a University of Saskatchewan professor, were requested to draft a proposal for Cabinet consideration. Their submission represented the "magnum" variety, outlining broad legislative powers over a wide environmental spectrum and the rearrangement of a number of existing government units, augmented by some new ones, into a large new government department. This was an approach similar to the one adopted by the federal government. Cabinet did not accept this proposal on the grounds of it being too ambitious and disruptive to other agencies.

A new team of officials were instructed to draft another proposal on a considerably more modest scale, more under the heading of "small is beautiful." Grant Mitchell, who was in charge of the Water Resources Commission, and David Shepherd, a biology professor of the University of Regina, undertook this assignment. This resulted in a new Department of the Environment (DOE), established in the spring of 1972. It was comprised of the existing Water Resources Commission plus an air pollution component transferred from the Department of Health. The only new units were a Policy, Planning and Research Branch and an Information and Extension Branch. In subsequent years, the department was rounded out with Land Protection and Mines Control branches as well as an Environmental Assessment Secretariat. The initial modest approach did not impress many, and the environmental lobby soon expressed its concern that the new agency did not have sufficient authority and resources to protect and manage the environment properly.

The new DOE Act had two interesting features. Firstly, it established an independent advisory council meant to advise the Minister on environmental issues on its own initiative or upon his request. This Environmental Advisory Council (EAC) had broad representation of the Saskatchewan scene and received funding to establish a secretariat, to carry out some modest programs. Besides representatives of the more traditional conservation agencies such as the Natural History Society, the Fish and Game League, and environment-oriented groups, the Council also had members from agriculture and forestry interests, rural and urban municipal governments, the academic community and industry. Particularly during the first few years it proved a very effective sounding board for government initiatives and was a valuable means to identify environmental issues and concerns of which the Minister should be aware or which required attention.

A second feature of the Act was the establishment of an Interdepartmental Coordinating Committee at the deputy ministerial level, representing a dozen related government departments and agencies. This Committee had as its main mandate to ensure that environmental considerations were incorporated in the planning and program development of other government departments. In turn, the environment department bounced its new plans off the other members for their assessment. Initially, some members did not take this seriously and considered the exercise only as an additional hindrance in doing their work. However, because the Premier's Office and Cabinet referred interdisciplinary issues to the committee for its consideration and/or advice, it developed into an effective vehicle of information exchange on a wide array of government concerns.

The occasional battle fought in this arena made it abundantly clear that the new "environmental conscience" was certainly not a universal phenomenon shared by all of government; politicians and public servants alike. Some considered the environmental movement to be based on gross exaggeration of issues and emotionalism rather than hard facts. This attitude remained over the years.

One of the first activities of the Department was a litter survey of a variety of community sites and along roads and highways. The high number of empty pop and beer bottles and cans was striking. In 1974, legislation was passed which banned the sale of carbonated beverages in non-returnable containers. The sale of pop and beer cans was virtually eliminated and the litter problem drastically reduced. The measure upset some people who were used to this convenience and retailers were particularly opposed to the legislation because of the handling of a significantly increased number of returned bottles. Even though the program was triggered by a litter problem, it was often regarded as a conservation measure, which received much praise during the energy crisis of the early seventies. The fact that the province did not have a cannery (but several bottlers) kept political flack to an acceptable minimum. Saskatchewan was the only province, and Oregon the only state, to develop such a program and were envied by many. In spite of many advantages and public appeal, the measure was under continual pressure to be cancelled because opponents saw it as regressive legislation, hindering progress.

Possibly the most significant commitment made in the New Deal for People was the requirement that all new industrial developments would be evaluated for their environmental effects before their introduction. In the past, too many developments or activities had been approved without adequate consideration of their impacts on the environment. The poisoning of streams and lakes by industrial waste, the irreparable damage to lands by poor forestry practices, irresponsible use of chemicals for pest control were just a few examples. To address such "environmental sins" which were often avoidable, proponents of developments or activities were to submit detailed plans of their proposals as well as ways and means to reduce or eliminate any potential impact on the environment.

The drafting of procedures, guidelines and regulatory requirements for an assessment process received high priority. There was additional urgency for quick action, since new electric power sources were required to meet rapidly rising demands, as identified by the Saskatchewan Power Corporation. Another potential candidate for review, the proposed pulp mill near Meadow Lake, ceased to be an environmental liability, because the new government cancelled the proposal due to unacceptable economics and environmental reasons. A number of environmental assessments and subsequent public hearings took place before all procedures were worked out and legislation passed.

The first environmental assessment to be carried out was for a coal powered, 300 megawatt power plant near Coronach. The proponent, the Saskatchewan Power Corporation (SPC), a Crown corporation, was requested to submit an environmental impact statement, which would subsequently be made available for public scrutiny and a Board of Inquiry. As things turned out, this assessment became a joint effort between the proponent and the Department. On the one hand it is likely that the Department was not clear and specific enough in outlining its requirements; on the other hand, the utility considered the process undesirable, because of additional costs in funds and time, and was therefore less than cooperative. The need for cooperation and consultation was essential since both parties were involved in a learning process. The experience proved successful to all concerned. As well, the Board of Inquiry made very useful recommendations for future inquiries regarding the scope of assessments, the need for the funding of interest groups for meaningful participation in inquiry procedures, and early public involvement in the assessment process.

The Board of Inquiry under the chairmanship of Leo Christianson (an economist who later became president of the University of Saskatchewan) made additional recommendations. A proponent, including the power utility, must demonstrate the need for a project. Long term power demand projections, as well as alternative sources of energy development, should be made

53

available by the corporation. Also, the scope of the assessment of power projects should be broadened to include all major power lines associated with them.

Subsequent assessments and public hearings were carried out on four more power proposals and a uranium mine. This experience enabled the various players to better determine their respective roles and decide what information was required for meaningful discussion and decision making. This culminated in the government's adoption of an Environmental Assessment Policy and the establishment of an Environmental Assessment Branch in 1976.

These experiences also formed a sound basis for the drafting of an Environmental Assessment Act, the first in Canada, which was completed in 1980. Much consultation with other agencies and interest groups was involved. Concerns were raised by development-oriented agencies and departments in the government. According to them, the powers of an environment minister would be far too extensive and could seriously retard economic progress. On the other hand, the environmental lobby pressured for a level of public involvement and government accountability which would have retarded the process to a snail's pace. Nevertheless, it was because of these efforts and experiences that an outstanding Act was passed which was one of the best in Canada.

The Act made it very difficult for government to allow projects to proceed without a proper environmental assessment. It forced government to be completely open about the process, and yet allowed for protection of proprietary information. As well, there were sufficient stipulations to move the process along and avoid unnecessary delays. The Minister had powers to carry out public consultations and to make limited funds available to interest groups who participated in the process. In addition, the Act allowed the Minister to request an assessment which could incorporate associated social, economic and cultural implications as well as the impact of the development proposal on the physical, natural environment.

Two rather large and controversial projects which the Department had to deal with should be discussed in a little more detail. A hydro power proposal on the Churchill River, the Wintego Project, actually involved two proposals. Besides the power project, there was a plan to designate the same area as a park. The environmental assessment was not carried out by the proponents, but under the joint supervision and management of a Canada, Saskatchewan and Manitoba study board. While the study incorporated extensive investigations on many aspects of the environment, it particularly stressed the socio-economic impacts. Great emphasis was placed on the early participation of interest groups, particularly the local residents whose hunting and fishing grounds would be flooded or otherwise affected. These efforts were only partially successful because the approach was new and at times awkwardly handled. The general public, particularly native residents, had difficulty accepting this new approach because of a traditional distrust of government. In the early stages, governments were blamed for a white-wash job since it was assumed, particularly by northern residents, that the decision had already been made to proceed with the power project. During the subsequent public hearings, the decision was made not to proceed with the power development. The tide then turned 180 degrees and the criticism became that the entire exercise was an environmental publicity gimmick. To those in government, it seemed that no matter what was done, the public refused to accept that the process was honest and above-board. The Board of Inquiry recommended (Churchill River Board of Inquiry, 1978) that the power proposal should not proceed for economic reasons. The government decided that the project would be shelved for the time being, not for economic reasons but because of concerns expressed by the residents of the area.

The Cluff Lake uranium mine proposal was interesting from a different perspective. After the environmental impact studies were completed by the proponent, the subsequent hearings under a Board of Inquiry (Cluff Lake Board of Inquiry, 1978) were not only to address the environmental impacts, but also to include whether Saskatchewan should continue to be in the uranium mining business. This represented the first time that a government policy and existing industry was under public scrutiny at government behest. The environmental assessment procedures related to the Amok proposal to establish a uranium mine at Cluff Lake had some interesting aspects. After the government received the environmental impact statements from Amok, an Order-in-Council was passed in February of 1977 establishing a Board of Inquiry under the chairmanship of Justice E.D. Bayda. The terms of reference of this Board not only dealt with the social, economic and environmental impacts of the project, but the Board was also asked to make general recommendations on the future expansion of the province's uranium industry. The Board established rules for public hearings which were somewhat formal, reminiscent of court procedures. However, within this framework the conduct was kept as informal as possible. To facilitate the meaningful participation of interest groups in the rather extensive public hearing and consultation process, the environment department made $100,000 available which was administered by an independent panel of specialists. Nevertheless, some considered the inquiry approach to be seriously flawed (Harding, 1995).

In May of 1978, the Board presented its report to the government. As far as the mine and mill proposal by Amok was concerned, the Board recommended that this could proceed subject to some conditions. These conditions involved changes in legislation, policies and administration of the Industry, as well as some technical matters. Highlights were the reallocation of the mine's pollution controls to the environment department, the establishment of an Environmental Protection Fund, and clarification as to who controls the industry, the province or Canada. Strong recommendations were made to ensure that the northern people would realize benefits from this industry. A Northern Development Board would play an important role in the coordination, initiation and direction of future economic and social development in northern Saskatchewan. As well, part of the revenues of the industry should be redirected to benefit northern people.

The opponents of the uranium industry supported their stand with four main arguments: inadequate waste disposal, nuclear proliferation, terrorism and moral/ethical issues (Harding, 1995). The Board felt that waste could be properly handled. Furthermore, they did not see that Saskatchewan's withdrawal from uranium mining and milling would have any influence on the potential for nuclear arms proliferation and terrorism. In view of the preceding arguments, the Board concluded that both the Cluff Lake development and the general issues of the expansion of the industry were officially acceptable. However, the Board did not make any recommendations regarding the subject (Cluff Lake Board of Inquiry, 1978).

A last environmental thrust to be mentioned is the attempted development of a provincial land use policy. Increased land use conflicts and the absence of a framework to resolve such issues, emphasized the need for such a policy. Some of the key issues related to competition between agricultural land uses with recreational pursuits. Clearing land of wooded vegetation and drainage of wetlands seriously affected wildlife populations. Urban sprawl on high class agricultural land was seriously questioned. Forestry activities had negative effects on game, fur and fish populations in northern Saskatchewan which jeopardized an important source of income to northern residents.

It was with a great deal of reluctance that the government embarked on this exercise, because it was politically touchy in a province dominated by agriculture and a population of highly independent entrepreneurial farmers. A committee was formed comprised of a wide variety of interest groups under the chairmanship of a well known rancher, Boyd Anderson. The first round of activities consisted of province-wide information meetings and discussions with hundreds of interested parties to define the conflicts and to discuss the need and scope of a policy. The next round was again made up of public consultations to define the elements of a land use policy. The third round of activities attempted to reach a consensus in implementation of a policy.

This process took several years of exhaustive work, mainly by members of the public, interest groups and departmental staff (in a supporting role). In early 1982, a final draft of the policy was submitted. However, after the election of a new government, the subject was shelved. Even though the outcome was disappointing, the extensive consultation and discussions which took place had definite educational values which benefited many.

There was another event which did not enhance the Department's image. Because public involvement and accountability was of such high priority in the Department, it came as a great shock when a reporter in Regina presented evidence of a "cover-up" regarding a 1,500 gallon PCB (polychlorinated biphenyl) spill which occurred in 1976 in a commercial plant in the city. When the spill was initially brought to the attention of the Department, corrective measures were undertaken as instructed by the appropriate authorities. Peculiarly enough, the event was never communicated to the Deputy Minister's or Minister's offices; no doubt a serious omission. The matter had just been treated as any other spill. The fact that no intentional "cover-up" was involved was unacceptable to the public. Immediately the pendulum swung to the other side and one press release after the other was made public regarding the progress on the containment of the PCB spill and monitoring programs. This created a high level of concern by the Regina public which came close to panic level when PCB traces were found in the Regina drinking water. After extensive and very costly investigations, it was found that the paint on the outside of the pipes inside a pumping station where the samples were taken, contained PCB which contaminated the samples. The drinking water to the public was therefore not affected. Nevertheless, the damage was done. Within a year the Department lost its minister, deputy minister and senior environmental protection official. In addition, a somewhat routine role of the Department had to be revitalized by making additional resources available to strengthen environmental protection programs.

Innovations

What really unique accomplishments can be made by one government which have not been tried, tested, worked out or approached somewhere else? The decade under discussion, particularly the first half, was a most exciting period to work in. New programs had to be developed which dealt with issues and concerns which were new and often had a strong regional character. There were no pat answers or models available which one could readily use. Neither was there any one "expert" who had the answers (even though there were those who thought so). Yet, new solutions had to be found and implemented. There was much fertile soil ready for new seed to take root. This new, favourable climate encouraged many ideas to be generated which had to be bounced off many stake holders, not only in the public arena but also within government.

A wide-open and honest public involvement and consultation process evolved. To make the process fair, meaningful and effective, financial and other assistance was made available to certain interest groups. This was unique! In addition, impact assessments were not restricted to the natural environment, but also included social and economic implications. This was also unique!

Lastly, public opinion and recommendations were not only solicited in well-defined, distinct projects, but for subjects and policies of major importance to the province. The uranium industry and land use policies are examples. This was new!

One could possibly include certain specific measures in this category, such as banning the sale of pop and beer cans, or unique aspects of environmental legislation. However, these did not have the impact of the previously mentioned points.

Great strides were made and significant results attained to better manage the environment. Unfortunately, some of it could not withstand subsequent political change and economic recession.

REFERENCES

Churchill River Board of Inquiry. 1978. *Churchill River Board of Inquiry, Report, June.* Regina, SK: Government of Saskatchewan.

Cluff Lake Board of Inquiry. 1978. *Cluff Lake Board of Inquiry, Final Report of the Cluff Lake Baord of Inquiry,* Hon. Justice E.D. Bayda, chairperson. Regina, SK: Government of Saskatchewan.

Harding, Jim, ed. 1995. *Social Policy and Social Justice: The NDP government in Saskatchewan during the Blakeney Years.* Waterloo, ON: Wilfrid Laurier University.

Carson, Rachel. 1964. *Silent Spring.* First Fawcett Crest Edition. New York: Fawcett Crest.

CHAPTER 3

Resource Rent and Taxation — Application of New Principles and Approaches in Saskatchewan*

by John S. Burton

Saskatchewan undertook some bold initiatives under the Blakeney government to ensure that the province on behalf of its people secured adequate returns from its resources. This had to be done by challenging the status quo of generally very modest revenues. Higher returns to the province as owner of much of the resource base were secured. In particular, it was determined that the province and thus its people should secure most of the revenue from windfall profits that occurred in the volatile economic situation of the 1970s.

Jurisdiction over resources in Canada is vested with the provinces but the federal government still has effective authority over resources in the territories and on a substantial amount of other land within the provinces. Additionally, much of the jurisdiction over commerce and trade is held by the federal government. In many parts of Canada a substantial portion of the ownership of resource lands (except for agricultural land) is held by the provinces, however, there is still a significant amount of privately held land.

The attitude of governments throughout much of Canadian history was "laissez-faire" with respect to resource affairs. The prevailing philosophy was that governments should only be concerned with the regulatory function and obtaining a modest amount of revenue.

Powerful lobbies in the mining, oil, and natural gas sectors/industries had no difficulty obtaining wide ranging concessions from both federal and provincial governments on taxation, royalty and other developmental

* Based on a paper presented to a Conference on Macro-Economic Planning in Zambia, University of Zambia, Lusaka, Zambia — April 28, 1984.

questions. The lobby persuaded governments for a long time that private industry could best undertake and run the industry. The role of government was largely to stay out of the way except when help was needed. Successive governments in most parts of Canada, when faced with the choice of development or revenue, usually chose development. The lobby reinforced this position by widely publicizing the benefits of development.

The strong position of resource industries was further enhanced by interprovincial competition for development. Thus, the mining, oil, and gas industries have long enjoyed tax advantages, modest royalties, and substantial assistance in development.

The first serious challenge to the power of the industry in Canada occurred in 1970 when the federal government undertook a major overhaul of income tax legislation. This would have done away with many of the concessions and advantages enjoyed by the mining industry. Organized lobbies reacted strongly to these federal proposals and eventually the Federal Government modified them substantially.

Having lost this initial battle, the federal government then found other ways to get more revenue from the mineral industry by developing direct levies on some activities, oil and gas in particular. In doing this, the federal government reversed its stance with the provinces of some years earlier when it had indicated it had no interest in obtaining direct revenues from the mineral industry.

Resource Taxation

Agriculture has always been the dominant industry in Saskatchewan, a landlocked province with long distances to seaports. The economy of the province is very vulnerable and subject to violent fluctuations due to prices, markets and weather. Manufacturing is relatively weak and service industries are often located in neighbouring provinces. Thus, whenever resources have been found and identified for potential development, the prospect of diversifying the economy has been eagerly welcomed. Noteworthy increases in government revenues have been anticipated but the benefits of new economic development have been generally of most interest.

Historically, revenue from resource taxation was not given high priority and the concept of resource rent (see Appendix I) was not well defined until the 1970s when world oil prices skyrocketed and other mineral prices also increased. In Saskatchewan, where virtually all of the resource industry was owned by non-residents of the province, primarily foreign investors, these events focused attention on the question of who should be the recipient of the windfall gains.

As a consequence, the subject of resource rent and taxation was then studied more intensively by academics, policy makers and administrators. Albert I.M. Church (1982) notes:

Nearly all phases of extracting and processing natural resources are subject to taxation. These levies include taxes on output (severance, privilege, and resource excise taxes, as well as royalty and lease payments to government as resource owner), on inputs to the production process (taxes on labour, materials and investment goods), on profits (corporate income taxes and net proceeds and lease payments), and on the resource *in situ* (property taxes on reserves and bonus lease payments).

Economic rent is defined as the amount by which the price of a good or service could be reduced (taxed) without motivating its owner to alter the use and employment of that resource.

... Unanticipated windfalls, however, represent economic rent because resource allocation decisions are made in their absence. There are three major sources of windfalls associated with natural resources — discovery windfalls, market windfalls and government policy windfalls.

This paper examines the Saskatchewan experience with five resources — oil, natural gas, potash, uranium, and forests. The Province is both the regulatory manager and the primary owner of these resources. The Saskatchewan government initiated and implemented some far-reaching policy changes that had a profound impact. Federal government policies also had some influence on the course of events.

Oil and Natural Gas

Saskatchewan is the second largest oil-producing province in Canada and also has a modest natural gas potential. However, it is far surpassed by Alberta, which is the major source of oil and natural gas in Canada. Saskatchewan accounts for 10–12 percent of Canadian oil production while Alberta accounts for some 85 percent.

Saskatchewan had a reasonable level of oil royalties that returned 10-15 percent of the gross value to the Province. That royalty scheme worked satisfactorily in the pre-1973 period.

From 1960 to 1973, world energy consumption rose at unprecedented rates — an average of 8 percent each year. During this time, Canada's consumption rate rose approximately 6 percent per year. The availability of cheap and plentiful supplies of oil from the Middle East was a key contributing factor, and resulted in a greater dependence on oil and gas as primary energy sources.

The events surrounding the 1973 "energy crisis" involved a realization that these resources are finite. As an essential scarce commodity in great demand, oil prices on the world market skyrocketed. Canada was profoundly affected by rapid changes in the market place.

Because of its geography, climate, and lifestyle, Canada has one of the highest per capita energy consumption levels in the world. It also has vast energy reserves — coal, uranium, hydropower, oil and natural gas. In 1973, Canada was one of the few industrialized countries in the world that was a net exporter of petroleum products.

Ontario and Quebec are the two largest consuming provinces, but are a considerable distance from the producing provinces. Oil must be moved by pipeline to these markets. In 1961, the Canadian government introduced a National Oil Policy which divided Canada into two consuming regions. Most parts of Ontario and all of Western Canada were supplied with domestically produced oil. For the Atlantic Provinces, Quebec, and Eastern Ontario, it was cheaper to import oil from the Middle East or Venezuela than to transport Canadian oil from the west.

> In the aftermath of the oil embargo and the OPEC price increases, the immediate adjustment problems facing Canada were quite different than those facing most oil-importing countries, and indeed as a net exporter, the immediate problem was not to ease the transfer of real and financial resources to oil-exporting countries, but rather to facilitate the transfer of income and wealth within the country, from oil-consuming provinces to oil-producing provinces in such a way that the legitimate aspirations of the oil-producing provinces could be realized while minimizing the disruption to the broader social and economic well being of all Canadians. (Energy, Mines, and Resources Canada, 1976, pp. 17–18)

Under Canada's constitution, the federal government had the responsibility to establish a national energy policy and to regulate the country's trade and commerce. The provinces, however, had jurisdiction over the production, sale, and direct taxation of their own resources. In 1973, jurisdictional disputes developed quickly over who controlled resources and, therefore, who was entitled to "windfall profits" or economic rent generated by world price increases that had nothing to do with increased costs of production. Both federal and provincial authorities agreed that economic rent should be retrieved from oil companies, but the questions of who should collect it and in what form were the subjects of contention between the two producing provinces and the Federal Government.

During the second half of 1973, all three governments moved to establish their rights to the economic rent from petroleum resources. The federal government levied a tax on Canadian crude oil exports — an action regarded by Saskatchewan and Alberta as direct interference in provincial jurisdiction over resources. The export tax rose from 40 cents per barrel in October of 1973 to $6.40 per barrel by February of 1974. Alberta also introduced new and sharply higher oil royalties. Their royalty structure made the distinction between "old" and "new" production in recognition of the fact that new oil reserves were expensive to bring into production and should therefore be taxed at a lower rate than existing supplies. Saskatchewan increased its royalty rates on crude oil and proceeded to levy a royalty surcharge that was designed to capture the net value of price increases.

Controversy over these actions quickly followed. At a federal-provincial energy conference in January of 1974, both sides had assumed strong positions. Saskatchewan and Alberta stated that resource control was an exclusive provincial responsibility. As owners of a depleting, non-renewable resource, the provincial governments planned to recapture the economic rent on behalf of their people, to ensure that the short-term benefits of oil and gas price increases were used to develop more diversified and stable economies. Having long been the "victims" of national policies that favoured the heavily populated and industrialized provinces of central Canada (Ontario and Quebec), Alberta and Saskatchewan were opposed to Ottawa's imposition of the export tax and a price freeze on western oil sold to the east because these actions effectively negated the one economic advantage which could be used to offset what were considered to be serious inequalities in other areas such as transportation, agricultural prices, location of manufacturing capability and other industrial development.

Ottawa, with strong support from provincial governments in Atlantic and central Canada, felt that it was in the national interest to protect consumers from rapid energy price increases and ensure that all Canadians, not just those living in producing provinces, received some of the benefits of higher petroleum revenues. The federal government, therefore, was resolved to continue its export tax, and to maintain domestic oil prices well below market levels, thereby forcing the producing provinces to accept considerably less than half the world price for its oil and gas. Federal revenues were used to subsidize oil prices in the portion of Canada dependent on higher priced imported oil.

By March, an agreement was reached whereby the oil producing provinces agreed to set a domestic price for crude oil at $6.50 per barrel plus transportation costs. This was still less than the world price of $9.60 per barrel but higher than the previously allowed price of $3.80 per barrel. The federal export tax remained in effect. As a result, the economic rent was being divided among consumers (in the form of lower gas prices), the federal government which received all revenue for oil exports above $6.50 per barrel and the producing provinces which received oil revenues up to $6.50 per barrel.

Over the next several years, conflict among the two levels of government continued, as world oil prices continued to increase. Several subsequent pricing agreements were negotiated between Ottawa and the producing provinces. Each time, the positions of the respective participants remained basically the same, with the producing provinces trying to get a domestic price comparable to current oil prices and with Ottawa maintaining its desire to cushion consumers from high energy costs and keep its share of the revenue intact.

Saskatchewan maintained its position as stated by Premier Blakeney at a federal-provincial conference in December 1976: "We intend to make sure that the revenue we have collected, as the legitimate price or 'Economic Rent' for resources belonging to the people of Saskatchewan, remains in the province for the benefit of those people." Saskatchewan and Alberta

63

both indicated they wanted to use these revenues to diversify and stabilize their economies. Saskatchewan also proposed an energy security fund which would reserve a specified portion of higher oil revenues for programs to achieve oil self-sufficiency. Implicit in this proposal was an unwillingness to trust multinational oil companies to do the job for Canada by letting them have the revenues concerned. While the proposal was rejected at the time, a modified version was later adopted by the federal government when it made a special levy which was turned over to Petro-Canada, the federal public oil company, to give it more equity capital to finance oil development programs.

Several events contributed to ongoing acrimony on these issues as Ottawa continued to challenge the provinces' constitutional rights over resources. First, the federal government announced its plans to disallow royalties paid to provincial governments as a deduction from taxable income. Second, it did not live up to other parts of the March agreement — whereby the Federal Government had agreed to provide other economic benefits (such as a $25 million transportation fund for Saskatchewan) in return for their agreement to keep domestic prices below world levels. Third, the Federal Government supported court challenges to Saskatchewan's oil royalty and potash prorationing legislation.

This jurisdictional wrangling had a disastrous effect on the Canadian oil industry, which was caught in the middle of the dispute. Although the concept of economic rent includes a fair return to the producer after the cost of production, the industry did not agree with either level of government's definition of what constituted a "fair" return. Oil producers put forward the position that they were not receiving a fair return, particularly to cover the high costs of exploration and development of new reserves (in the expensive Arctic offshore or the oil tar sand deposits). In addition, both governments were attempting to tax the same revenues, and the resulting double taxation produced further hardships for the industry.

Because the oil industry was experiencing serious financial pressures and uncertainties due to federal and provincial government policies, exploration and development activities dropped sharply. Ultimately all governments introduced revisions of their royalty/tax policies to alleviate some of these difficulties. Both Alberta and Saskatchewan introduced rebate plans to return all or a portion of the industry's increased taxes which resulted from the federal government's policy of nondeductibility of provincial royalties. In addition, the two producing provinces modified their royalty structures, provided drilling subsidies, and implemented other measures to make exploration and development of new reserves more "attractive" to oil companies. The Federal Government also amended its taxation system to achieve similar objectives.

The principal features of the revised royalty scheme developed after a protracted period of negotiations were: first, adjustments to overcome the burden of double taxation incurred during the period of federal-provincial conflict; second, the province captured a substantial portion of the economic rent from better producing facilities; third, incentives for exploration and development; fourth, allowances for higher costs incurred in producing lower grades of oil; and fifth, allowances for marginal depleted oil wells.

Eventually pricing agreements were reached (although none were of any duration and renegotiation of the terms was required every six to eighteen months), and all levels of government had "fine-tuned" their tax structures and royalty rates to deal more effectively with the needs of the oil industry and the fluctuations of the world market.

During the latter half of the 1970s, several significant circumstances further shaped the direction of Canada's energy policies. First, governments began collecting economic rent on natural gas resources by substantially increasing the price to consumers and on exports to the United States. As a fuel source, however, natural gas still remained much cheaper than oil.

Second, emphasis was placed on encouraging Canadians to conserve energy through measures such as purchasing smaller, more fuel efficient cars, home insulation programs, home heating conversion programs (from oil to natural gas), use of alternative energy sources, and allowing consumer oil and gas prices to rise closer to the world price. Third, oil exploration and development activities increased as rising prices made previously "expensive" reserves more economically feasible to develop. Fourth, Petro-Canada, the country's nationally owned oil company began operations in 1976, primarily to provide a catalyst in forming joint ventures to develop new offshore and Arctic oil supplies and to inject more Canadian ownership into the oil industry.

Despite all these initiatives in conservation and development Canada became a net importer of petroleum products by 1976. New upheavals in the Middle East in the late 1970s underscored the need to ensure security of supply for Canadians by developing energy policies designed to make Canada energy self-sufficient.

Accordingly, in 1980, Ottawa introduced the National Energy Program, and negotiations began again with the producing provinces. The NEP included a wide set of proposals aimed at achieving three main goals: "security of oil supply" and eventual independence from imported oil; "opportunity" for greater participation by Canadians, particularly in the petroleum industry; and fairness in petroleum pricing and revenue sharing. However laudable the objectives of the NEP may have been from some perspectives, it was not accepted by the Alberta Government or the oil industry.

Following the failure of oil pricing negotiations between Ottawa and the provinces (between Alberta and Ottawa in July 1980), the federal government established the NEP in the face of vigorous objections from Alberta. Alberta retaliated by introducing significant production cutbacks, thereby reducing greatly revenue to Ottawa and forcing the country to import more oil to make up the shortfall. Canadian consumers were losing more by having to use higher priced foreign oil and gas than they would have under Alberta's proposed policies. Eventually Ottawa and Alberta came to terms, and a modified pricing policy was agreed to in return for Alberta's removing its production cutbacks. An "uneasy truce" had been arranged, but the NEP remained as a strong reminder to the Western Provinces of their continuing struggle to achieve a more equitable balance of power within Confederation.

The most obvious result of the many years of federal-provincial disagreements in energy matters was their hampering of Canada's ability to become energy self-sufficient. This became obvious when the target date for self-sufficiency was set back from the late 1970s to the 1990s. At the same time, the energy issue gave some power to Western Canadians, enabling them to have some say in national affairs. Provincial control over resources became a central issue in the development of a new Canadian constitution, and this principle was reconfirmed in the constitution adopted in 1982. As a result, energy issues became a focal point around which the Canadian style of government moved from a federal state with a strong national government closer to a federal state run by consensus of the national and ten provincial governments.

Following a change of government in Saskatchewan in 1982, a royalty holiday, and other measures welcomed by the private sector, brought about a significant upturn in oil activities for a period of years. The Conservative government made a choice for short-run gains instead of longer term benefits. The former government clearly took the stand that it was not necessarily advantageous to exploit depleting nonrenewable resources as rapidly as possible.

A further word is also necessary on natural gas. Saskatchewan does not have enough natural gas potential to serve its own needs on an economic basis in the long-run. Thus, Saskatchewan's policy for many years was to obtain only a portion of its domestic natural gas requirements from within the province and the rest was obtained from plentiful supplies in Alberta. The primary focus of natural gas policy was to serve the domestic requirements of the province.

The government decided to step up natural gas activity in the 1980s with the objective of doubling production in five years. While there may have been some benefits from lower costs for supplies and higher royalties, the principal motive appeared to be increased economic development. It was contended that reserves were sufficient to supply two-thirds of domestic needs "for many years."

During the 1970s, oil was the major ingredient in inflation and certainly complicated international dealings. It brought about a major confrontation between the federal government and western provinces as well as providing the impetus for a significant shift in political and economic power within Canada. It was the objective of oil-producing provinces to capture the windfall gains to enable them to do things that had been beyond their means previously.

Potash

Saskatchewan potash production commenced in 1962. A schedule of potash royalties was approved with a relatively low level of return to the Province (2–3% of the value of production). Earlier attempts to set royalties at a higher level met with industry resistance. Rates were set at a similar level to those in New Mexico, the one other place in North America where potash was then produced. The concept was to allow potash companies to recover a larger portion of their capital investment in the short-term and then increase royalty rates at a later date.

This was followed by a guarantee to maintain those royalty rates for all firms to 1974 and to 1981 for the two firms that overcame critical technical difficulties. The latter was in recognition of the large expenditures required to overcome the technical problems.

Following a change of government in 1964, existing royalty rates were guaranteed for all firms to 1981. The new government was committed to rapid economic development and encouraged rapid expansion of the industry. By 1968 it was clear that overcapacity was developing and within a year there was a full-scale crisis involving sharply reduced prices and imminent plant shutdowns. The answer was a government production control and price regulation plan. It left Saskatchewan a residual supplier in world potash markets with its plants operating at 50% of capacity compared to 85% in the rest of the world.

The new government in 1971 was concerned about the state of the Saskatchewan industry and the prospect of continuing low returns to the Province. It found an easy way of nominally increasing revenues without violating the royalty guarantee by imposing a fee on the production control and pricing plan. But it had considerable difficulty in unravelling the existing state of affairs and in developing new approaches. Reasons for this included scarcity of expertise, political sensitivities, constitutional constraints and, of considerable importance, resistance by the existing bureaucracy to meaningful change. A number of options were considered such as the establishment of a marketing board for potash.

The first real breakthrough came in late 1974 when a property tax type plan was implemented to tax potash reserves. This was done in a way that would not violate the royalty guarantee and was designed to produce a significant amount of revenue for the Province. It was developed with some knowledge of the composite state of financial affairs of the 12 potash operations in Saskatchewan, but there was no specific information on the state of each of these operations or of the impact of the new tax on them.

So the government required each operation to file regular financial statements. This met with severe resistance from the companies and it was only when a crisis developed later that those in the poorest condition broke down and submitted statements.

67

The government also announced that it would be interested in acquiring a share in the ownership of existing mines through negotiations but would insist on participating in expansions or new mines.

In less than a year, a full-scale crisis erupted, with companies refusing to pay their taxes, most refusing to submit financial statements, court challenges to the government's programs and federal interference on a number of matters. Either the provincial government or the industry had to give way.

In this context the provincial government announced legislation in November 1975 enabling it to nationalize part or all of the potash industry. Those powers were never used formally but did serve as an effective tool enabling Saskatchewan eventually to acquire through negotiation (and subsequent expansion) some 40% of the Saskatchewan potash industry.

After the controversy had settled down, negotiations resumed between the provincial government and private industry on royalty levels. It was clear now that the government was determined to get more revenue from the resource and the industry now knew there was a limit to the Government's tolerance. The Potash Corporation of Saskatchewan, as an instrument of government policy, was generally supportive of the government's objectives but nevertheless had some points of difference with the Department of Mineral Resources as it pursued its own mandate. This is one small example of the complexity of government, involving conflicting interests and objectives within the public sector.

Eventually a new tax system was concluded with the potash industry in 1979. A Potash Resource Payment Agreement was negotiated between the Province and each potash producer, public and private. This new levy was substituted for certain existing taxes. It ended a complex tangle of court battles.

The new levy was substantially less than the 1974 tax plan would have yielded but the net effect was still substantially higher revenues for the Province than before 1971. A substantial portion of this economic rent now accrued to the benefit of the owner — the Province. On the other hand, a portion of the economic rent remained with the industry. Where that industry was publicly owned, the portion of the economic rent retained by the industry would accrue to the public benefit. It should also be noted that the property tax plan was probably punitive for some firms because of the inadequate information available in establishing the system.

In one instance, the old tax system resulted in approximately 55% of the profits being paid in taxes while, under the new system in the same circumstances, it resulted in just over one third of profits being paid in taxes. The Province paid a price for peace and stability in the potash industry.

The new payments included first a "base payment" placing a small levy on each unit of production with a small escalation feature. This was based on the concept of a basic return to the Province for the removal of each unit of the resource. The second feature was a "graduated payment" based on each mine's net operating profit. Thus the system was sensitive to prices, costs, and profits, while also maintaining the principle of a minimum return to the Province for the exploitation of the resource regardless of the profitability of the operation.

There are lessons for both the public and private sectors in the Saskatchewan potash battle. The private sector came to realize that it was not sovereign, that it could not hold governments to ransom, that it could not operate in the same secretive fashion as in the past, and that economic rents really did belong to the owners, in this case the public authority.

The public sector, too, had lessons to learn. The first was that it is unwise to surrender virtually all rights to economic rent for the sake of development. While there may be short-run benefits, eventually other considerations of the public interest come to the fore. There may be advantages to concessions for limited periods of time but there should be a clear termination point for them. Another need is to have clearly spelled out rules and requirements from the beginning so there is no argument later, e.g. over access to financial statements.

The only way of ensuring that all economic rent goes to the state is through public development. There may be sound and even overwhelming reasons for surrendering a portion of economic rent for the sake of development but the price to be paid in doing so should be clearly understood. When the nature of the resource and its comparative standing lead to a position of strength for the public, it makes a substantial difference in determining the course of action that can be taken. When a political jurisdiction is bargaining from a weak position, as Saskatchewan was not too many years ago, it is almost inevitable that major concessions have to be made if development is to be achieved (unless there is some external source of assistance). While concessions may be necessary, the important thing is to develop a strategy for overcoming inherent weaknesses and developing the necessary political and economic strength.

It is useful to summarize the principal reasons for the potash nationalization policy: to capture resource rent; to ensure orderly expansion of the industry; to give Saskatchewan some market power and to change the old structure whereby most potash mines were adjuncts of foreign-based operations which managed their Saskatchewan operations from the perspective of corporate interest rather than Saskatchewan's interest; to ensure that secondary economic benefits associated with potash activity accrued to the benefit of Saskatchewan as much as possible; and to avoid and overcome the problems of transfer pricing.

Uranium

Saskatchewan's uranium production commenced in 1953 and was one of Canada's major sources of this product. In the early 1970s, new finds were developed and several huge deposits were located.

Until 1976, the royalty structure was a 12 ½ percent levy on the profits of existing mining operations. New mines had a three-year tax holiday and then a graduated scale up to nine percent of net profits. Since the existing operations were no longer very profitable, revenues to the province were minimal.

It was clear that the royalty system was inadequate for the new developments underway and anticipated. Thus a new royalty system was developed. The prime objectives of the new system were to ensure a minimum return to the Province for the extraction of the resource; to provide the producers with an adequate rate of return on invested capital, recognizing the relative riskiness of uranium exploration and development; and to capture for the Province the majority of any windfall profits that might accrue.

The first objective was achieved by levying a basic royalty of three percent of the gross value of sales. The second was achieved by providing that the producer would obtain his original investment back plus the cost of the investment before he started to pay graduated royalties.

Windfall profits were garnered through the graduated royalty system. It was levied on operating profit — income after operating costs and capital recovery — and operated as follows:

When the Ratio of operating profit to capital investment is:	The Graduated royalty is:
Below 15%	0
15% to 24.9%	1. 15% of operating profits in this bracket;
25% to 44.9%	2. 1 plus 30% of operating profits in this bracket;
Above 45%	3. 1 and 2 plus 50% of operating profits in this bracket.

In addition producers paid federal corporate income tax — then 27% of taxable income — and provincial corporate tax at 14% of taxable income.

While negotiations were lengthy, uranium royalties were resolved easier than in any other sector because they were put into place before major new facilities came into production, companies cooperated in providing information and were prepared to accept the new era in resource rents. The experience gained in dealing with other royalty problems enabled the government to achieve its objectives while being sensitive to the situation of the industry.

Forests

Over one-half of Saskatchewan is designated forest land; virtually all of the forest is owned by the Province. It is, however, scattered, slow-growing, and generally not of equal quality to forests in many other parts of Canada. A modest level of sawmilling activity was maintained for many years which produced a nominal amount of revenue for the province. Large tracts of timber land remained untouched.

Saskatchewan yearned for a pulp mill in order to exploit this resource. During the 1950s and early 1960s the government of the day actively worked for pulp mill development. Due to financial limitations, it looked to private sector development. The government was willing to make some concessions in order to get development, but there was a limit to the concessions and, despite several promising prospects, development never came. Development did not occur in part because forest companies had better forests elsewhere to turn to which were more economic to develop than the Saskatchewan forest. More attractive concessions were also offered by other jurisdictions.

In 1964, a change in government brought to power a Liberal government which was committed to private enterprise development and had made political commitments for more economic development. Because it was prepared to make much larger concessions than the CCF government, it was not long before a pulp mill was started by a large international forest company, Parsons and Whittemore Inc.

This company obtained a very low set of royalties, guaranteed for a period of 25 years, got generous aid otherwise, and was given total lease rights on a large tract of forest land. Clearly, greater priority was given to the benefits of economic development activity than ensuring that the Province, as owner of the resource, got an adequate economic rent and return from the exploitation of the resource. Additionally, lack of experience in this industry by the Province probably contributed to more give-aways than were necessary. Sooner or later, Saskatchewan would have warranted a pulp mill as more economic stands were depleted to meet growing world demand for pulp and paper. Saskatchewan's turn would have come. It came sooner than might have been expected because of the special concessions granted. Fortunately, the developing company was a competent operator.

The trade-off was the benefits of economic development occurring sooner than would have otherwise been the case versus the cost of foregone economic rent for the utilization of the resource. It would be an interesting economic study to determine whether the province was better off getting development sooner rather than ensuring a higher level of government revenues together with lower levels of financial assistance for the new operation. A plausible case can be made for earlier development in this instance because of the need for new development in the province. In hindsight, it should be noted that earlier development also avoided sharp increases in capital costs occasioned by inflationary pressures.

In 1971, the newly elected NDP government faced serious problems in the forest industry. A second pulp mill agreement provided for another mill with the same low royalties and other generous assistance. It would have allowed poor forest practises in an area with a fragile ecosystem. This agreement was cancelled at some cost to the province. The pulp mill already in operation also caused concern. Financial arrangements were a burden for the Province and unsatisfactory, cost-cutting forestry practises, involving large clearcut operations, had been allowed. Good saw logs that could have been used to make lumber or plywood were being chopped up for pulpwood, a product with less economic value. Some other forest industry agreements entered into prior to 1971, containing unacceptable royalty, financial concession and special assistance provisions, also required attention.

Drastic action was taken in 1973. Legislation was passed that gave the government the power to change contracts made with forest companies in the previous several years. One set of contracts with a large sawmill was changed to ensure better royalties, reforestation, use of wood supply and forest practises.

In the case of the pulp mill, forest practises were improved, better utilization of timber was achieved and other improvements made. At that point, the government ran out of political will to finish the job. There was concern lest further action might jeopardize the large number of jobs involved. Royalties stayed the same. Lease arrangements remained intact. By 1979 and 1980, it was clear that the operation was very profitable and that royalty revisions were overdue. Legal studies determined that the government would have extreme difficulty forcing royalty revisions even with the legislative powers it obtained in 1973. The only alternative was to negotiate changes from a weaker bargaining position.

But the course of affairs changed. The private owner negotiated a sale of its interest to another private company, Canadian Forest Products Ltd. (Canfor), a British Columbia forest company. However, the government had first option and bought the operation with the idea of eventually developing a joint venture with the new private company that would also include some other forest operations already owned by the Government. It would also make it easier to revise royalties before having to deal with a new owner with the same royalty agreements in place. Unfortunately these negotiations failed because of lack of agreement on price. Thus the government became the unwilling owner of much of Saskatchewan's forest industry and royalties were still unchanged.

Meanwhile, studies proceeded on a desirable new royalty regime based on the concept of economic rent. Old, fixed-level approaches were deemed inappropriate in periods of rapid commodity/resource price changes because they made easier a transfer of economic rent or extraordinary profit from the resource owner (the Province) to the resource extractor. Resource income taxes or profit sensitive royalty levies were regarded as suitable alternatives. Objectives for a forest royalty system were set: collect larger and more appropriate levels of rent; be responsive to the cyclical nature of the forest industry; place an equitable burden on individual forest firms; retain the feature whereby at least a minimum basic fee for the harvesting of public forests is collected; be simple to understand and implement; be constitutionally sound and remain deductible from federal income taxation.

In contrast with the other resource sectors examined, forest affairs were left unfinished when the Blakeney government left office in 1982. An aggressive stance in dealing with forestry affairs in the period following 1971 was not maintained as uncertainty and difficulties mounted in coping with an increasingly complex situation.

Government ownership of some sawmills, a plywood mill, a wood treatment plant and some special small northern mills on the one hand, and private ownership of the pulp mill, some sawmills, a pressed board plant and other miscellaneous operations was complicated by overlapping and conflicting rights to wood supply. Sharply differing royalty rates, unsatisfactory reforestation requirements and heavy forest fire losses contributed to a situation difficult to unravel. In addition, the regulatory function was divided between the Renewable Resources Department and a new Department of Northern Saskatchewan with jurisdiction over most government affairs in the northern half of the province. Then, Crown Investments Corporation, the holding company for Crown corporations and other government investments, became heavily involved when pulp mill negotiations got underway and exceeded their jurisdiction in some areas.

At the political level, Ministers, who were very aggressive in dealing with forest management issues and new forest development following 1971, became uncertain and reluctant to take further action as they recognized the difficulties caused by their earlier actions and further problems that would come with corrective action. Thus a combination of political and administrative problems hindered a satisfactory resolution of affairs.

Several lessons can be learned from this experience. First, forest management, reforestation, and royalties must be considered on an integrated basis and not separately. Second, when an industry sector has limited economic strength there are definite advantages in developing links or ties with an entity that has more economic power. Third, don't make a bad deal at the outset. Fourth, when concessions are made, don't allow them to remain fixed for too long a time period. Fifth, take care to ensure that best possible economic utilization is made of the resource. Sixth, ensure that long-range economic benefits and goals are given adequate priority alongside shorter-range objectives.

Conclusion

A number of questions arise out of the Saskatchewan experience with resource rent and taxation.

• How does government deal with "knowledge" issues?

First, it is essential to develop internal expertise. This requires a learning stage and process. A disciplined approach is critical since "a little knowledge is a dangerous thing." Second, management of and knowledge of production activities is essential but proved to be not as much of a problem as anticipated since it was possible to hire the necessary expertise. Third, sound financial management is crucial and requires dedicated people. Fourth, marketing strategy is critical. If the resource position is weak, there may be advantages in developing links or ties with stronger organizations. If the resource position is strong, it is likely a better strategy to develop in-house capability and management of affairs. Marketing Boards may be useful mechanisms in some jurisdictions but proved difficult to develop in Canada.

- **How can royalties be made sensitive to profitability, investment risk and the implications of extraction?**

First, a base royalty can be key; second, early recovery of capital costs may be warranted; third, if applied, a substantial portion of profitability should be captured after capital costs are recovered; fourth, an adequate knowledge base is essential; fifth, strict control of allowable costs in determining profitability is necessary; sixth, tough negotiators are needed; seventh, flexibility during negotiations is a must.

- **What is the role of state ownership in relation to resource rent policies in achieving public objectives?**

In Saskatchewan, public ownership played a significant role but not an exclusive role. There was a degree of public ownership in each of the resource areas discussed in this chapter ranging from a public monopoly in natural gas distribution to a public company in a totally competitive environment in oil operations. The Government was prepared, however, to use the prospect of public ownership as a bargaining lever in dealing with private owners in order to protect the public interest.

- **Is transfer pricing a problem in managing resources?**

First, experience has shown that multinational organizations with complex structures and diversified activities have many ways of transferring value to other jurisdictions in order to obtain best advantage. Pricing policies, sales commissions, management contracts, technical contracts, patent and process royalties and many other methods can be used to transfer value. Second, ownership of the resource and the resource development activity by itself is not enough. Skilled and dedicated people are essential. There are numerous examples throughout the world of resource industries being transferred to the public sector. Much of the management remained in place without an adequate evaluation of their capability and willingness to function in the public sector. Fortunately, in Saskatchewan, there was an adequate level of management and technical expertise "in-house" which helped to ensure satisfactory implementation of public policy.

- **What are the key requirements in bargaining with multinational resource companies?**

The essentials include a good knowledge base; skilled and tough negotiators; flexibility in negotiations; an adequate understanding of the benefits involved and the price paid for concessions on issues under negotiation;

74

insistence on full revelation of affairs by companies (Saskatchewan companies provided sharp contrasts in performance as already outlined).

Take note of Saskatchewan's range of experiences. With forests, the province had a very low rate of royalties; changes were attempted, and partially implemented; but the situation remained unresolved. In Oil and Natural Gas, there were adequate royalties pre 1973; new royalties were introduced on windfall profits post 1973; federal-provincial confrontation was a major factor; there were industry problems; royalties were revised, and compromises made. In uranium, old royalties were reasonable, but not much revenue was produced; new royalties were introduced before new production started; they captured windfalls, but were sensitive to the industry. In potash, there was a low rate of royalties; royalty increases were attempted; government — industry confrontation ensued; a nationalization policy was introduced; new royalties captured only part of economic rent.

Saskatchewan's experience demonstrates that when a government wants to change royalties and return on its resources, the process of change will likely be turbulent and controversial. The political and economic pressures on the government are a significant factor in determining its bargaining strength. The skill with which the government manages the situation is also of material importance.

On the other hand, the attitude of industry is of major importance. Saskatchewan provides some contrasts. Potash companies attempted to defeat the government totally in its attempts to change an unsatisfactory regime. Their attitude suggested that the companies regarded themselves on a par with sovereign governments. They were not prepared to recognize changes that were being demanded by society. They paid a heavy price for their failure. In contrast, uranium companies were cooperative and forthcoming. The outcome was a satisfactory arrangement for both government and industry. Oil and gas companies resisted changes but recognized that society, through its governments, ultimately decided the new regime. Things were complicated by the federal/provincial confrontations and oil companies still exerted considerable power by curtailing exploration activity in Canada.

Changes in resource arrangements and taxation must be viewed in the context of the macroeconomic and political situation. Flexibility and adaptability are necessary requisites for dealing with the variety of issues that arise. A basic rule should be, Keep it as simple as possible. Don't make a bad deal at the outset, is the best way to avoid trouble. It is essential that the necessary expertise is available for developing and implementing policies.

Three further observations are pertinent: first, economic rent has to be considered in the context of the total management of the resource and policies for the development of the resource. It cannot be considered in isolation. Second, there are indications that some multinational resource companies recognize that the rules have changed and that nation states are insisting on a higher level of return for the exploitation of resources than was the case in the past. Third, a major component of a comprehensive strategy for resource activities has to address the question of economic spin-offs. A first consideration is location of support activities for the resource industry to ensure maximum benefits to the jurisdiction concerned. Second is to ensure that processing, refining, and fabricating of the resource together with research and development is located advantageously.

Further changes in resource policies are a certainty. Saskatchewan's experience since 1982 demonstrates that those changes won't necessarily follow the pattern the Blakeney government developed. The right wing government elected in 1982 reversed many of the policy thrusts developed in the 1971–82 period. Since 1991, the NDP government has done little to reconstruct previous policies.

The setting for future changes is a turbulent world with growing demands for resources and uneven distribution of those resources. Enormous economic power in the hands of multinational and transnational resource companies, changing views within government of how to obtain best benefits from resource development, and changing views about the role of government in society contribute to a complex mix of factors. The outcome of the interaction among these forces cannot be predicted with certainty. What is certain is that clear leadership at the political level in setting goals and objectives is key to success.

REFERENCES

Church, A. 1982. "Economic Rent, Economic Efficiency and Distribution of Natural Resource Tax Burdens: Copper and Coal." *Natural Resources Journal* (July).

Energy, Mines, and Resources Canada. 1976. *An Energy Strategy for Canada: Policies for SelfReliance*. Ottawa: Government of Canada.

Wilkinson, B. 1978. *Trends in Canada's Mineral Trade Implications for an Industrial Strategy*. Kingston: Centre for Resource Studies, Queen's University.

Appendix I: The Concept of Resource Rent

Minerals are a gift of nature, whose exploitation yields a return beyond the necessary factor payments of labour and capital required for their discovery and extraction. The additional return is due to the limited quantity of mineral resources, thus minerals yield a **scarcity rent**. This rent element is the target of mineral taxation particularly when property rights are vested in society as a whole.

A **resource rent** is a kind of scarcity rent related to a depletable natural resource. Different resource rents arise because some deposits are richer, closer to markets or have lower extraction costs. A surplus beyond costs of exploitation will always accrue because developers have the option of postponement.

Decisions to extract resources depend on the expectations of cost and revenue and on the discount rate. As lower cost ores are depleted, the differences between costs and prices will widen. Exploitation of resources will be timed to take place when the current cost/price gap has grown sufficiently to offset any advantage from further delay.

In theory, if pure rent is requisitioned by government, it has the additional attraction of being "costless" in that it does not impose a penalty on output or allocation of resources. Thus a community, for reasons of both economic efficiency and natural justice, has the right to tax resource rents apart from "normal" taxes (corporate income and royalty taxes).

In markets subject to a high degree of seller concentration companies also earn **monopoly profits** that are well above normal profits because selling prices are noncompetitive. Producing countries through skilful tax policy should be able to appropriate monopoly returns.

Taxation of windfall profits, occurring when a group of nations collectively dominate supply and act in concert, provides another type of potential rent. For example, Canada, although not a member of OPEC, has taxed the windfall rents received by its domestic oil producers since the 1973 oil price increases. Windfall profits are returns higher than normal returns due to unusual circumstances.

A resource tax which is too severe will have a high payoff but will alter long-run decision making and will reduce the present value of mineral returns to the host country.

> It is no easy task to determine the economic rents for any one mine or oil pool, let alone to construct a standardized tax structure to appropriate all, or a majority of rents, on the one hand, and to avoid, on the other hand, dipping into the return required for the investment to take place and for new domestic exploration to continue (Wilkinson, 1978)

It is a widely held view that for different reasons of managerial efficiency (if the company views the tax as too high it will restrict output), the marginal tax rates must be kept well below the levels required to capture available rents.

Resource rent taxes are difficult to design due to technical, measurement, philosophical, and political problems.

Governments must use other vehicles in addition to taxation of economic rent to ensure that citizens receive a "fair" share of their resources. If there is a significant level of foreign ownership, nonresidents may be able to appropriate a large part of the available surplus.

4 Innovations in Agriculture

by Gerry Gartner

POLITICAL AND ECONOMIC SETTING

Historical Setting

From the beginning of settlement, the Canadian prairie presented a formidable challenge to those who chose to make it their home. Its harsh and variable climate tested the mettle of many a settler who was lured by the promise of "free land" and a new beginning, only to be confronted with drought, grasshoppers, disease, and the vagaries of unstable world grain markets. Externally, they faced powerful economic forces which dominated their markets for products and farm inputs. Nowhere did these circumstances exist in a more acute form than for those who settled in Saskatchewan.

Yet those who survived the early physical and economic perils built a vast network of communities clustered around railway delivery points. These centres became the focus of most economic and social activities for surrounding farm families.

Despite their independent-minded spirit, farm families and communities banded together through various forms of self-help initiatives as a source of greater power and strength with which to face adverse circumstances. That spirit of cooperation grew in intensity as the prairies became fully settled and the forces of exploitation reached new heights. Battle lines were drawn against the rate gouging of the railways and the monopolistic buying practices of the private grain trade.

The movement to develop countervailing market power, and to seek redress became known as the Agrarian Reform Movement — a movement which took a variety of forms depending on the nature of the measures required to rectify the disadvantaged position in which farm families found themselves. The CCF (Cooperative Commonwealth Federation) became the vanguard for political action to regulate the grain trade and establish central selling through the Canadian Wheat Board. Legislation was sought to protect farmers from the railways with the institution of the Crowsnest Rates, which were to give producers stable and favourable freight rates for the movement of grain to export position.

Political action to address issues beyond their direct control were complemented by initiatives of their own to achieve greater countervailing power in the marketplace and to introduce an element of competition into areas where little previously existed. Cooperative institutions such as the Saskatchewan Wheat Pool, were erected to replace and to compete with private elevator companies for the grain delivered by farmers to delivery points. Consumer retail cooperatives and machinery manufacturing cooperatives were formed to combat the unfair trading practices of the farm input sector.

The Postwar Period

After the crushing blows of drought and depression experienced during the "dirty thirties", the postwar period brought refreshing prosperity to rural Saskatchewan, albeit short-lived. Moreover, farmers had now to contend with other factors in addition to the chronic problems of unstable markets and production conditions.

As markets and growing conditions temporarily improved in the 1940s and 1950s, farmers were in a position to modernize and improve their living and working conditions by rapidly adopting new technology. Tractors replaced horsepower, and a vast network of roads, power, and telephones released farmers and communities from the confines of their local trading area. Moreover, farm mechanization replaced manual labour. It enabled a farm family to farm more land, thereby triggering consolidation of farms into fewer, larger units.

The process of mechanization and farm capitalization further exposed farmers to the physical and economic elements inherent in their lives and added to their vulnerability. In recognition of this grim reality, farmers called for new and varied forms of government action to stabilize their precarious situation. Saskatchewan and other prairie farmers road the roller coaster of price and income fluctuations throughout the 1950s and 1960s as best they could. Those who were able to diversify into livestock enterprises could stabilize their income to some extent, but even livestock markets experienced wild price swings within the Canadian market.

Farm organizations called loudly for strong federal measures to cushion producers from the vagaries of world markets, and to price farm products at parity with the good years of the 1920s. National governments of the day responded weakly to the pleas of farmers and their organizations with a special credit program administered by the Farm Credit Corporation and the Agricultural Stabilization Program. These measures proved inadequate in the minds of producers. Ad hoc acreage payments were made in the late 1950s by the Diefenbaker government to inject much needed funds into a cash-starved region.

In total, federal initiatives did little to address the scale of the farm income problem emerging out of the postwar period. With each cycle the income and price swings grew wider, and the toll on farmers increased proportionately.

Because of their limited jurisdiction and finances, provincial governments largely confined their assistance to extension education programs to improve

79

farm management practices, and to incentives to diversify production into other non-grain enterprises. Ironically, a side effect of this assistance (to the extent that it was successful) was improved farm productivity among individuals that collectively aggravated periodic market gluts and drove prices even further down than normally would have occurred. In addition, the programs accelerated the adoption of new technology and farm mechanization, thus placing farmers on an economic treadmill in which they were forced to produce more even to stay at their past income levels.

It was clear that the agricultural production policy of making "ten blades of grass grow where only one grew before" may have resolved a production problem at the individual farm level but was creating more than offsetting problems at the aggregate, industry level when their product faced an inelastic market demand. Besides worsening the "low income problem," it failed to address the more acute remaining problem of instability in production and farm prices.

Knowing that they could do little to stabilize and/or improve farm prices, provincial policy makers turned their attention to program solutions to protect producers against the uncertainties of prairie weather.

In Saskatchewan, crop insurance was the 1960s brainchild of Dr. Phil Thair, an Agricultural Economist at the University of Saskatchewan, a farm boy who grew up in the "thirties" on the Regina plains. Working with Jake Brown, the first economist in Saskatchewan's Department of Agriculture, they together formulated the first crop insurance program to protect farm income to the extent possible from year-to-year fluctuations in production caused by adverse weather conditions. The essential feature of their first innovative and pioneering effort was to build up a fund through premium contributions from farmers and governments during high yield years, and to pay out indemnities when yields fell below historical averages for the areas in which a farmer lived.

The successful launching of the Saskatchewan Crop Insurance Corporation provided important lessons to government and administrators for the future. First, programs targeted directly at chronic farm difficulties would be welcomed with open arms by the farmers. Second, direct involvement of farmers in tailoring the program to their personal needs was a further guarantee of success. In this case, producers from various farm regions were represented on the Board of Directors and were charged with policy responsibility. This close representation sensitized the program to general program needs of farmers, yet assured flexibility in terms of addressing the varying conditions throughout the provinces.

Pre-Election Farm Circumstances

Through the 1960s, the wide swings in production and prices for crops and livestock enterprises continued unabated. With increased mechanization and a lesser degree of self-sufficiency, the need for a constant and stable cash flow took on increased prominence in maintaining farm viability. Farm indebtedness rose sharply with each drop in economic fortunes. Moreover, many farmers were reaching retirement age and the desire to transfer ownership to younger generations became a priority. The prospects of a life filled with economic risks and hardships did not provide a satisfying future for the younger, educated rural generation, particularly when the urban economy offered an attractive alternative.

A severe blow to the farm community came with the supply glut and depressed prices of the late sixties and early seventies. Farmers searched desperately for solutions within the farm to survive. Some turned to livestock (mainly hogs and beef) to consume the vast supplies of cheap grain. Soon, an oversupply of these products drove their prices to rock bottom. Off-farm employment was sought by farmers and their spouses where skills matched local opportunities. Those in poultry originated the current supply management system by creating marketing boards to stabilize their product prices. Others turned to the only alternative available to them — abandonment of the farm and migration to urban centres to start a new life for their families.

The bitter attitude of farmers in this environment was heightened by the creation of the federal "LIFT" program. This program paid farmers to set aside land from production until more buoyant markets returned. This poorly conceived program went against the "grain" of prairie farmers whose mind-set was to produce crops. The job of the Federal Government and the Canadian Wheat Board was to sell their crops and to do so at a good price!

Again, the government of the day did nothing to intervene and to address the obvious needs of desperate farm and rural people. This was the rural setting which prevailed at the time of the 1971 election. The NDP read the situation well and campaigned on an aggressive interventionist platform which struck a responsive chord in the hearts and minds of the rural voter. The fury created by the insensitivity of the provincial government to their cause, when coupled with the folly of the federal "LIFT" program paved the way for a warm reception for any alternatives which might alleviate the desperate farm economic situation.

Another major irritant befell those young farmers wishing to expand small units, take over the home farm or re-enter the industry after accumulating savings while working in towns and cities. Vast amounts of foreign capital began flowing into the prairies. Farmland was an attractive haven to escape taxation abroad. Large blocks of farmland fell victim to foreign investors who wished only to preserve their capital. With luck, they would even make a capital gain as farmland prices rose in the "good times". The growing presence of foreign investors drove up land prices beyond the affordable levels of local farmers. Residents matching prices with foreign buyers soon found the error of their decision because returns did not justify the high purchase price. Moreover, farmers and their communities were deeply concerned that these absentee landlords contributed nothing to rural areas at the same time as more and more rural youth left the land to pursue other alternatives open to them.

The NDP Agricultural Election Program of 1971

The NDP responded to the acute farm situation with a range of agricultural programs designed to tackle the problems of low and unstable farm incomes, intergenerational transfer and land tenure. The agricultural and rural component of their campaign platform was a potent populist response developed by party members with a deep and abiding concern for preserving the family farm and the rural way of life. It was based on the premise that adjustment to new production methods and modern transportation and communication systems could be made a positive force in strengthening the economic and social fabric of rural Saskatchewan.

The NDP election victory of 1971 represented a ringing endorsement of their election platform in general, and their array of interventionist agricultural programs in particular. The time had come to work their full impact on the farm scene.

The four-year time frame was extremely restrictive for implementing a program complement of such massive dimensions. There were no historical models to follow, nor was there an administrative base on which to build. Besides, the high profile afforded these programs during the election raised expectations to high and often unrealistic levels.

The most significant feature of this period was the volatile nature of the political mood of farmers which shifted rapidly with the economic situation of the day. Such was the case especially with the rural electorate. With the coming of "good times" shortly after arrival in office, broad acceptance of radical solutions to farm problem began to weaken as a more conservative, individualistic attitude accompanied improved grain sales and prices. The implications of this phenomenon were most noteworthy respecting the public acceptance of the Land Bank Program, the flagship of agricultural programs put forward during the 1971 election.

LAND BANK PROGRAM
— STATE INTERVENTION INTO THE LAND MARKET

The Land Bank Program was the most bold and innovative component of the program package to be implemented during the first term of the new government. It was charged with the formidable tasks of arresting the trend to farm consolidation, strengthening submarginal farms, and fostering intergenerational farm transfers. With an agricultural land base of over 65 million acres (over 26.3 million hectares) and some 80,000 farmers, this would prove to be a daunting administrative and financial task. Never before in the history of Canadian agriculture had a provincial government so directly intervened in the allocation and exchange of land as a means of achieving its objectives.

Throughout its life, the program and the government were haunted by what might be called a schizophrenic attitude towards land tenure by the prairie farmer. On the one hand, farmers possessed a burning desire to own land as part of their individualistic character. On the other hand, particularly during desperate economic times, they expected government action to "right all the wrongs" which befell them, not recognizing that the drive to own their land may be inconsistent with a strategy to maintain their farm viability. In their minds, leasing of land was only a means to an end — that being to own all the land they farmed. The Land Bank Program tried to accommodate this unique mindset in program formulation. Only to a limited degree were they successful.

Formative Years

The new government recognized well the political sensitivities and administrative hurdles it had to overcome in order to successfully implement a program of this magnitude in the sensitive area of land tenure. The most novel departure from the normal administrative structure for government programs came with the establishment of the Land Bank Commission. The Commission consisted of a small group, appointed by Order-in-Council not only to formulate detailed operational policies but also to administer the various program elements. Gib Wesson, a man with many years' experience in crown land administration with the Saskatchewan Department of Agriculture, was appointed Chief Commissioner. They were a unique blend of the usual Board of Directors and public administrators responsible directly to the Minister of Agriculture. The rationale for such a structure was to facilitate high level policy decisions in rapid order, and to tightly integrate policy formulation with implementation in an area that required a high degree of political sensitivity.

The Commission rapidly recruited and established a field staff of 12 counsellors to deliver the program which, by its nature, required direct contact with farm clients.

The basic strategy of the Commission in making its contribution to stabilizing rural population was to create the opportunity for farm people, who might not otherwise have a chance, to establish and operate viable farms. The major vehicles for expediting this strategy consisted of purchasing land from older generation farmers or absentee owners who wished to sell — thus building a "bank" of land to reallocate on a discretionary basis; leasing purchased land to new and existing farmers on small marginal units at favourable rates with the option to buy when farm income circumstances permitted; and facilitating the transfer of land between generations within a family through purchase and leaseback of all or part of the unit.

Armed with a start-up budget of some $20 million the Commission set about rapidly developing appraisal procedures, lease and purchase policies, eligibility criteria and counselling services for farm families involved in the program. Sights were set on appraising 1,000 farms per year and assisting 700 vendors annually. By the end of 1973–74, the commission's objective was to have an effect on about 1.5 per cent of the province's farms.

Program Innovations

Needless to say, the Commission would have fallen well short of its lofty targets if it had not been for the introduction of another innovative arrangement for implementing its program. This initiative consisted of leveraging the wide range of extension, financial and land administrative services from the Department of Agriculture. Regionalization of its extension services and a broadening of its capability in the area of farm financial management greatly eased the workload and multiplied the capacity of the Land Bank Counsellors whose job it was to provide a comprehensive range of services on a farm-by-farm basis.

Where farm development work required financing of livestock enterprises to make viable those farms on submarginal land, the newly established Farmstart Program was integrated into the formulation of viable farm development plans for younger or beginning farmers. This flexible farm credit program, in addition to complementing the effort of the Canadian Land Bank Commission, added impetus to the government's efforts to diversify the production base of rural Saskatchewan.

The horizontal knitting together of diverse agency and departmental expertise became central to the successful implementation of the Land Bank program. Although not without its difficulties at the outset, these linkages strengthened as the program became established. Administrations in sister agencies made the adjustment from the traditional independent extension model to one of a team approach which brought together various technical capabilities to achieve a common purpose.

A further innovative aspect of the Land Bank program was found in how the program would finance its activities. It was clear at the outset that the program would require massive amounts of budgetary expenditures if it was to have a significant impact on farm revitalization and population retention. In the interests of keeping the financial outlays within manageable proportions, the concept of capital recycling was established as the basis for financing the program. The basic idea was first to "grubstake" the Commission with start-up capital. Then, once it had established its initial "bank" of land, the revenue received from the resale and/or leasing of that land would serve as the capital base for its next round of land purchases. It was hoped that a balance would be struck between land purchases and revenues received to enable the program to become self-financing.

Administrative and Political Report Card

From a public administration standpoint, the Land Bank program scored high in terms of its effectiveness in marshalling a massive delivery system throughout a vast geographical area and client population. Caseload was in the thousands and many a young farmer would not be actively producing if it had not been for the "leg-up" provided by the Land Bank program.

However, from the standpoint of financial administration, its revolving fund concept did not materialize as planned, for a number of reasons. First, the program was positioned in a time of rapidly rising land prices driven by improved market and production conditions for grains and oilseeds. Competition with larger and well established farmers for available land was intense, and attractive prices had to be paid particularly for small parcels.

Second, leaseback terms were extremely favourable and biased the decision making of farm clients in favour of continuing to rent rather than purchase. In addition, the cash flow generated was slow to increase among most newly established farmers, and was inadequate in many cases to pay off land debt and provide a living at the same time.

As a consequence, the Land Bank capital fund was in a continuous shortfall or deficit position. This created a frustrating situation for central financial agencies who were called on annually to provide larger and larger amounts of funds to maintain the program momentum with little prospect of seeing the capital returned.

The program scored high in terms of contributing to farm family retention and stabilizing rural population. Many hundreds of younger generation farm families would have long left the farm if it was not for the comprehensive and ample assistance of the Land Bank. However, within the mix of young farmers assisted, the composition was less than what was desired. The program fell short of its objective to establish new farmers on totally new operating units. The bulk of those helped were beginning farmers on small or submarginal units who needed a larger land base or an additional enterprise in order to be viable. The related category that benefitted most from the program were those who relied on the Land Bank to facilitate the transfer of the farm within the family.

From a political standpoint, the Land Bank became a liability particularly during the later terms in office. Accusations of "state farming" and "making tenants of farmers" had always haunted the program. These criticisms grew with the years as the political mood of farmers shifted to the right. Even though the Land Bank attempted to "follow" the land market in its purchase activities it was accused of "leading" the market and pricing land beyond the reach of competing, established farmers.

Despite the fact that the program was active in less than one percent of the available land, the perception was created that the province would soon have a state owned and operated farm sector. The province's total agricultural base is more than 65 million acres (26.3 million hectares). Those perpetrating this myth failed to point out that the province had for many years administered over 8 million acres (3.2 million hectares) of crown land on a continuous basis.

Like the ongoing crown land program, lease and sale of land was an inherently difficult exercise, despite the development of detailed allocation criteria designed to provide benefits to those in greatest "need". Because the amount of available land was fixed, for every parcel available there were up to 30 applicants who felt their need was greater than others. The sheer arithmetic fall-out from the allocation process in itself became a major political liability, defensible as it was (one farmer was happy while 29 others were unhappy!).

In its final years the program was downplayed on the political scene by the government despite the fact that its administrative effectiveness improved with time. With the change in government, the program was dismantled and every attempt was made to sell its land inventory to lessees but with little success. Administration of the program was folded into the Agriculture Department's Lands Branch as part of its ongoing responsibility to administer the province's crown land program.

Many another provincial government viewed the bold and creative initiative in Saskatchewan with mixed emotions. They were tempted by the potential impact it could have on retaining farm families and stabilizing rural population. Provinces such as Manitoba and Alberta were experiencing very much the same economic circumstances as Saskatchewan. However, they shied away from taking the Land Bank approach because of the massive financial implications of administering a program with any degree of effectiveness. An even more significant factor in their hesitancy was the recognized political stigma attached to the program's approach to achieving its objectives.

Alternatively, governments such as Manitoba later chose a more subtle but less effective means of fostering intergenerational transfer and young farmer retention by establishing a special program within its farm credit agency. Most other provinces have adopted the Manitoba model, recognizing that its administrative effectiveness may be less, but more manageable in terms of the political profile of its efforts. Its approach is to act as the financial intermediary to facilitate the financial transaction between the buyer and seller of farms. In some cases a leaseback is part of the transaction if the buyer has insufficient equity to immediately amortize the outstanding debt.

The more passive role in achieving the smooth intergenerational transfer of farms has now received wide acceptance among provincial lending agencies. In addition, the federal Farm Credit Corporation has recently established a vendor mortgage program with leaseback provisions as a regular feature of its farm lending operations.

FARM LAND OWNERSHIP PROGRAM

The Blakeney government knew from the outset that it was on much firmer political ground when it came to restricting the ownership of farm land by foreign owners. The growing activity of American, and then European interests to acquire farmland raised a cry from every community affected. Failure by the previous administration to act provided a vacuum for the new government to enter with another bold initiative.

The *Saskatchewan Farm Land Ownership Act* sharply restricted the amount of land that foreign interests could own in the province, unless the individual was prepared to emigrate and actively farm as a member of the community. Amendments were made to the Act over time and to close off loopholes as real estate interests and foreign buyers tried to skirt the law. Minimum acres allowable were reduced over time and further restrictions were placed on the definition of "foreign ownership".

The program was administered by a very small staff complement, guided by a Board of Directors (mainly farmers) and under the able chairmanship of Jake Brown — by now an Agricultural Economics professor at the University of Saskatchewan. Their work involved the onerous task of vetting all potential land transactions within the province, developing qualification criteria and rejecting those who failed to meet the eligibility criteria established under the Act. It meant a close working relationship with provincial land titles offices through which all title transfer applications (domestic and foreign) had to come for processing.

Although the program was well received on the home front, it encountered many obstacles and challenges externally. First, this new and unusual initiative ran headlong into a constitutional dispute with the federal government. Whose authority would prevail — provincial authority respecting property rights, or federal authority respecting citizenship? Finally, after much debate and court action, the provincial authority was determined to be preeminent.

Some support for the program declined when the province introduced further restrictions to improve its effectiveness. The amendment broadened the definition of foreign ownership to include Canadians outside the province who owned land in the province but who no longer actively farmed, and those wishing to acquire land but not actively farming it themselves. The former category in particular raised the wrath of those related to the absentee Canadians who loudly chastised the government for its parochial stance.

The public demand to eradicate this major irritant to farm viability endured through years of the Blakeney government. The program's administrators were under constant pressure to ease the restrictions of the program. Not only did they hold the line, but they continued to fine-tune the program, including the working out of procedures in cooperation with Canadian Immigration officials for the processing of legitimate applicants who had serious intentions of migrating and taking up residence on Saskatchewan farms.

The program scored well in achieving its basic purpose — taking the pressure off the farmland market from an external source so that younger farmers could more fairly compete for available land. Its most notable success was to eliminate extremely high prices in districts where large land units were targets of foreign investors.

The Saskatchewan and similar Prince Edward Island actions in managing the foreign ownership issue became the foundation for similar thrusts in Manitoba and Alberta. Fortunately for them, much of the work to gain public and legal acceptance had been accomplished through the Saskatchewan experience. Equally important was the fact that the bulk of the administrative procedures and "spade work" was in place, ready for others to emulate.

MARKETING BOARDS AND COMMISSIONS
— PRODUCER POWER IN THE MARKET PLACE

Early in the first term of office, the Saskatchewan Department of Agriculture was reorganized to bring extension staff into closer contact with their farm clientele through massive regionalization of the service.

Less visible, but of even greater significance was the increased priority placed on market development and restructuring. Young, aggressive professionals were recruited to begin the task of assisting the various commodity groups identify market opportunities, and to organize their efforts in putting forward effective marketing thrusts. These marketing specialists acted as catalysts by mobilizing commodity groups and private sector interests to seek out markets not normally pursued on their own.

Hog Marketing and Stabilization

One aspect of this overall drive to enhance producer marketing initiatives was to establish central desk selling agencies to achieve increased bargaining power for producers in the market for their produce. Rather than having individual farmers sell their products and compete separately in the market with a few buyers, the central desk selling agency acted as the sole negotiator and seller on their behalf.

The Saskatchewan Hog Marketing Commission was a prime example of government and producer cooperation to establish countervailing power — long overdue in the minds of producers who, for years, had struggled as "price takers" to survive the wild price and production cycles that long characterized their industry.

In the early 1970s the time was ripe for radical action to respond to the long-standing grievances of farmers when placed at the mercy of a few buyers for their produce. A vote of producers gave overwhelming support to the Commission option — central desk selling with no supply management power. Producers chose this option because they saw export opportunities for their pork and decided not to restrict available product when neighbouring provinces chose to do otherwise.

Following the favourable vote, a producer Board of Directors was elected to hire a General Manager and to start building the structure of the marketing concept. Jim Morris was hired out of the Department of

Agriculture as the new General Manager — a young and aggressive marketing specialist. Together with Harry Jae-Elder, the Commission Chairman they worked intensively to develop the marketing policies and handling arrangements for marketing Saskatchewan hogs through the new agency.

The Commission's formation was vigorously opposed by local and regional meat packing plants who saw their favourable market position eroded. Threats and product boycotts were common practice during the formative years as part of the strategy to undermine the initiatives of the Commission. Fortunately, parallel action was taken in neighbouring provinces. By coordinating their marketing strategies the agencies were successful in preventing buyers from playing one group of producers off against the other.

Price negotiations and delivery policy remained a contentious issue. After much trial and error, the Commission established a basic formula pricing system that closely tracked large markets, such as Winnipeg and Toronto, and priced their product accordingly, with an adjustment for the transportation differentials between markets. This pricing policy kept local prices in line with competitive alternatives. In turn, it was a fair system for packing plants who had to face neighbouring firms in the Canadian market for fresh and processed pork products.

Local assembly points were constructed throughout the province to enable hogs from a wide geographical area to converge and be marshalled to their final destination by truck transport. Producers were paid by the Commission who in turn received payment from the buyers. Soon after its establishment producers were paid on a quality index basis which provided a premium for better quality carcasses. Compared to the old live-weight system, producers viewed this arrangement as a vast improvement in that it also eliminated a major grievance against packers — that of downgrading the carcass quality of animals sold.

The day-to-day administrative costs of the Commission were financed by a small check off on each hog sold through the Commission. Part of this levy was also used to finance the market promotion activities of the Commission.

Having firmly established itself as a permanent fixture in the hog marketing landscape, the Commission turned its attention to its other mandate — market development. The Commission looked to the vast Pacific rim as the opportunity to broaden its market and production base. Unfortunately, penetration of Asian markets proved more difficult than first anticipated. The region was the stronghold of U.S.A. and Danish marketing interests who were not prepared to give way without a fight. While Canadian hogs were much preferred for their quality, the Commission was not able to obtain prices that made the venture viable over the long-term.

After several unsuccessful attempts to establish a firm foothold in international markets, the Commission turned its attention to a major problem within the industry — income instability. The Commission knew it had limited capacity to achieve major price increases to enhance producer returns. They were part of a national market and prices could not exceed transportation costs for any length of time before imports from other regions would undercut their bargaining position.

With limits to their price bargaining power, the Commission searched for new and imaginative means of stabilizing farm income. Why not apply the insurance principle used to stabilize income due to crop hazards to hog production? That question was soon to be answered.

The Commission and provincial government together constructed what was to be the first farm income stabilization program designed around the insurance principle. Producers welcomed the new initiative because it finally gave them the level of income protection they required to stay in business while riding the swings of the market. Producers quickly opted for the new provincial scheme and abandoned the meagre federal stabilization program that responded slowly and inadequately to their immediate needs brought on by rapidly changing market conditions.

Unlike the national program which was based on a five-year running average of costs and prices, the new Saskatchewan Hog Assured Returns Program (SHARP) was a cost-based initiative that guaranteed producers returns on their variable costs plus a significant return to fixed costs.

The plan was administered by the Commission and financed by producer premiums and matching government contributions. The support level was compared quarterly with the average market price for hogs marketed during that period. If prices fell below the support price, a payout was made to producers for the hogs marketed during the quarter in question. If the price was above the support level, premiums accumulated in the insurance fund to be drawn on in future, less favourable periods.

After several years of observing the successful operation of the SHARP program, producers in other provinces lobbied vigorously for a plan of their own. Reluctantly, the neighbouring province of Alberta, then Manitoba came forward with similar schemes modelled on the insurance principle.

Permanent plans replaced ad hoc emergency assistance to bail out hog producers in other provinces. By the mid 1980s all provinces with significant hog production levels had insurance programs in place structured basically along the lines of the SHARP program. It ultimately became the model for reformulating the federal stabilization program and the melding of provincial and federal schemes into a national tripartite program that provides vastly improved income protection to the broad base of Canadian producers.

Beef Marketing and Stabilization

Bolstered by the success achieved in meeting the stability needs of hog producers, the government turned its attention to applying the same marketing and stabilization measures to beef production. Those who remembered the bitter struggle to establish a beef marketing board in the 1950s approached the new challenge with some trepidation. This earlier attempt to establish central desk selling was defeated by the charge led by the Saskatchewan Cattleman's Association. However the new government had the support of smaller mixed farming groups such as the Saskatchewan Cow-Calf Association and the National Farmers Union. To gain broad producer support, the government tied the marketing and stabilization program together as a package.

After considerable negotiation and consultation, the Saskatchewan Beef Commission was established in 1980. The Saskatchewan Cattleman's Association remained philosophically opposed to the central desk selling powers of the Commission but welcomed the stabilization component of the government offer.

The program gained wide acceptance because of its attractive stabilization features. Producers signed on and agreed to market their cattle through the Commission in order to gain the income protection afforded by the stabilization scheme whether or not they were supporters of central desk selling.

The Beef Commission was administered and structured very much along the lines of the Hog Commission. The main difference between the two was that the Beef Commission did not have the mandate to market all cattle sold in the province. (The government knew its limits before incurring the wrath of right wing elements in the industry!) As a result, it could not point to any price enhancing effect of its power in the market place. Its appeal rested almost totally on its attractive stabilization scheme. This in itself had the benefit, like hogs, of keeping producers viable in times of weak prices, thus playing its full role in maintaining a solid livestock base in the province.

With the change in government, the option to sell in the open market was added as an alternative for those who wanted to participate in the program, yet wanted to market their cattle on their own account.

The hog and beef marketing initiatives can be labelled a success in their own right. Finally, after so many years of agitation and action, producers had developed and implemented programs directly tailored to meet their long standing needs.

FARMSTART — CREATIVE FARM FINANCING

The Saskatchewan venture into farm financing was driven by two imperatives. First, traditional lending programs of the federal Farm Credit Corporation were too land-based and rigid repayment schedules failed to reflect the cyclical nature of farm income and the related ability to service debt. Despite continued pressure to increase their flexibility, the federal agency was slow to adjust their lending policies to foster diversification. The second and most compelling reason for creating Farmstart was to complement the efforts of the Land Bank program, whose clients were young, beginning farmers with a limited land base to serve as collateral for any borrowing requirements.

In close parallel with the work involving the formation of the Land Bank program, Agriculture departmental staff and central agencies developed the program framework that would meet the financial needs of young and beginning farmers, whether they be Land Bank clients, or those who wished to further develop their farms through livestock and other means which did not require a land base.

By filling the gap left by other public (and private) lending institutions, program architects fully realized they were putting the government at substantial risk, for two reasons. First, the client group possessed little equity, even in land. If default occurred, there was only the salvage value of livestock and/or machinery to repossess. Second, due to limited experience of most potential clients, the productive potential of the new producers was questionable.

To safeguard against these inherent risks, a number of important steps were taken. In terms of the program design, flexible repayment terms were established as the central feature of the lending program. For instance, repayment of principal did not start on livestock loans until the first offspring were marketed; the amount of repayment could be tied to market prices as a measure of the farmer's ability to pay.

A further step to minimize the risk inherent with this farm group was to appoint farmers with superior management ability to the Farmstart Board of Directors. Chaired by John Gronsdahl, a former Farm Management Specialist with the Department and now farming in southern Saskatchewan, the Board was responsible for not only assessing the financial viability of various loan proposals, but also to determine the management capability of the client. Where management and skill requirements needed to be enhanced, the loan was made conditional on receiving training or assistance from Departmental extension specialists now strategically located throughout the province.

At the administrative level, Farmstart loan officers were deployed throughout the province as part of the decentralization strategy of the Agriculture ministry. This overall deployment saw Land Bank, Farmstart, and extension staff working out of the same offices, and linking together to serve the differing needs of common clientele. Through this interdependent structure, Farmstart loan officers were first able to initiate loan proposals in a focused manner, monitor loan performance, and bring other resources in conjunction with the Land Bank staff if client viability was at risk.

The Farmstart program was thus launched from a firm foundation of sound program design and effective administrative features to safeguard against undue risk to the government. The program filled a critical void in the farm lending area in terms of enabling the government to meet effectively its objectives respecting the Land Bank program, but also more broadly in terms of the general diversification of the province's production base.

The program continues today through two subsequent administrations. Over almost two decades, thousands of young and beginning farmers have thrived because of the new and flexible lending policies of Farmstart. Its innovative approaches to farm lending did not go unnoticed by both private and other public lending institutions within and outside the province. Today flexible repayment terms sensitive to enterprise production characteristics is commonplace. Most significantly, the Farm Credit Corporation has finally shifted away from its traditional dependence on land as the basis for loan security to one that includes all farm assets. By so doing it no longer discourages diversification and has eased the pressure on provincial lending agencies for higher risk loans associated with diversification.

SASK TRADING CORPORATION

The Saskatchewan Trading Corporation was added to the family of Crown corporations in 1975. Its mandate was to act as a commercial vehicle to actively buy and sell local products into international markets on its own account, or to serve as an export agent for groups of producers, processors and manufacturers who wished to pool their individual efforts to meet a world market demand.

In the course of pursuing export opportunities, Industry and Commerce as well as Agriculture staff were often frustrated in the early 1970s with the lack of ability to expedite actual sales contracts in markets for certain products where an obvious demand existed. Loosely organized production groups often recognized these export opportunities, but for various reasons were not prepared to make the quantum leap from serving a local or regional market to the high risks of international markets. Moreover, their associations did not see commercial trading as part of their responsibility, nor did they have the staff capability or experience to carry out this function effectively.

After much Cabinet discussion, and even more trepidation on the part of the Crown Investments Corporation, the Trading Corporation was launched with a "grubstake" of $100,000 and a staff of five seconded from Agriculture and from Industry and Commerce. The Board of Directors consisted of five businessmen who had considerable experience in export marketing, particularly in those areas where potential opportunities were foreseen by departmental marketing staff — breeding stock, farm machinery, specialty crops and seed.

During its early years of operation, the Corporation incurred only small losses until its cash flow was strengthened by its gradual build-up of sales, largely in the market for breeding stock. Its early attempts at direct buying and selling on its own account met with only limited success, and in a few years was discontinued. However, the Corporation was more successful in its role as agent for commodity groups such as cattle breeders, where many large volume sales were negotiated and expedited by the Corporation.

93

The revenue base and sphere of activity was broadened in the late 1970s when the Corporation captured a series of CIDA contracts which it staffed and managed on a fee-for-service basis. Tied to these projects was often the opportunity to link the sale of Saskatchewan-grown or manufactured goods. During this latter period the Corporation underwent a name change to AgDevCo, to more properly reflect its area of emphasis and the elimination of its direct trading activity.

Under the Devine administration, AgDevCo continued to play a prominent role as a contractor with CIDA for international development, expanding into turnkey projects utilizing local expertise and manufacturing technology. Its role as a commission and sales agency declined as producer and manufacturing groups and individuals gained increased confidence and took on more direct responsibility for export sales. Finally, in the last years of the Devine government, AgDevCo was totally privatized by sale to local interests who were involved in many of the CIDA ventures.

The success of this pioneering venture into international markets must be measured by more than the profitability of its balance sheet, albeit very positive over its corporate life. Its true success lay in the catalytic role it played to lead private sector interests into the treacherous waters of international markets, and enabled them to expand their production and market base.

FARM LAB — FARMERS LEARNING FROM FARMERS

The process of developing and applying new production technology to prairie agriculture went through a number of evolutionary phases throughout its history. Beginning with the experimental farm service, the federal government took on the role of crop and animal research. Early work began on developing crop varieties that were adaptable to the harsh prairie climate, along with the testing of different tillage practices to improve crop yields and control weeds. Geography and manpower severely limited the effectiveness in mustering any extension effort, in addition to their basic research responsibility. Colleges of Agriculture also undertook research to supplement that of the federal government in addition to their central teaching role.

Provincial governments, with their constitutional authority in education, soon developed extension services in their agriculture departments to bridge the gap between basic research at the federal government and university levels, and the educational needs of farmers. This rural educational service expanded rapidly in the postwar period at a time when technology became available in a variety of forms, and in great abundance. With new production tools at their disposal, the need for educational services to learn their application became more important.

The United States extension model was widely adopted by most provincial agriculture departments, including Saskatchewan. This educational approach consisted basically of a one-direction, top-down process in which the extension specialists attempted to inform farmers how to use the latest in production technology. With the advent of the new government in 1971, the Saskatchewan Department of Agriculture underwent a major restructuring. One very decentralized division was dedicated to enhancing and broadening the extension services throughout the province. The prime objective was to increase the proximity of extension personnel to local farmers and the region, thereby improving the sensitivity and flexibility of their programs to better suit the unique needs of various districts.

The management of the vast amount of new technology had become a complex task for both the farmer and extension people alike. The general knowledge and skills of the Agricultural Representatives had to be supplemented by specialists in various fields. Their special knowledge in various aspects of farm production and management was called upon to assist in communicating highly technical information.

The old extension model, even in its modern form, had its shortcomings. A "credibility gap" still existed between the farmers on the land and the university and federal researchers. Even though the provincial extension services had bridged this gap to some extent, farmers were still frustrated by instances of the lack of application of research findings to the particular needs of their locality. Moreover, the farm population by now was well-educated and innovative in their own right as part of their adaptive heritage. Frequently and loudly, they questioned the program efforts and their effectiveness, often pointing to experiments of their own which questioned "scientific" claims.

A broad concern by all was the chronic deterioration of the soil's natural productivity due to the loss of organic matter. Periodic drought and erosion was taking its toll on the production capacity of a once rich soil. By the late 1970s more and more farmers and researchers were calling into question the merits of strongly held views about traditional tillage practices. None was more vocal than Dr. Don Rennie, head of the Soil Science Department at the University of Saskatchewan. The target of his criticism was the practise of summer fallowing — leaving fields idle supposedly to control weeds and conserve moisture.

Soon this scepticism spread throughout the farm and research communities. With it came a call for expanded research and extension efforts to evaluate old and new production practices focused largely at soil and moisture conservation. Unfortunately, the groundswell of agitation for increased research and extensive efforts coincided with the latter years of the administration when public expenditures, including university research funding, were being sharply constrained. New and creative methods had to be found to address the substantive need for enhanced applied research along with improved evaluation techniques at the farm level.

The government response came in the form of the Farm Lab Program — a program designed to achieve a new level of cooperation between the research, extension and farm communities. The essence of the program was a two-way flow of information and communication — a drastic shift in approach compared to the old extension model.

The new scheme was the brainchild of Gordon MacMurchy, a former Minister of Education and Municipal Affairs, and then Minister of Agriculture. MacMurchy held a deep and abiding faith in farmers' ability to find solutions to their problems, and held high regard for their innovative approach to problem solving. He applied that capability to the creation of a unique form of community college while Education Minister. That program featured a strong element of self-help and learning from the skills of fellow community people. This same approach was applied to the problem at hand. MacMurchy could often be heard to say, "farmers are researchers and experimenters in their own right — maybe the scientists can learn something from them as well."

At the farm level, Farm Lab Associations were organized around producers in districts with similar production problems. Their task was to prioritize production issues and to select those requiring greatest attention. At the university level, a special long-term funding arrangement was negotiated with the College of Agriculture. Approximately 50 per cent of new funds were earmarked to conduct field-scale experiments with Farm Lab associations, with the balance devoted to research staffing and related applied research.

Dr. George Lee was appointed to coordinate the university components of the program — appointing specially dedicated research staff and assigning them to respective Farm Lab groups to design and implement scientific investigation within the districts on actual farms. Together with the farmers involved, a collaborative effort and learning experience was created in a form and magnitude never seen before.

The early success of the program throughout the province did not go unnoticed by Agriculture Canada researchers. This highly capable group was starved for funds due to federal austerity measures, so they sought out opportunities for linking their programs with local initiatives. Where successful, they gained funding in return for more closely tying their efforts and skills to relevant problem solving at the farm level.

At its peak in the early 1980s the Farm Lab program consisted of 12 Associations successfully operating a variety of on-farm experiments and demonstrations geared to the specific needs of farmers in their community.

The Farm Lab program was the last of the innovative programming efforts of the era. The program proved to be a "win-win" situation in every respect in that: it responded directly and effectively to farm production needs; it created a structure that marshalled the resources of the farmer, the extension service and the researcher in a manner that had the capacity to develop solutions to real farm needs; and it provided a solution to the research funding problem by closely earmarking funds for specific use by university departments.

Most importantly, it created in the minds of those involved a new sense of relevance and purpose as they addressed production challenges throughout rural Saskatchewan.

Although the program underwent a name change with the new government of 1982, its structure and purpose remained intact. Neighbouring provinces moved to adopt the Farm Lab model to achieve greater effectiveness of their own extension efforts, but in a less dramatic and more gradual way.

A by-product of this evolution to a new extension model was to restore the credibility of agricultural researchers and extension personnel in the minds of farmers. Mutual respect for each other's special talents and complementary ability was greatly enhanced by the process which bound them closely together to solve various production problems.

CONCLUSION

This chapter has described a few of the many agricultural innovations from the 1971–1982 period. Time and space do not permit a full presentation of all efforts to introduce new approaches to program delivery in the agriculture area.

Its purpose is to demonstrate the manner in which change was developed and introduced to achieve greater program effectiveness in addressing the needs of the farm community. All possessed a strong element of bold action and risk-taking as the government ventured into untested areas of public involvement.

The political side effects were mixed. Predictably, initiatives of a new venture brought the usual negative public reaction, particularly from those with vested interests in the status quo. After the difficult "run-in" period, political endorsement can be closely correlated with the proper positioning and timing of various initiatives. The Land Bank and farm ownership programs were prime examples in this regard.

REFERENCES

Government of Saskatchewan. 1972–82. Department of Agriculture. *Annual Reports.*

Government of Saskatchewan. 1973–82. Saskatchewan Land Bank Commission. *Annual Reports.*

Government of Saskatchewan. 1974–82. Saskatchewan Farmstart Program. *Annual Reports.*

Government of Saskatchewan. 1974–82. Saskatchewan Hog Marketing Board. *Annual Reports.*

Government of Saskatchewan. 1981–82. Saskatchewan Beef Marketing and Stabilization Board. *Annual Reports.*

Section III

Innovations with a Social Justice Focus

5 Indian and Native Policy in Southern Saskatchewan

by Jerry Hammersmith and Bob Hauk

For the Blakeney government, one of the fundamental differences between Indian and native policy development in southern Saskatchewan, where aboriginal people were a minority, and northern Saskatchewan, where they were the majority, was simply that in the South the government was not pro-actively attempting to achieve an ambitious agenda. Instead, it was largely responding to strong Indian and native agendas.

During the 1970s, aboriginal Canadians began to exercise the levers of political power for the first time. Mobilized by the Trudeau government's 1969 White Paper, Indian leaders across Canada began to focus on fundamental political and economic issues. On many of these issues, the Indian leadership found a relatively sympathetic non-Indian public. It was thus possible to make considerable progress in convincing at least some Canadian political leaders of the need for special and unique approaches to Indian policy.

This chapter will illustrate the progress of the aboriginal leadership in Saskatchewan in convincing the provincial government to move forward in two key areas: education and land entitlements. Three major themes will emerge through the analysis. One theme revolves around the element of expectations. It will be argued that government and public expectations for innovation and accomplishment in aboriginal policy were not high, at least at the beginning of the Blakeney administration. As a consequence, the accomplishments of the administration are magnified when set against these modest expectations. This theme becomes all the more clear when compared to the high expectations for northern policy.

A second theme is who leads in the policy development process. In northern Saskatchewan, government led the process of trying to develop new policies and programs and often received a negative reaction from stakeholders who felt inadequately involved. By contrast, it will be argued in this chapter that aboriginal leaders set the agenda for government with

101

respect to issues south of the Northern Administration District. The strong leadership role played by Indian and Metis organizations and leaders, together with a sympathetic provincial administration resulted in the development of a number of innovative policies and programs.

This second theme of who sets the policy agenda can be expanded into some reflections about the role of government-Indian organization partnerships in creating innovative policy. In Saskatchewan, a very strong partnership existed between the provincial government and the Federation of Saskatchewan Indians, and innovative policy was created through this alliance. Relations between the Province and the Metis Society of Saskatchewan, however, were characterized by confrontation and no partnership ever developed between the two organizations. Policy for Metis and Non-status Indians was therefore made in an incremental way: no policy innovations have been found which resulted from this testy, adversarial relationship.

The Political Climate for Indian and Aboriginal Issues

The late 1960s and early 1970s were a time of unique political opportunity for aboriginal people. A coincidence of legal cases, policy issues and developments, public attitudes and economic developments with potentially significant impact on Indian communities resulted in unprecedented mobilization of Indian organizations. For the first time, Indian organizations found that they could wrest significant concessions from the Federal Government. A brief description of how this unique political climate evolved is essential as a foundation for this chapter.

Until World War II, Canadian policy toward Indians was ruled by the assumptions which had prevailed during the colonial and treaty settlement periods: Indian culture was considered morally and economically inferior to Euro-Canadian culture and Indian numbers were declining. The biggest favour the dominant culture felt it could provide the subordinate culture was to assimilate it as quickly and completely as possible. The events of World War II began to undermine these assumptions. Canadians began to notice that they were fighting a war against institutionalized racism and barbarity which had at its foundation the same kinds of assumptions about the moral inferiority of groupings of people based on race which underlay our policy toward Indians. Moreover, once again Canadian Indians had volunteered for service overseas in numbers far exceeding their proportion of the Canadian population. Finally, it was obvious to many observers in government and church organizations that most of the policies and programs based on these assumptions were not having the effects desired by policy makers.

A special joint committee of the Senate and House of Commons was appointed in 1946 to review the Indian Act. Although some incremental changes to the Act were passed in 1951, the changes were made in response to government requirements, and ignored the advice of those few Indian leaders who were allowed to make representation to the committee (Dyck, 1991, pp. 104–5).

While Canadian policy toward Indians remained relatively static during the 1950s and 1960s, the underlying political climate began an important shift. The civil rights movement in the United States began to raise the awareness of all Canadians about minority group treatment and about the consequences of not dealing with minorities who had been structurally disempowered. There were growing signs that the "Indian problem" would not go away. A significant rise in the number of Indians began in stark contrast to the dramatic decline in Indian population during the period prior to World War II. Since more of the Indian population was also migrating to urban centres, the consequences of failed Indian policy were becoming much more visible to all Canadians.

Another contributing factor was that, as the resources boom of this period gathered momentum, more of the mid-Canada corridor (where a significant portion of Indians lived) became attractive to developers. The consequences for Indian communities living near these developments were almost never positive. At best, Indian communities could hope to be mostly ignored, perhaps receiving a few low-paying jobs, primarily during the construction phase of such projects. At worst, Indian communities were completely uprooted and moved, sometimes to places where their physical health, and especially their mental health, was seriously endangered. In most of these cases, intruding developments also negatively affected what was left of a traditional lifestyle which, while marginal, at least provided some community members with basic necessities and some sense of dignity. As Canadian society generally continued to grow wealthier, the disparity between cultures became increasingly unconscionable.

The federal government again determined to wrestle with its Indian policy, this time by commissioning the Hawthorn report. Released in 1966, the report detailed the deplorable socio-economic conditions which existed for Indians. It also suggested for the first time that, because of Indians' aboriginal and treaty rights, they deserved far better treatment than they had received from the Canadian state, and they in fact deserved to be treated as "citizens plus." (Hawthorn, 1967–68) Based on Hawthorn report findings, the Pearson government made a commitment to review and make changes to the Indian Act.

Into this environment came Pierre Trudeau. Making statements about a "just society" and "participatory democracy," Trudeau marched to victories in the 1968 Liberal leadership convention and federal election. These phrases resonated well with the political climate of this period: the public had become sympathetic to the plight of minorities who had been mistreated and there was no more visible minority than Canadian Indians. The Pearson government's commitment to review the Indian Act turned into a Trudeau government's comprehensive search for a new Indian policy. The review included a series of consultations with Indian groups and the bureaucratic stakeholders. As they had done previously, Indian groups clearly articulated a desire to maintain and strengthen the identity of Indians, and to establish an Indian land claims commissioner to deal with unresolved land claims.

When Jean Chrétien, Minister of Indian Affairs, introduced the White Paper on Indian Policy in 1969, Indian groups were dismayed and shocked. The paper recommended that the separate status of Indians be abolished, that Indians begin to receive their services from governments in the same way as other Canadians and that the Department of Indian Affairs be wound up within five years. Indian claims to aboriginal rights were dismissed as being so vague that they could not possibly be responded to in a specific way. Indian demands to establish a land claims commission were rejected: government perceptions were that Indian land claims really represented Indian grievances over other issues and that a claims commission was therefore an inappropriate policy approach. Government's assumption in this paper was that the sorry state of Indian peoples and their communities was primarily a product of the special legal status which Indians had, and that if Indians were simply treated in a manner equal with other Canadians, all their problems would disappear (Miller, 1989, pp. 224–27).

The Indian reaction to the White Paper was swift, unequivocal and united. Indian leaders everywhere denounced the White Paper as an attempt to wage "cultural genocide" on status Indians. Within three months of introducing the White Paper, Government agreed to fund Indian-controlled land claims research, a request Indian organizations had been making for years. When this announcement failed to halt the backlash against the Paper, government began to back even further away from their proposed policy. In June 1970, the Prime Minister meeting Alberta Indian chiefs to receive their "Red Paper" proposals, committed to them that no federal proposals would proceed without Indian approval, and that there was no longer any deadline for federal changes to policy (Miller, 1989, pp. 231–32).

Perhaps the most enduring legacy of the federal White Paper was the tremendous mobilization and politicization of the Indian community which ensued. For the first time, provincial Indian associations worked effectively together within a national Indian association. Indians and their Band Councils across the country realized that if they worked together, they could alter or even halt federal policy initiatives. The credibility of their provincial and federal associations multiplied many times over, and this political capital was to become a significant resource for the provincial and federal associations in the decade which followed.

Political capital was parlayed into economic resources. Indian associations received significant core funding from the federal government. They even began to deliver some government programs. The provision of core funding allowed the provincial and national associations to hire full-time, professional employees. Staff contributed to the further advance of Indian interests with governments, resulting in more funding and more credibility with local Indian leaders. As Noel Dyck identified:

104

... in three years, government funding had changed Indian associations almost beyond recognition.... By 1972 each of the three provincial Indian associations on the Prairies, for example, had annual operating budgets of more than a million dollars; their leaders headed programs to provide community development, health liaison, communications, sports and recreation, economic development liaison, and various educational services to reserve communities; they published newspapers, ran fleets of leased automobiles, and chartered aircraft to transport delegations of band chiefs to Ottawa. (Dyke, 1991, p. 111)

Education: the Catalyst for Renewing an Indian Political Vision

By 1970, two years after David Ahenakew's election as Chief of the Federation of Saskatchewan Indians and one year after the 1969 White Paper, education issues had become a major focus for provincial and national Indian organizations. Provincial organizations in Saskatchewan, Manitoba and Alberta were on the leading edge of the call for "Indian Control of Indian Education." Indian leaders and Indian professionals who were products of those systems, characterized both government and church-administered Indian education systems as examples of the weak, ineffective and oppressive failures of "settler colonialism."

Saskatchewan Chiefs in 1970 mandated a Saskatchewan Indian Education Task Force to identify, assess and analyze the results of government and church-administered education systems. The Task Force was not only to assess "Where we are," from an Indian perspective, but also identify "Where we want to be" and "How we will get there."

The Saskatchewan Indian Cultural College was established by Saskatchewan Chiefs in 1970 with a mandate for researching and teaching Indian culture, values, arts, music and languages. The Centre quickly became an international collector, library, clearing and distribution house, for Indian history, literature, the arts, social sciences and humanities. With the involvement of and under the direction of Indian Elders, the Centre inspired and in many ways led the identifying, recording, renewing and revitalizing of Saskatchewan Indian culture, values and languages. An Indian view of Indian history was finally being collected, documented and communicated for Indians, to Indians and by Indians. The Indian past and present was beginning to become part of an Indian vision of an Indian future in a modern world.

The Saskatchewan Indian Cultural College itself was a first in Canada. After overcoming initial Department of Indian Affairs resistance, the College inspired the establishment of a number of similar institutions across Canada. Based on the Saskatchewan model, the Department of Indian Affairs developed a "Cultural Centres and Institutions Program."

Through the Federation of Saskatchewan Indians and its Saskatchewan Indian Cultural College, Chiefs co-operated with the University of Saskatchewan to initiate the Saskatchewan Indian Teacher Education Program (ITEP).

Initially resisted by governments, teachers' and trustees' associations, ITEP was the first of a number of programs, known as "TEPs," established in Canada over the years, all based initially on and inspired by the ITEP model. Convinced by FSI leadership, vision and perseverance, governments, teachers, trustees and academics eventually became supportive and appeared to "run to stand in front."

The next step led by the Chiefs of Saskatchewan, through the FSI, was the development of the Saskatchewan Indian Social Work Education Program (ISWEP). As had been the case with the Cultural College and ITEP, a minority of bureaucrats, professionals, University and Technical Institute academics initially resisted the basic premises and goals of ISWEP. As they had with the Cultural College and ITEP, this smug minority eventually claimed this visionary innovation as their own.

In 1975, directed strategically by the Chiefs, Ahenakew and the FSI Executive addressed itself to the establishment of two more Indian educational firsts in Canada — the Saskatchewan Indian Community College (SICC) and the Saskatchewan Indian Federated College (SIFC).

SICC had a mandate to deliver Adult Basic Education (ABE), Technical and Vocational training on Indian reserves and Federal Crown land in both the Northern Administration District (NAD) and the south. While administratively and financially distinct, SICC was academically integrated with the provincial Community College system. An accommodation was reached between a provincial policy calling for Cabinet appointment of Community College Board members and an FSI policy calling for District Chiefs' selection of the SICC Board. It was agreed that the names of nominees, selected by the Chiefs in each of 6 Districts, would be provided by the FSI Executive to the provincial Cabinet and then be appointed by Order-in-Council to the SICC Board. This policy accommodation stands in interesting contrast to the very firm position which the Province took in northern Saskatchewan when native northern groups wished to appoint their own nominees to northern community college boards.

Also in 1976, with Ahenakew's leadership, the FSI successfully negotiated the terms and finalized the establishment of SIFC, the first Indian-controlled, degree-granting institution in Canada. SIFC, while administratively and financially distinct, was academically integrated with the University of Regina. This meant that while courses and programs confronting Indian issues, needs and goals would be planned, initiated and delivered under SIFC management, they would require input, assessment and approval through standard U of R processes. Courses and programs would be accredited and degrees granted in the name of the University.

The process of creating SIFC is revealing of how Indian policy processes developed. In 1975, the recently-appointed President of the University of Regina, Dr. Lloyd Barber, who had been the first Canadian Indian Land Claims Commissioner, agreed to co-operate with Ahenakew in attempting to find means to negotiate federation of an FSI-driven institution with the U of R. Barber appointed a small U of R faculty group, chaired by then U of R Secretary, Teal Lowery, to work with a small FSI group appointed by Ahenakew.

In response to Ahenakew's request to Gordon MacMurchy, the provincial government assigned Dr. Alex Guy, Deputy Minister of Continuing Education, to assist the process. Guy was to provide the provincial government's perspective in facilitating the federation of this Indian-controlled professional college with the U of R.

As they had with the Indian Cultural College, ITEP, ISWEP and the SICC, Ahenakew[1] and his 1st Vice-Chief, Sol Sanderson, sought and secured the input, approval and endorsement of the appropriate professional and administrative bodies, and secured provincial government funding (with federal funding of SICC. When SIFC became a reality, all stakeholders had "bought in," endorsing the outcome of a policy development process within which they perceived themselves as having been included, a process which all stakeholders felt had benefitted from their individual input.

Led strategically by the Chiefs, the FSI's Education Task Force formed the basis of the renewal and the development of a modern Indian vision, mission and strategy. The creation of the Cultural College, ITEP, ISWEP, SICC and SIFC resulted in the development and maturation of an FSI management and administrative capacity later applied to several other areas. This was a development model, emulated with varying degrees of success by native organizations in Saskatchewan and other jurisdictions.

The Process of Land Entitlement in Saskatchewan

The political climate for Canadian Indian demands to resolve land claims issues was identified earlier in this chapter. Even before the federal government released its controversial White Paper, delegates to a national meeting in May 1969, which was considering Indian Act reform, decided to form a national committee on Indian Rights and Treaties. The committee began to conduct research for the National Indian Brotherhood. This committee was the beginning of an unprecedented wave of historical research into Indian land claims and Treaty rights (Daniel, 1980, pp. 220–21).

---

[1] The contributions of David Ahenakew, in leading the FSI in establishing the Indian Education Task Force, the three colleges and two programs, was recognized by presentation of an honorary Doctor of Laws degree by the University of Regina in 1975. Further recognition was accorded Chief Ahenakew and, through him, all the Indians of Saskatchewan when he was named a Member of the Order of Canada in 1978. The Government of Canada recognized not only his leadership in the educational field, but also his leadership in the field of land entitlement, Indian government and other Treaty issues. Ahenakew was also recognized for his strategic leadership and for operational leadership in building and developing the management capacity of Indian organizations and institutions.

This response to a federal request to consider Indian Act reform is interesting and revealing. Indian organizations have consistently responded that no changes to Indian status or to how Indian people and their communities receive their government services could be entertained until the matter of outstanding land claims was resolved.

In the fall of 1969, as the Indian reaction to the federal White Paper was building to a crescendo, Lloyd Barber was appointed as a one-man Indian Land Claims Commission. The initial reaction of Indian organizations was generally negative: an Indian had not been appointed and Indian organizations had only just begun what they perceived as a lengthy process of fully researching and documenting the extent of Indian land claims. Subsequent to the Barber appointment, and in response to the very negative reaction of Indian organizations to the White Paper, these organizations secured federal funding to conduct Treaty rights research. The issue of land claims remained relatively quiet while these organizations began the process of documentary and oral historical research to identify the Indian meaning of the Treaties, and the historical basis for land claims.

Several major development projects proposed in northern Canada quickly pushed Indian land claims into the forefront. In November 1972, the Indian and Inuit associations, representing native peoples in the James Bay area, succeeded in temporarily halting work on the James Bay hydroelectric project (Daniel, 1980, pp. 223–24). This legal action drove home the point to the Quebec government that a negotiated settlement with the associations would be preferable to protracted court battles.

The real turning point for government land policy relating to land claims can be traced to the decision in January, 1973 by the Supreme Court of Canada in the case of *Calder vs. Attorney General of British Columbia.* In this case, testing the aboriginal land claim of the Nishga Indians, the claim was rejected, but only on technical grounds. Six of the seven judges made it clear in their ruling that the concept of aboriginal claim had some validity. As one individual involved in the James Bay negotiations commented:

> From reading these decisions one cannot help but draw the conclusion that the courts were giving the parties involved a message: *"Negotiate and Settle."* (John Ciacci, quoted in Knoll, 1987, p. 27)

In April that year, the federal government was confronted with another court injunction delaying a major development. This time the Chiefs of the Mackenzie Valley Indian bands filed a caveat against roughly one-third of the Northwest Territories as a response to the proposed Mackenzie Valley pipeline proposal. Justice William Morrow of the Northwest Territories Supreme Court ruled there was sufficient doubt aboriginal title had been extinguished that no development should take place pending final settlement of the dispute between government and the Mackenzie Valley Indians. This time, the injunction was to hold up development for two years and led ultimately to the precedent-setting Berger Commission — Mackenzie Valley Pipeline Inquiry (Daniel, 1980, pp. 222–23).

In July 1973, the federal government issued a "Statement on Claims of Indian and Inuit People." This statement recognized two broad categories of claims. Comprehensive claims applied to those areas where Indian rights and land claims had not been extinguished by treaty. The other category, specific claims, applied to those situations where government already had lawful obligations, based on treaties, and issues that had arisen since treaty-making related to the administration of Indian lands and assets. It is within this context that FSI leadership, management and research capacity dealt with Treaty Indian land entitlement in Saskatchewan.

Since all of Saskatchewan was covered by treaties, the land claims issue in Saskatchewan for Treaty Indians, has always been an issue of specific claims. Treaties had provided for 128 acres of land per person to be recognized as a basis for bands to establish reserves. Some bands had not received the land to which they were entitled. Indian bands whose land was desired by the new wave of immigrants or by the railways faced pressure to surrender their lands, often under questionable legal circumstances. While government from time to time recognized that there was a debt of outstanding land claims, no progress was made in settling this debt.

The Natural Resources Transfer Agreement of 1930 created an additional complicating factor: there was now a third party, not contemplated in the Treaties, to Indian land entitlements: the provincial governments. The 1930 Agreement clearly spelled out primary federal responsibility for settling outstanding claims, and identified unoccupied Provincial Crown land as a primary source of land for making these settlements.

In the 1971 election campaign, the New Democratic Party as part of its platform, had promised to:

> provide substantial grants and technical assistance to Indian organizations to enable them to undertake a thorough study of treaty rights, aboriginal rights and other special rights which Indian people may possess by reason of their being Indians. (New Democratic Party of Saskatchewan, 1971)

Identified in the Party's detailed election platform, this promise was never identified as one of the major election planks.

David Ahenakew said[2] that "during the Blakeney years, the development of an FSI-provincial government relationship based on mutual respect, trust and a mutual understanding of our Treaties yielded many positive results." According to Ahenakew, the province supported innovative Indian leadership and direction by providing significant assistance in funding recreation, communication and research activities. He said that the province provided a level of core funding to the FSI, matching what the federal government

---

[2] In a personal interview on June 16, 1993.

provided through the Department of Secretary of State. Significant financial assistance was also provided for research assistance to the FSI's Indian Rights and Treaty Research Section.

By early 1974, the Federation of Saskatchewan Indians was beginning to get some sense of the potential magnitude of Indian land claims. Its research efforts originally had focused on how Saskatchewan Indians interpreted the meaning of the Treaties and this research was directed at establishing what overall understanding all bands had of the treaties. However, this early research, together with the specific requests from Indian bands for the Federation to help them pursue specific land and other claims resulted in the Federation establishing a Claims Development Section within its Indian Rights and Treaties Research Branch. The FSI document proposing this Claims Development Section identifies clearly that individual bands were driving the process (Federation of Saskatchewan Indians, 1974).

For Saskatchewan bands, specific claims were fit into one of two categories: "Unfulfilled Land Entitlements," referring to those bands who, at the time of treaty signing had not taken up their full land entitlement; or "Illegal Surrenders" referring to bands such as Ocean Man, Pheasant's Rump, Chacastapasin and others. Some of the lands of these bands had been surrendered illegally by the Canadian government, and subsequently sold by the government to third parties.

Over the course of the next year, the impetus toward determining a fair entitlement process continued to move forward. The James Bay Agreement, signed in November, 1974 reminded stakeholders in Saskatchewan that outstanding land claims required some resolution. As specific band claims came forward, issues were surfacing about how to determine the size of the claims, and then how to move the land selection process forward. None of the issues was simple and a great deal of research by the FSI Claims Development Section, both in Saskatchewan and Ottawa was required.

The unresolved issues of which formula would be used to determine the size of bands' entitlements and of which government jurisdiction had what responsibility for supplying land to fulfill the entitlements prompted the FSI to request the then Federal Minister of Indian Affairs, Judd Buchanan, to write Premier Allan Blakeney. Buchanan solicited the Saskatchewan government's co-operation in resolving these issues and arriving at a process which would allow for resolution of land entitlements. Blakeney responded promptly, promising to support the federal initiative, and designated G.R. Bowerman, Minister of Northern Saskatchewan, to be responsible for co-ordinating the provincial policy (Pitsula, 1989, pp. 191–94).

It made sense to many, including provincial politicians and civil servants, that if Treaty Indians could enjoy a fuller life on larger and more viable Indian reserves, the pressure to migrate off-reserve would be reduced. The growing pressure on the Province to provide resources to Treaty Indians living off-reserve would therefore be reduced. At least at the policy level, support for positions taken by the FSI helped to align the Province with an important political constituency, and to distinguish this government from the discredited and distrusted federal government. This question of political constituencies is significant, since Saskatchewan's Treaty Indian population was and continues to be the largest as a proportion of any provincial population in Canada at approximately 12%.

There were positive, co-operative relationships, serving the goals of both the FSI and the provincial government, between some members of the Provincial Cabinet and the Federation of Saskatchewan Indians. Initially, this had been focused mainly on education by Chief David Ahenakew and Gordon MacMurchy. After 1974, the relationship included Ted Bowerman, the provincial minister responsible for Treaty Land Entitlement. This relationship allowed the Federation to exert significant influence over provincial policy positions whenever they affected Treaty Indians. It may also help to explain why the Government of Saskatchewan took a position on the land entitlement issue which was vigorously opposed by provincial governments in Manitoba and Alberta.

The August 1976 proposal, which came to be known as the Saskatchewan formula, suggested that land entitlements be established by multiplying the band population at December 31, 1976, by 128 acres, and then subtracting the acres the band had already received. The Saskatchewan formula would have resulted in a land transfer of approximately 1.3 million acres (over half a million hectares). The Province further recognized that since unoccupied Crown land was no longer readily available in the southern part of the province, occupied lands could be transferred so long as the interests of current parties were satisfied. Finally, the proposal offered the possibility of revenue sharing in resources and joint development of currently disposed land as an alternative where land transfer was difficult or unacceptable to the band in question (Pitsula, 1989, pp. 195–96).

The Federation of Saskatchewan Indians immediately accepted the Province's proposal and even praised it for its "good faith and commitment." Again, such a response and language suggests a very close relationship between the Province and the Federation. Receiving a reply from the federal government was another issue. A series of letters and phone calls finally produced a response in April 1977; however, no formal public response was made until August that year, fully one year after the Province had offered its proposal. The new Minister of Indian Affairs announced his support for the Saskatchewan formula, indicating that the Government of Canada was prepared to purchase private lands if necessary to fulfill entitlements, and recommended the formula to the governments of Alberta and Manitoba (Pitsula, 1989, p. 196).

The Saskatchewan formula represented an important policy innovation. It represented the first time that a provincial government had responded favourably to specific Indian land claims with an offer to settle these claims

111

by providing Provincial Crown land as part of the entitlement. Moreover, the provincial formula, which essentially was the FSI's formula, was by far the most generous offer which had been proposed to that point in time in the case of specific claims policy.

The mid-1977 period was the last time for nearly a decade and a half that there appeared to be agreement over how the Saskatchewan land entitlement issue was to be handled. Within a few months, provincial and federal officials began a long process of disagreeing about almost all aspects of the agreement. Initially, the backtracking appears to have been a reaction by federal officials against the Saskatchewan formula principles because of their concern with the generosity of the formula and the implications of applying this formula to Alberta and Manitoba (Pitsula, 1989, pp. 197–98).

By the mid-1978 period, provincial resistance to the land selection process was beginning to surface. As provincial departments began to become involved in responding to the selection requests of individual bands, more and more caveats were entered. The Department of Mineral Resources expressed opposition to transferring mineral-bearing lands to Indians. The Minister of Natural Resources advised against putting provincial parks on the table, since transfer of these lands would fan an anti-Indian backlash in the white population. The possible transfer of commercial forest land was also resisted, both by provincial officials and private forest companies. Community groups opposed the idea of transferring recreation areas to bands. Finally, opposition to the transfer of community pastures was expressed by pasture patrons and by local politicians involved with rural municipalities, who feared a loss of tax revenue if Crown land was transferred to bands (Pitsula, 1989, pp. 201–2).

The change of federal government in 1979 put the entire land entitlement process on hold for a year, until the Liberals returned to power in 1980. For a brief period, the issues which had separated the two levels of government appeared to have been resolved, and the Province's political will to push the entitlement process had stiffened. By April 1981, the Province had committed to transfer 18 parcels of land comprising just short of 200,000 acres of land. Not surprisingly, this action provoked a response from community pasture patrons and from the Saskatchewan Wildlife Federation (Pitsula, 1989, pp. 220–26).

A change in the leadership at the Federation of Saskatchewan Indians, with the election of Albert Bellegarde in 1978, followed, after Bellegarde's death, by the election of Sol Sanderson in 1981, had some impact on this process as well. Sanderson began to call for additional lands and for broader recognition of hunting and trapping rights. This may have been partly as a response to the rising tide of resistance in rural Saskatchewan to Treaty Indian land entitlement.

In April 1982, the election of Grant Devine's Conservative Party put the entitlement process on hold for nearly a decade. The Conservatives had supported the opposition by rural municipalities and community pasture patrons. They fired the provincial land entitlements coordinator and did not fill the position. Although 21 band claims had been validated prior to 1982, only one band had received its full entitlement, and less than 10% of the total acres selected had actually been transferred or were in the process of being transferred (Pitsula, 1989, p. 207).

Relations with The Metis Society of Saskatchewan

While the FSI continued throughout the 1971 to 1982 period to lead innovation in provincial Indian policy, with the provincial government supporting these initiatives, the same kind of relationship was never fully developed with the Metis. In 1971, when the Blakeney government took office, the Metis were represented by the Metis Society of Saskatchewan (MSS). Partly to embrace and include the needs and goals of non-status Indians who were not represented by either the FSI or MSS, the Metis Society reconstituted itself as the Association of Metis and Non-Status Indians of Saskatchewan (AMNSIS) in 1974.

Neither the MSS or AMNSIS ever developed the kind of clear community-based and community-driven vision, mission and strategy which characterized the FSI. Indian Chiefs and Elders had been able to direct the FSI Executive in developing pragmatic operational plans and management capacity based on recognition of Treaty rights and the driving role of Band Councils, Elders and Chiefs. This community-based foundation provided the FSI leadership with the credibility which neither MSS nor AMNSIS was ever able to achieve.

MSS and AMNSIS appeared driven more from the top than the FSI. Perhaps these apparent differences made the provincial government appear less confident in and trusting of the Metis leadership than they were of the Indian leadership. By repeated public endorsation of what he called "the politics of confrontation," Jim Sinclair, the President of MSS and AMNSIS throughout this period, distinguished himself from the "politics of negotiation," endorsed and practiced by Saskatchewan Chiefs and David Ahenakew.

Confrontations, demonstrations and public exchanges of personal criticism between Sinclair and the provincial government characterized much of the MSS/AMNSIS relationship with the provincial government. This made it increasingly difficult, if not impossible, for ministers like Bowerman and MacMurchy to develop the kind of win-win relationship with the Metis they had developed with the Indians. Both the Metis and the government were frustrated by what appeared a "win-lose" Metis-provincial government relationship. Both found it even more frustrating when it was contrasted with what appeared a "win-win" Indian-provincial government relationship. In retrospect, it is clear that the FSI-provincial relationship was a partnership, an alliance between two political organizations both of whom perceived that strong benefits could be obtained for themselves through this alliance. A critical aspect of this partnership's success is that the political constituency for these two organizations was mutually exclusive to a large degree. The Province recognized and respected the FSI-federal jurisdiction over reserve communities, and did not attempt to compete for influence with or control over this constituency. The MSS/AMNSIS-Provincial relationship clearly was not such a partnership. The most vivid evidence of this dysfunctional relationship is again provided from a northern setting.

In the summer of 1973, the MSS presentation to Cabinet called for northern municipal government organized around community-driven, Regional Councils which would, in turn, drive a Northern Territorial Council. The Northern Territorial Council would be directly involved in and would influence DNS policy development and programming. Many elements of this proposal were very close to Bowerman's September 1971 Cabinet Paper and the resolutions passed by the NDP at its November 1971 convention. The ingredients for an innovative, native-led policy process and results similar to the process and results which were occurring with the FSI, were present early in the government's first term.

However, by 1973, the government had already decided on an incremental approach to the development and operation of the single agency. Having already decided on a government-led incremental agenda, government simply ignored the opportunity presented by MSS for a co-managed, innovative agenda. The evidence suggests that government may have already become so preoccupied with the difficulties in implementing its own northern agenda that it did not realize it was walking away from a potential joint agenda, consistent with its own public pronouncements of 1971 and early 1972.

A key element in the breakdown between the MSS and the Government was trust, or the lack of trust. The MSS leadership had always viewed government initiatives with distrust; they took the early pronouncements of provincial politicians at face value. Hence, the idea of a northern territorial council became interpreted as a northern council with powers of control over provincial affairs in the north. When the Northern Municipal Council (NMC) became reality in May of 1973, with the powers of a rural municipality operating within the Northern Administration District, the MSS response was to set up a "Watchdog Committee." This committee was to monitor the government's handling of the NMC and ensure that the terms of the legislation were implemented fully. What occurred very quickly however, was a dramatic difference in opinion about the role of the NMC. While some government officials, including the Minister, had initially discussed the possibility of the NMC taking over responsibility for many of the municipal functions being provided by government, including a $2.8 million budget, government quickly became nervous about the administrative capacity and political trustworthiness of the Council and its members. As government backed away from its position of turning over program delivery responsibilities to the Council, the MSS and others quickly reacted with public condemnations of government. By late 1973, the relationship between the Province and MSS had deteriorated beyond the point of repair. The lack of an effective partnership between government and the Metis and Non-status organization meant that policy initiatives for this constituency from 1973 on had the character of following very much in the footsteps of Treaty Indian-led initiatives.

A further irony, perhaps illustrating the mutual distrust developed over 10 years, is that when the government finally proposed in 1982 a new Northern Municipalities Act, a structure similar to the one proposed by MSS in 1973, AMNSIS rejected it, calling it an attempt to "divide and conquer." Perhaps the incremental and the control paradigms modelled by government had been adopted by AMNSIS.

During its 1975–78 term, the Blakeney government did cooperate with and support an AMNSIS initiative in the establishment of the Gabriel Dumont Institute of Applied Studies and Research (GDI). GDI was created for the educational, cultural and social development of Metis and non-status Indians in Saskatchewan. The provincial government contracted with GDI to provide for four functional areas: research and development; library and resource centre; educational resource development; and land claims and research.

A further contract was signed to have GDI become the specific delivery agent for Saskatchewan Urban Native Teacher Education Program. Subsequent arrangements with the Universities of Regina and Saskatchewan, as well as with the Saskatchewan Institute of Applied Sciences and Technologies, have seen GDI taking a lead role in the delivery of both professional and technical education programs in native communities.

This AMNSIS initiative, like earlier FSI innovative policy developments which required new policy and program initiatives, originated with a native organization. Government's role was to respond to a pro-active native agenda, rather than to set its own agenda for native issues. Initial reactions from the public service to innovative native initiatives, had invariably been to deny them as either "unnecessary" or "too radical."

Perhaps by 1976 the Indian Cultural College, the SICC, the SIFC and their emulation across the nation, together with the public recognition of Ahenakew by the University of Regina, had taken native-managed and directed educational institutions out of the "innovative" category. This made the AMNSIS proposal for GDI appear less "radical" and more within the realm of incremental change.

Epilogue and Reflections

The NDP and government made commitments to innovation in northern policy making, program development and service delivery, and created a public expectation for innovation in the north. Neither the NDP nor the government had ever made similar commitments to innovation in native policy.

Government's commitment was to incremental change and, in the case of Treaty Indians, a very simple promise to support financially the research activities of the FSI. Perhaps that is why the significant positive change and developments in Indian policy, though not as noticeable as the changes in northern Saskatchewan, were more frequently celebrated. The development of Indian-controlled post-secondary educational institutions was a first in Canada, and formed the basis for on-going development of human resources in the Indian community. The "Saskatchewan formula" for land entitlements was precedent-setting in Canada. Until then, no provincial government had gone so far to recognize the requirement for provincial co-operation to facilitate the land entitlement process.

The differences between northern and native policy development, and the legacy left by the NDP administration in these areas, reflect the differences between incremental and innovative policy development. Agenda-setting is the clearest issue. In the case of northern policy development, white southerners were clearly setting the agenda. The rather turbulent arguments about innovation versus incrementalism were fought out within the civil service for the most part. Northern organizations were largely marginal in these debates, and certainly did not force government's hand in any significant way. The organization which had the greatest stake in northern Saskatchewan was the Metis Society. It was mostly reacting to government's agenda and was marginal in determining policy outcomes.

In native policy setting, the agenda was clearly influenced much more by native organizations. The FSI in particular had a clear agenda, and government responded to and supported it. When government decided to be supportive of the native agenda, great strides were made.

Some significant differences in the relationship between the Province and native organizations are observable. The relationship between the Province and the FSI was a mature one, characterized by trust, mutual respect and recognition of credibility. To some extent, these characteristics could develop because the two political organizations did not perceive themselves as fighting over the same constituents. Particularly after the Indian reaction and mobilization following the White Paper controversy in 1969, the Province recognized and respected the Treaty Indian desire to hold the federal government responsible for the moral, legal and economic debt to Indian people.

At the same time, several prominent and influential Cabinet Ministers felt a very strong need to be supportive of Indian aspirations in whatever way was possible. This recognition translated initially into "hands off" funding, and later into active support for Treaty Indian initiatives in a variety of areas. Although there were occasionally tensions between the Province and the FSI, these were almost always dealt with through private negotiation and compromise which allowed both organizations to save public face. Clearly there was an active and well-functioning partnership between

116

the two organizations and this synergy translated into policy innovations which occasionally have been emulated by other jurisdictions in Canada.

The Province's relationship with MSS/MNSIS could almost be characterized as the antithesis of its relationship with the FSI. There appeared to be an opportunity in northern Saskatchewan to establish a positive partnership. The controversy which developed over the structure and function of the Northern Municipal Council broke whatever trust had existed previously in this relationship. Where each organization had been suspicious of the other before, the Metis Society after the NMC debate viewed the provincial government with hostility and deep cynicism. The Province, put in the position of having to respond to public criticism in the form of demonstrations and sit-ins, reacted by publicly calling into question the credibility of the Metis Society and its leadership. When the Province did respond to AMNSIS education initiatives in the mid-1970s, these initiatives were perceived as copies of a model which had been pioneered as a result of the FSI-Province relationship. Within the generally antagonistic relationship which existed between MSS/AMNSIS and government, policy innovation was impossible.

One final observation about the relationship between innovation and partnership between government and native organizations: the partnerships which have been described were both personal and limited. The best evidence of this is provided through the land entitlement analysis. For the Province's part, the land entitlement process was driven through the political will of a few Cabinet Ministers and key officials. During the post-1977 period when opposition to the land entitlement process began to surface, other Cabinet Ministers and officials in the departments most affected by land entitlements began to raise objections to the process as well. While these objections appear to have been stifled somewhat after 1980, they were never completely eliminated, and some bureaucratic resistance remained throughout. This suggests that regardless of the political will of politicians, the civil service can remain a source of inertia favoring, incrementalism over innovation.

REFERENCES

Daniel, R.C. 1980. *A History of Native Claims Processes in Canada, 1867–1979.* Ottawa: Department of Indian and Northern Affairs, Research Branch.

Federation of Saskatchewan Indians. 1974. Discussion paper on claims development in *Report to All Chiefs' Conference.* Unpublished.

Dyck, N. 1991. *What is the Indian "Problem": Tutelage and Resistance in Canadian Indian Administration.* St. John's, Newfoundland: Institute of Social and Economic Research, Memorial University of Newfoundland.

Hawthorn, H.B., ed., 1967–68. *A Survey of the Contemporary Indians; Economic, Political, Educational Needs and Policies.* Ottawa: Queen's Printer.

117

Knoll, D.C. 1987. "Unfinished Business: Treaty Land Entitlement and Surrender Claims in Saskatchewan." *Saskatchewan Indian Federated College Journal* 3:2, 21–52.

Miller, J.R. 1989. *Skyscrapers Hide the Heavens: A History of Indian-White Relations in Canada*. Toronto: University of Toronto Press.

New Democratic Party of Saskatchewan. 1971. *New Deal for People*, NDP pamphlet. Regina.

Pitsula, J.M. 1989. "The Blakeney Government and the Settlement of Treaty Indian Land Entitlements in Saskatchewan, 1975–82." In *Historical Papers*, edited by D. Johnson. Ottawa: Canadian Historical Association, 190–209.

CHAPTER 6 Saskatchewan's
One Province
Library System
by Keith Turnbull

An Innovative and Unique System

There are ten public library systems in Saskatchewan. Eight regional libraries with headquarters in smaller centres (with the exception of the Wheatland Regional Library centred in Saskatoon) serve the rural areas with a network of branch libraries and bookmobile stops in towns and villages. There are also two large urban public libraries in Regina and Saskatoon. The newest system, Pahkisimon Nuye,ah, was begun in 1990 to serve the North.

The Saskatchewan Provincial Library coordinates interlibrary loans, provides back-up reference services, maintains a central location file, and houses a back-up reference collection for the Province. *The Public Libraries Act 1984* mandates the Library to serve as the central coordinating agency for public libraries in the province, to facilitate cooperation among public libraries and other libraries within and without the province, and to deliver certain services to libraries. The Provincial Library also allocates provincial government grants. Although the urban public libraries are funded primarily from municipal taxes, the regional libraries are dependent on provincial funds for over 50% of their revenue.

The One Province Library System was innovative in that it was able to get all players in the public library sector to work together while recognizing differences of geography and population density. Services long taken for granted in Saskatchewan are still subject to debate in other parts of Canada. A case in point is the reciprocal borrowing agreement. All public libraries in the province agree to honour each other's library cards. Anyone living within the boundaries of a library system can use not only any branch library in that system, but any branch of any other system in the province. Books borrowed from one branch library can be returned to any other branch. Books are then sent "home" by courier or mail. Thus, a resident of Maple Creek vacationing at Loon Lake can use her Chinook

119

Regional Library card in this branch of the Lakeland Library Region and return it, free of charge, to the library in Maple Creek.

Another unique aspect of the system is the extensive interlibrary loan system. Because of the relatively small size of local library collections, interlibrary loans are encouraged. A simple form is filled out by the patron. If the book is available in Saskatchewan or anywhere in Canada, it should eventually get into the hands of the person who needs it.

The system contains elements familiar to library users in all parts of Canada. What makes it unique is the scope of the system and the equality of access to information that it gives to all residents of the province. For example, in 1974, when the last regional library was set up, 55,317 interlibrary loans were handled by staff at the Provincial Library (Saskatchewan Provincial Library, 1974). By 1980, this had increased to 72,543 (Saskatchewan Provincial Library, 1980). In the same year, 1980, the Library Services Branch of Alberta Culture, serving 2.5 times the population, handled 12,098 interlibrary loans. Although library development across Canada has been significant since the 1960s, nowhere has it resulted in such a comprehensive system.

A Brief History

The process leading up to creation of the One Province Library System, as it came to be known in the 1970s, began during the twenty years of the CCF government, from 1944 to 1964. The idea of a cooperative library system, providing information to a population which has very limited access to library collections and services, was a logical extension of the cooperative ideology of the CCF. Allan Blakeney had been the minister in charge of libraries during the formative years and he maintained a vision of what library services could mean to a province like Saskatchewan.

The library system continued to develop during the Thatcher years and carried on with its growth throughout the 1970s. By 1971, four of the eventual seven regional libraries were established and in operation and a fifth had budget approval. But it was only after 1971 that a full scope One Province system was realized.

Because Saskatchewan has a small, dispersed population living in municipalities with very limited tax bases, people can only enjoy reasonable access to library service if resources are shared. This is the cornerstone of public library policy in Saskatchewan.

Karon Selzer, who wrote her library science thesis on the history of the Provincial Library states that "In 1914 an appropriation of $3,000 was made to inaugurate a system of travelling libraries ... (consisting) of boxes containing sixty to eighty books which were loaned to a group or community for a period of one year. Books were sent to every part of the province, to forestry stations, Hudson's Bay posts and homes for the infirm, with the only cost to the recipient being the return freight" (Selzer, 1979, p. 2).

During the Great Depression, user fees were established and borrowers were charged 10 cents per circulation, to make up for reductions in government appropriations. This effectively put the service out of reach of many rural residents, but the service did not die. Rather, it strengthened public support for more substantial library services which would benefit everyone. As early as 1933, the Canadian Commission of Enquiry's "Libraries in Canada," a study of library conditions and needs, stated "Saskatchewan is a most hopeful and promising province for a comprehensive and creative library experiment." In 1944, according to Selzer, with the election of a new provincial government, that experiment could begin (Selzer, 1979, p. 3).

In 1945, the Open Shelf Library was reorganized and became the public information library. In 1946, the government passed the Regional Libraries Act and appointed a supervisor of a regional libraries division, reporting to the legislative librarian. In 1950, the first regional library on the prairies, the North Central Saskatchewan Regional Library, was organized.

The (Saskatchewan) Library Inquiry Committee report of 1967 stated that "The most important single action in the improvement of library services was the creation, in 1953, of the Provincial Library ... As a result there came into being a provincial agency capable of coordinating library services at all levels. This factor, combined with relatively substantial grants for the regional library and the provision of consultative and demonstration service, enhanced province-wide interest in the provision of better libraries" (Library Inquiry Committee, 1967, p. 13).

The Provincial Library was composed of the old Travelling Library, the Public Information Library, the Technical Services Division and the Regional Libraries Division. A bookmobile demonstration project travelled the province to generate more interest and work began in the southeast of the province to garner interest in another system. By 1964, when the CCF government was defeated, momentum for libraries was building quickly, and would continue to build.

By June of 1966, as pressure mounted for the development of a province wide plan for library service, Premier Ross Thatcher appointed the Library Inquiry Committee, which was directed to investigate the adequacy of existing library facilities, to study the organization and administration of library services, to examine financing of libraries, and to make recommendations for the future (Library Inquiry Committee, 1967, p. 1). The study was thorough in its needs assessment and consisted of public hearings, field surveys, private interviews and the solicitation of consultants' views. In the end, the report's findings could not be denied. Although watered down before it became law, much of the intent of the report did see the light of day when a new Public Libraries Act was assented to in 1969. This act was to remain in force throughout the eleven years of the Blakeney government.

The South Eastern Saskatchewan Regional Library, headquartered in Weyburn, began in 1966. The Wheatland Regional Library, centred in Saskatoon, was organized in 1967. Two more areas were ready for development by the spring of 1968. The largest of these, the Parkland Regional Library, started in 1968 when establishment grants were approved in the provincial budget. The Provincial Library continued the groundwork to get the remaining three regional jurisdictions ready to begin operations, but no further action occurred until the spring of 1971 when, with an election call imminent, the Thatcher government approved grants for the establishment of Chinook Regional Library in the Swift Current area.

The system developed over many years. The CCF government of 1944–64 laid the groundwork for a province-wide, accessible library system that would stand the test of time and be maintained by later governments of both the right and the left. By the time the NDP gained power in 1971, the stage had been set for a rapid expansion to complete the One Province Public Library System in Saskatchewan.

The Blakeney Years

Public libraries have often been considered "frills" by politicians facing demands for roads, electrification, farm subsidies and employment opportunities. By contrast, studies done in Ontario (*One Place to Look; the Ontario Public Library Strategic Plan*) and Alberta (*Giving Voice to the "Quiet Majority"*) show that a vast majority of citizens see libraries as essential services. This is also true in Saskatchewan, with its long history of cooperative library development.

Saskatchewan had a well-organized lobby on behalf of public libraries. Women's Institutes, Home and School Associations, Boards of Trade, cooperatives and other organizations were powerful advocates for library development. This was vital, because every city, town, village and rural municipal council in the province was required under the Act to sign an agreement to belong to a regional library, and pay a per capita levy. Virtually every community had to be visited and the council sold on the idea of a library.

The Provincial Library hired consultants, usually young, energetic and motivated to action, to "sell" libraries to councils and set up regional library operations. Hiring of such consultants was central to the success of the program.

I was one such consultant. Fresh out of Library School, with one year's experience as a clerk with the Edmonton Public Library, I found myself in Saskatchewan, on the cutting edge of library development in Canada. My job was simple — to build library services where none had existed before, and mesh these with existing services. Harry Newsom was the Provincial Librarian. A man of enormous energy and vision, he had been the driving force behind the Library Inquiry Committee report of 1967.

In the spring of 1971 we began to visit communities in the southwest corner of the province, laying the base for the Chinook Regional Library. We were greeted with enthusiasm, warmth, tea and cookies — and sometimes scepticism.

Towns and village councils were, on the whole, more supportive than rural municipal councils whose residents might have to travel many miles to get to a library. In some cases we were dealing with councils with budgets so small that we were literally competing with sewer, water or gravel on the main street. But these were not a hard sell. People in towns and villages had a very clear understanding of the importance of information and being linked more closely to events in the rest of the world.

Rural municipal councils could be tougher. Don Meadows, the Provincial Librarian at the time, loved to recall a meeting with such a council in eastern Saskatchewan, where he was told explicitly that "Books is bullshit."

Nonetheless, within a year of starting, we could look back at an 80% success rate in signing up municipalities, and this percentage was the same in every part of the province. Recognizing that a great majority of people wanted library services, The Saskatchewan Library Association launched a campaign for legislation to make it compulsory for the remaining municipalities to join library systems. The Association felt that libraries were as important as schools, and nobody had a choice as to whether or not they belonged to a school district. Without full participation, and with municipalities having the right to opt out of a regional library, stability and funding would always be a problem.

In the end, key officers of the Library Trustees Association balked at the idea of compulsion, and the provincial government was not prepared to institute a change of this magnitude. Many viewed this as a major setback. It created a rift between the Library Association and the Library Trustees Association which lasted for several years.

Provincial Library staff had taken their turns as officers of the Saskatchewan Library Association and had helped to organize library support groups including the Library Trustees Association. Subsequent years proved the value of such strong support groups, even if they were not always in agreement with one another.

One of the main reasons for the successful development of the library system is that we were not afraid to act, without worrying too much about political constraints. We lobbied, argued, fought for better budgets without concern over whether or not we were stepping on the toes of our political masters. For its part, the government did not put many restrictions on us. Because staff were not afraid, our energies were directed very effectively.

Provincial Library staff worked with native peoples and their organizations, offering advice on how best to approach government and how to set up programs. They were actively involved in recruiting staff for both the Saskatchewan Indian Cultural College and the Gabriel Dumont Institute.

123

In the mid 1970s a library consultant position was specifically established to work with Aboriginal peoples. Today, the new Pahkisimon Nuye,ah system in the North serves a predominately Aboriginal population.

Close links were also established with the Francophone community, the multicultural community in general, and numerous community organizations throughout the province. There was little concern over whether or not people were government "bureaucrats" or public library workers employed by boards. We were all in it together, and worked together as a team.

The Provincial Library moved beyond public library coordination when, in the early 1970s, it moved to incorporate records of governmental and other special libraries into its union catalogue. Consultative help was provided to all types of libraries. This was outside the official legislated mandate of the Provincial Library, but it was welcomed by Departments which suffered from isolation and a lack of resources to serve all the needs of their staff.

By the autumn of 1971, only months after the election of the NDP, the Chinook Regional Library was providing services to about thirty branches in the Swift Current area. By the fall of 1973, the Lakeland Library Region (North Battleford) and the Palliser Regional Library (Moose Jaw) were fully operational. This brought to nine the number of library systems operating in the province, effectively blanketing the entire province south of the Department of Northern Saskatchewan (DNS) line, and including all cities, the vast majority of towns, villages, and rural municipalities.

As an agency of government, the Provincial Library allocated grants by formula to regional and large public library systems. Grants increased from $1,066,800 in 1971 to $6,288,200 by 1981, a 490% increase. A formula put in place in 1975 moved grants away from a per capita basis and onto a more equal basis, recognizing distances, population density and basic costs of running a headquarters operation regardless of the size of the population served. This allowed regional libraries serving less densely populated areas to raise their levels of service to those achieved in more heavily populated areas.

While other provinces were still struggling with the questions of whether or not rural areas could be best served by regional systems or by less formal library federations, and whether or not government agencies should "interfere" with library development, Saskatchewan was quietly on its way to building a province-wide, coordinated system with a clear governmental role, and clear roles and responsibilities defined for all its parts.

The principle was simple and effective: centralized administration and decentralized service based upon the needs of the population. Planning and commitment made the program viable. The key was the Provincial Library, set up not as an arm of another department such as Education or Culture, but as a separate entity dedicated to organizing and delivering public library services. Also, there was a wing of this agency whose sole reason for existence was to develop libraries and to address problems such as equity in service delivery and provision of grants.

Other provinces did not move as quickly or decisively, perhaps because of fragmented programs or a reliance on central provincial library offices which did not have the mandate, resources, staff or ideology to treat library services in the same manner as, say, education or health care. In 1994, Saskatchewan's sister provinces of Alberta and Manitoba still did not have library systems in all of their rural areas, nor do they have the comprehensive resource sharing network which is enjoyed in Saskatchewan.

By 1982, it was estimated that as many as half of the residents of Saskatchewan were using libraries on a regular basis, borrowing over 6.5 million items and requesting about 200,000 interlibrary loans annually. Virtually every centre of over 300 people had a library open at least fifteen hours a week. The system employed about 600 full-time and 300 part-time paid staff, many of them in the rural areas at a time when rural communities were in decline and when jobs were scarce.

This was quite an accomplishment in such a spread-out, thinly populated province. For those of us who were part of it, however, there was nothing onerous about the task, at least not in the early years. Getting there was more than half the fun. The foundation proved to be strong. After nine years of Conservative policies, difficult world prices for grain, and a crippling recession, the provincial library system was still viable and thriving as people demanded ever greater access to information and knowledge.

REFERENCES

Calder Bateman Communications. 1991. *Giving Voice to the "Quiet Majority."* Final report to the Alberta Public Libraries Marketing Task Force, April 26. Edmonton: Alberta Public Libraries Marketing Task Force.

Campbell, J. 1992. *The Saskatchewan Provincial Library*. SLA Forum, April. Regina: Saskatchewan Library Association.

Library Inquiry Committee. 1967. *Library Service in Saskatchewan*. Regina: Province of Saskatchewan.

Ontario Strategic Planning Group. 1990. *One Place to Look; the Ontario Public Library Strategic Plan*. Toronto: Province of Ontario.

Saskatchewan Provincial Library. 1974. *Annual Report*. Regina: Government of Saskatchewan.

———. 1980. *Annual Report*. Regina: Government of Saskatchewan.

Saskatchewan Library Association. 1988. *Library Association Echo Valley Library Forum*. Regina: Saskatchewan Library Association/Saskatchewan Library Trustees Association.

Selzer, K. 1979. *A History of the Saskatchewan Provincial Library*. Edmonton, Alberta: Faculty of Library Science, Major Project.

7 Use of Paraprofessionals: The Saskatchewan Dental Plan

by Steve Wolfson

Introduction

In September 1974, the Government of Saskatchewan began operating a universal dental program for children, the Saskatchewan Dental Plan (SDP). Universal dental care for children was not in itself innovative. It had existed in Newfoundland since 1950 and Prince Edward Island since 1971. In 1974, Quebec and Nova Scotia also introduced children's dental programs. What made the SDP unique in North America was its innovative approach to delivering services. The other provinces' programs, with the exception of Prince Edward Island,[1] were based on a private practice, fee-for-service model. For the 11 years the SDP existed, children in Saskatchewan received dental care in school-based clinics and the main provider of this care was a government-employed dental paraprofessional called a dental therapist.[2]

Precursors to the Saskatchewan Dental Plan

Poor dental health in Saskatchewan, particularly among children has been recognized for many years. Since the 1930s proposals have been made for a children's dental program. At different times these proposals advocated

---

[1] In Prince Edward Island care was also provided by government-employed salaried staff and a paraprofessional was used. Compared to the Saskatchewan dental therapist, the PEI expanded duty hygienist could not perform as wide a range of duties and a dentist was required to be present at all times.

[2] Throughout this article the term dental therapist will be used to describe the Saskatchewan paraprofessional. When the program started the New Zealand term dental nurse was used but this was soon changed to dental therapist. One objective of changing the name was to encourage more males to enter the profession. This strategy did not succeed and the profession remained virtually all female.

three distinct approaches to delivering care: private practice fee-for-service, government-employed dentist, and government-employed dental therapist.

A private practice fee-for-service model for a children's dental program in Saskatchewan was first proposed by the Canadian Dental Association (CDA) in the 1930s (Barker, 1985, p. 25). They recognized the poor dental health of the children in Saskatchewan and outlined an approach to dealing with the problem.

In 1954, the College of Dental Surgeons of Saskatchewan (CDSS) started a drive for the establishment of a dental school in Saskatchewan. One of the main arguments for the school was that it would create sufficient manpower for a private practice fee-for-service children's dental program. The CDA and the CDSS have promoted this approach throughout the years and continue to do so.

In the 1940s, the newly elected CCF government was concerned about the problem of children's dental health (Barker, 1985, p. 25). They advocated the use of government-employed dentists to provide dental care. In 1946 two health regions in the province began to offer dental services for children using salaried dentists. However, these programs failed because there were too few dentists available.

It was clear that the government would need to look for other means of improving the dental health of children. In November 1948, a division of dental health was established in the Saskatchewan Department of Health. Dr. A.E. Chegwin was appointed Director. In 1951, the Saskatchewan Health Survey Committee reported that dental disease was "the most extensive health problem in Saskatchewan."

The Dental Therapist Option

The first recorded mention of a dental therapist option was in an interdepartmental memo dated July 31, 1952 (Barker, 1985, p. 44). It recommended that the province set up a training school for dental nurses. The school and the program that would follow were to be based on the New Zealand children's dental program.

The New Zealand program had been in operation since 1932. When faced with a severe dental health problem and too few dentists, New Zealand developed the concept of a dental nurse (dental therapist). New Zealand dental nurses are high school graduates who have completed a two-year technical training course. Working alone in school dental clinics throughout the country, therapists provide basic restorative and preventive dental care for children. The dental program is universal and without charge to the patient or family. Children from preschool age until the age of 13 are treated in school clinics.

In 1954 and 1955, Dr. Chegwin and his division outlined a rationale for a dental therapist option and recommended that a pilot project be undertaken. However, this proposal did not find favour in the government

127

because of opposition from the profession and because of the deeply in-grained belief among politicians that dentists provide dental care.

A second opportunity to promote the dental therapy option came in 1959. The committee that recommended the introduction of medicare also recommended that a New Zealand-type children's dental program be inves-tigated (Barker, 1985, p. 48). They said that at some future time the province would want a universal dental program. Dr. Chegwin and Dr. Murray Acker, the Director of Health Research seized this opportunity and put together another, stronger proposal. They took it directly to Premier Tommy Douglas. Mr. Douglas was in favour. This led to a committee being struck with the CDSS to study the mounting of a pilot project leading to training and a children's dental program.

The profession successfully managed to stall the process. Finally, in 1962, they agreed to take part in a mission to New Zealand to observe the school dental program. Upon return from New Zealand the president of the CDSS recommended that the profession accept the idea of the dental therapist. However, the council of the CDSS and the CDA executive blocked his recommendation.

In 1963, the new Minister of Health, Allan Blakeney, was not inter-ested in taking on the dental profession, after having just concluded a bitter fight with the medical profession over medicare (Barker, 1985, p. 53). Mr. Blakeney's main concern was to fight off the dental profession's push to start a dental school.

Although the Liberals, elected in 1964, had a bent toward free enterprise, some in the government including Premier Thatcher wanted to solve the dental health problem. In 1965, after 15 years of arguments about a dental school, the premier decided the issue on his own, without consulting the relevant departments. Mr. Thatcher also informed his Minister of Health, David Steuart, that he wanted a "concrete program" aimed at recruiting recent dental school graduates to set up practice in Saskatchewan.

On July 18, 1966 the Department of Health announced a five-point program (Barker, 1985, p. 55). The first four points dealt with attracting more dentists to set up practice in Saskatchewan including a bursary program, rural practice establishment grants, buying places in other dental schools for Saskatchewan students, and the establishment of a dental school at the University of Saskatchewan.

The fifth point was a surprise. The department said it would seek the opinion of the CDSS on the advisability of instituting a course to train dental therapists. This position was the result of the combination of a Minister who was not happy with the dental profession's half-hearted at-tempts to solve the children's dental health problem and a deputy minister, Dr. Clarkson, who liked the dental therapist concept. In the July 18th press release, Dr. Clarkson called dental therapists, "a solution to the treatment of routine problems in children."

The dental profession continued to resist a plan using dental therapists. The plan they presented in August of 1967 was essentially the CDA's 1938 plan with hygienists providing prevention in schools and referring treatment to dentists in private practice. The plan spoke against dental therapists saying that they would ignore prevention, have a short working life and they would hurt rural practices that were dependent on children.

In November 1967, Dr. Tom Curry became director of the Division of Dental Health (Barker, 1985, p. 61). He favoured dental therapists. This support combined with his considerable powers of persuasion had much to do with the establishment of the SDP and its final design.

A Pilot Project

Dr. Curry was in favour of mounting a pilot project. The site chosen for the pilot was Oxbow. However, Dr. Curry first had to sell the idea to the dentists in the area. Dr. Curry was a persuasive man. One of his colleagues described him as "... a political fellow, typically Irish, mixing blarney and sense." His meetings with the dentists were held over meals in local hotels which included generous amounts of alcohol.

At these meetings Dr. Curry sold the project on the basis that the closest dentist to Oxbow was in Estevan which was 35 miles away. The therapists would only see children and these children were now getting virtually no care. The therapists would provide dental health education in both the clinic and the schools. Finally, he stressed that it was just a little project in a small little area of Saskatchewan and there were no long-range plans for expanding it after the experiment was completed in three years.

At the annual meeting of the CDSS in April of 1968, a resolution was passed saying that the CDSS would cooperate with the government in the pilot project. After the 1967 election, however, the Premier had slashed government spending. The Department of Health closed small hospitals, cut program budgets and introduced hospital and medicare user fees. Dr. Curry had to go to Ottawa for funding of the pilot project.

The Oxbow Project was finally begun in 1969. A 50-foot mobile home was used as a clinic. It contained three fully equipped dental operatories, a waiting area, a mechanical room, a staff room and a bathroom. The clinic was set up near schools in Oxbow and two other surrounding communities. It was staffed by two British-trained dental therapists, one receptionist, one dental assistant and one supervising dentist.

There were two main objectives of the Oxbow Project: first, to determine whether parents would allow their children to attend a dental clinic where services were provided by a dental therapist rather than a dentist, and second, to assess the quality and quantity of dental care provided by a dental therapist.

From early on it was obvious that the Oxbow Project was a success. Parents were pleased to enrol their children to receive care from dental therapists at a nominal cost. Also, the children were comfortable with the therapists. Their work was assessed by dentists in private practice and the quality of care was found to be fully acceptable. Another important finding was that the clinic was most successful when the trailer was placed adjacent to the school.

Toward a Provincial Children's Dental Program

The NDP defeated the Liberals in June 1971. The NDP promised in their campaign to establish an insured dental care service, initially for those under 12 years old. This promise, however, did not ensure that a program would become a reality or that the program would use dental therapists.

Walter Smishek, a long-time advocate of a strong government health policy and the only left-wing member of the party in the Cabinet, was appointed Minister of Health. He had an interest in showing fellow Cabinet members that meeting past commitments and seeking almost radical change could produce substantial political benefits. By September 1971, Mr. Smishek was able to convince his Cabinet colleagues to introduce the Saskatchewan Dental Plan. According to the Minister, the program was approved despite tight financial restraints because it met various goals of the government (Barker, 1985, p. 85). It was grabby and would be remembered by voters at election time. It would help revitalize rural Saskatchewan. Also, it could help produce a rational health system.

Although approved in principle by Cabinet, the design of the program had not been finalized. The CDSS was still opposed to any use of dental therapists. Mr. Smishek met with the CDSS and was noncommittal on nurses and the timing of the program. This seemed to satisfy the College and it gave the government time to determine their preferred approach to delivering the program without interference from the profession.

Within the Department of Health, the Research and Planning Branch headed by Duane Adams had some concerns about the proposed school-based, dental therapist model for the program and felt more time was needed to study the issue. The Deputy Minister, Dr. Louis Skoll, on the other hand, was in favour of Dr. Curry's proposed use of dental therapists. A planning stalemate developed, which was broken in March 1972 by a Cabinet directive stating that the Premier wanted the program operating by September 1974 (Barker, 1985, p. 102). A compromise was necessary in order for the program to be ready in time. Research and Planning agreed to go along with the school-based dental therapist model. Dr. Curry agreed to let Research and Planning put together the detailed plan for the program.

Sid Smith of Research and Planning Branch was assigned to direct the writing of the planning document. By the beginning of December, the Department had completed a detailed proposal for a dental care program for children. It outlined a plan that closely resembled what would eventually become the Saskatchewan Dental Plan. The proposal detailed two main reasons for establishing the proposed plan, poor dental health of the province's children and insufficient dental manpower to cope with the problem. (Department of Public Health, 1972)

A 1971 dental survey of six school units revealed that among 7 year olds 76% required restorative dental treatment and 39% required the extraction of one or more teeth. On average, each 7 year old had 3.2 temporary teeth that needed restoration. The story was much the same in the 11 year olds: 75% required restorative care and 26% needed one or more teeth extracted. In addition to this survey, the Oxbow Project had shown that the average child needed three hours of dental care to take care of their restorative and preventive dental needs.

The proposal showed that there was insufficient dental manpower in the province to meet the dental needs of children. There were 185 dentists in Saskatchewan or a ratio of one dentist to 5,000 people. This was the worst ratio in Canada. In addition to too few dentists, the distribution of dentists favoured the cities. One-half of the Province's dentists were located in Regina and Saskatoon though these two cities held only 30% of the province's population. It was estimated that a 50% increase in the number of dentists practising in Saskatchewan would be needed to provide sufficient services for children aged 3–12. The report also stated that even if dentists could provide the needed care, the financial burden would be too great for a large proportion of families.

This proposal was submitted to a Minister's Advisory Committee on Dental Care for Children chaired by Dr. K.J. Paynter, the dean of the College of Dentistry at the University of Saskatchewan. The other committee members were Mrs. J. Bell, Dr. A.W. Geisthardt (representing the College of Dental Surgeons), Dr. Michael Lewis, Mr. G. McGuire and Mrs. L. Tuchscherer. The committee submitted its report to the Minister of Health on March 31, 1973. The committee endorsed the government's proposal with a few suggestions for minor changes. However, Dr. Geisthardt did not agree with some of the main principles of the proposal and submitted a minority report outlining his concerns.

The government's proposal recommended that all children be treated in school dental clinics unless they had complex dental needs that were beyond the scope of the Dental Plan's staff. In such cases, they would be referred to a dentist in private practice. Dr. Geisthardt felt that parents should be able to choose between having their child treated in a school clinic or by a dentist in private practice and the government should pay for the care in either case. The other main area of the proposal that Dr. Geisthardt disagreed with concerned the dental therapist. He felt that dental therapists needed to be supervised directly by a dentist who was on the premises during treatment. The proposal called for dental therapists to be able to work with no dentist present. Supervision would be done by supervising dentists who would make regular visits to work with the therapists.

In the end, however, the dental profession was unable to pressure the government into making significant changes in the program. According to Barker (1985, p. 109) there were a number of reasons for this. First, they did not react strongly when put off by the government partly because they were busy in their practices and had little interest in politics. Another reason for their low interest in the issue was that they felt they had little at stake. Few dentists were interested in the children's market and thus very few dentists were worried about losing it. Also, many dentists in the province were in favour of using dental therapists in some capacity. Finally, the dental profession had very little power to exert pressure. A work stoppage on their part would not affect the dental program. The public was not likely to support the profession because they were upset by the poor dental coverage in rural areas, the profession's support of fluoridation, their prosecution of denturists, and the pain and general unpleasantness associated with dentists.

The last attempt by the profession to stop the implementation of the program came in late 1974. The CDSS changed the regulations under the dental practice act so that dentists from the United States would have to take the exam set by the National Dental Examining Board. This was at a time when the SDP had been unable to recruit a sufficient number of Canadian dentists and had hired five dentists from the States. The Government threatened to amend the Dental Professions Act and the CDSS backed down (Barker, 1985, p. 207).

The training of dental therapists began before the planning document was complete. Dr. Graham Keenan, a New Zealand dentist and former instructor at the New Zealand nurse training school, was hired to begin a training program as part of the Wascana Institute in Regina. He recruited six New Zealand dental tutors to come to Saskatchewan. Dr. Michael Lewis was also hired to teach part time and to assist in the planning of a children's dental program.

In April 1974, Dr. Curry resigned. Dr. Michael Lewis was immediately hired and became the first and only Executive Director of the SDP.

The Program

In September 1974, the Saskatchewan Dental Plan began operations. All children in the province born in 1968 (six-year-olds) were invited to enrol. These children were the first of many to participate in a dental program that was unique in North America. In the time it endured, the SDP became known around the world as one of the most advanced and successful dental care programs for children.

The program that was finally established in many ways resembled the New Zealand program; however, some key changes made the program more appropriate for the situation in Saskatchewan.

As in New Zealand the vast majority of the work was performed by dental therapists working in school dental clinics. The training of the dental therapists in Saskatchewan was modified to take into account the most up-to-date standards for children's dental care in North America. Among other things this meant that Saskatchewan dental therapists were trained to use high-speed drills, place stainless steel crowns, and provide freezing for more parts of the mouth. Dental therapists were taught to use rubber dams for all restorations. This not only provided more safety and comfort for the patient but it kept saliva out of the filling material thus extending the life of the filling.

In New Zealand the dental nurse works alone. The Saskatchewan Dental Plan was based on a team consisting of a dental therapist and a certified dental assistant. One dentist supervised between 8 and 10 teams. Working in teams meant that care could be provided more efficiently. Among other advantages the patients would spend less time in the dental chair and away from class. Having a teammate was also thought to help dental workers cope with the stress of the job.

For administration, the SDP was organized into six regions with a central office in Regina. Central office staff included the Executive Director, and an Associate Director who specialized in administration, Clifford Millions.

Each region had a complement of supervising dentists, who visited dental teams regularly. They helped the teams with any problems they encountered, periodically examined patients, talked to parents about specific dental problems, and made sure that the quality of care was up to Dental Plan standards. Each region had one administrator who facilitated administrative operations for the region. To assure that all equipment and clinics were well-maintained, each region had its own dental equipment technician.

From the outset, the Dental Plan was committed to establishing a management information system. Information was gathered primarily in two areas, dental health and services provided. A number of different programs were designed so that the data gathered could be used for annual reports, as management tools for field staff, and to help program managers gauge program effectiveness and staff productivity.

The Effectiveness of the Program

In 1980, Dr. D.W. Lewis (no relation to Dr. Michael Lewis) of the University of Toronto conducted an evaluation of the first six years of operation of the Saskatchewan Dental Plan (Lewis, 1981).

In the first year of operation, 14,342 six year olds were eligible for the program; by the sixth year 142,182 children ages 4–13. Of those eligible an average of 83% had enroled in the program. Dr. Lewis found the participation rates to be high. They were 20% higher than the three other universal provincial dental programs which used fee-for-service delivery systems and about the same as that found in PEI that used salaried staff. Dr. Lewis estimated that 90% of the children eligible for the Dental Plan were either receiving care from the Dental Plan or a dentist in private practice. Thus the proportion of children receiving care in Saskatchewan was higher than any other large geographic area in North America.

Being enroled in the program was not the only important factor; children's needs must also be met. Of those enroled in the Dental Plan in the sixth year, 88% had all their dental needs, as identified by the staff of the Dental Plan, cared for.

Another indicator Dr. Lewis used to gauge the success of the program was parent satisfaction. In March of 1978, a phone survey was conducted of 600 families that had children in the Dental Plan. The parents showed overwhelming support for the program. Overall satisfaction with the program was expressed by 89% of those surveyed. When asked specifically about their satisfaction with the work of the Dental Therapist, 89% of those living in cities and 94% of rural residents were satisfied. Of those questioned, 79.5% were in favour of expansion of the program.

Another important factor for the Dental Plan was cost effectiveness. The Dental Plan was able to take advantage of economies of scale as it expanded. Also, as the backlog of dental needs was met and patients reached a maintenance level of care, each dental team was able to treat more patients. The cost of care per patient fell from $163 in the first year of operation to $68 in the sixth year, in real dollars, not accounting for inflation. Dr. Lewis states that this decrease in cost of delivering care to patients occurred without any sacrifice to the quality of care provided.

In a 1976 study by Ambrose, Hord and Simpson, the quality of restorations provided by dental therapists was compared to the quality of restorations provided for the same patients by dentists in private practice. They found that the work of the dental therapists was as good as, if not better than, the work of local dentists. (Ambrose, Hord, Simpson, 1976)

The most important factor when looking at the quality of the program is the impact it had on the dental health of enroled children. Over its lifetime, the Dental Plan produced dramatic improvements in their dental health. The total number of decayed, missing and filled permanent and baby teeth for six-year-old children declined from 6.5 in 1974–75 to 2.9 in 1985–86. In addition, there was a major shift in the proportion of this total that represents treated disease, that is filled teeth. In 1974–75, 17% of the total (6.5) were filled and in 1985–86, 62% of the total (2.9) were filled teeth (Department of Health, 1987). Also, the proportion of six year olds that were totally free of dental caries (no decayed, missing or filled teeth) increased from 12% to 32%. In 1978, 7.5% of the 13-year-old population was caries free, while in 1985 this figure had increased to 24.0%.

Adolescent Dental Care

As some of the children in the Dental Plan approached adolescence, it was felt that they would benefit from getting into the habit of receiving treatment from a dentist in private practice prior to the time they left school and were no longer covered by the Dental Plan. In the 1981–82 school year, a portion of the adolescents were assigned to private dentists. By the 1985–86 school year, 32,982 adolescent patients were assigned for treatment by private practice dentists.

An innovative approach was taken to funding care provided for adolescent patients by dentists in private practice. The College of Dental Surgeons was paid a capitation fee for each child assigned to private practice. It was then up to the College of Dental Surgeons to establish a fee schedule and control the cost of care provided by individual dentists so that the cost would not exceed the total capitation budget.

Another innovative aspect of the program was the government's insistence on ensuring the quality of the dental care for which they were paying. A quality assurance team was established consisting of three dentists representing the College of Dental Surgeons, the College of Dentistry of the University of Saskatchewan, and the Provincial Government. The team travelled throughout the province examining patients. Without knowing who had provided the work, they assessed the quality according to a set of established guidelines. Thus, they were assessing the work provided by dental therapists and for the first time ever they were making a systematic review of work provided by dentists in private practice.

The vast majority of the work inspected had been done over the years by dental therapists. Although several cases were discovered which showed a pattern of sub-standard care, none of these were found to be the work of therapists.

The Impact of the Program beyond Its Patients

The College of Dental Surgeons dealt with the cases that were brought to its attention by the inspection team. It can be assumed that an improvement in the quality of care provided by the practitioners in question to their adolescent patients would also have some benefit to the other patients in their practice.

As part of the care for children, staff made frequent contacts with parents. Parents were encouraged to visit the clinic so that the treatment and preventive needs of the child could be explained. This process greatly increased the dental health knowledge of a significant number of adults in Saskatchewan. As these adults became more aware and as their children's needs were being met by the SDP, they became more interested in seeking dental care for themselves. Not only did the demand for dental care by adults increase, they were now demanding more sophisticated dental services. As this happened, more dentists in private practice began to offer more complex services such as root canals, crowns, bridges and orthodontics.

The standards of care set by the SDP influenced standards of care in the private sector. One illustration of this is the SDP's use of stainless steel crowns to restore badly broken-down baby molars. These crowns were the accepted standard for this procedure in North America but they were rarely used in Saskatchewan. When the SDP began operations, some private

135

practice dentists advised parents of SDP patients that a stainless steel crown was a poor type of restoration. Despite this resistance, the SDP continued to place stainless steel crowns quite successfully and with the understanding of parents. Private dentists soon dropped their opposition to the procedure and many began using these crowns in their own practices.

The use of X-rays is a good example of a change that was made. When the plan started it used the then-accepted standard that all patients should have routine X-rays taken at the time of examination. There was, however, a growing belief that the amount of radiation children were exposed to should be minimized. A new set of standards was put in place that reduced the use of X-rays without compromising the dental health of the children. As a result, the use of X-rays was reduced from an average of 2.41 films/patient in 1974–75 to .57 films/patient in 1979–80. Dr. D.W. Lewis, in his evaluation, reported that this change did not lower the quality of care provided.

It is likely that this change in standards for X-rays had some impact on dentists in private practice; however, their use of X-rays on adolescent patients was significantly higher than the use of X-rays by the Dental Plan on the same age groups. In the 1985–86 school year the Dental Plan staff provided 408 sets of two bitewing X-rays per 1,000 adolescent patients while dentists in private practice provided 817 sets of two bitewing X-rays per 1,000 adolescents.

The SDP established a number of standards for care that were adopted by private practice dentists across the province in varying degrees. These include the use of rubber dams, fissure sealants, and lead aprons and later cervical collars to protect patients during exposure to X-rays. When Vietnamese refugees began to arrive in Saskatchewan, there was a concern about the transmission of hepatitis to dental therapists and dentists as well as its spread among patients. The SDP introduced procedures for sterilizing instruments that would ensure that viruses transmitted by blood (including AIDS) would be killed. Dental Plan staff began to wear rubber gloves and masks for all patient treatment. This has since become the standard for care across North America.

A Program Observed around the World

The SDP generated interest well beyond the borders of Saskatchewan, from across Canada and around the world. Many made special trips to visit the program and observe it first-hand. Others stopped by for a day or two if they were passing through Saskatchewan. Many others wrote with specific questions or just to obtain the latest annual report.

People were interested in all aspects of the program from the management of equipment, information and personnel to the impact of the program on the dental health of the children. In virtually every case, the interest stemmed from the innovative approach the SDP took to aggressively improve the dental health of the children of Saskatchewan.

In 1976, Manitoba announced a children's dental program. The Manitoba program excluded the city of Winnipeg but otherwise it was almost identical to the SDP. Manitoba arranged for therapists to be trained in Saskatchewan. The people developing the Manitoba program consulted with the managers of the SDP, and adopted many of Saskatchewan's procedures and management systems.

The Demise of the Saskatchewan Dental Plan

In June 1987, all of the approximately 400 employees of the dental plan were called into locations around the province and told that the government would no longer provide dental care using salaried staff. The Saskatchewan Dental Plan would be privatized; all care would be provided by dentists in private practice. This marked the end of the innovative concept that was the SDP.

The Dental Plan's demise must be linked at least partly to its success. The government's rationalization of the change included the fact that there was now very little decay occurring in children and 75% were caries free. In addition, there were now enough dentists and they were more equally distributed in the province so that dentists could now handle the care. Finally, the change was put forward as a cost-saving measure. The Dental Plan was inefficient because staff could only treat patients during school hours and there were no patients for them during school holidays.

The Progressive Conservative Government and the College of Dental Surgeons later claimed that the privatized children's dental program achieved higher participation rates and lower costs than the SDP. If this is so, it would contradict the experience of other dental care programs throughout the world. Since children no longer receive care in schools, it would be expected that utilization would decrease, particularly in rural communities where there is no dentist and amongst urban low income and single parent families. There are no clear answers to these discrepancies since no independent evaluation of the privatized program has, at this time, been made.

Other questions that have yet to be answered are how much of the motivation to privatize the program was related to provincial politics, dental politics and the politics of gender.

It is easy to understand why the Government might have been anxious to put an end to the SDP. For one thing, the SDP was a program that was seen very much as an NDP program. The NDP, in their unsuccessful election campaign of 1982, had promised to extend dental care benefits to all people in the province. Another irritation for the private sector-oriented PC government was that the SDP was the most high-profile example of a socialized health program within the government. It was a program that sent government workers into virtually every community in the province that had a school to provide health care services at no direct charge to families.

In terms of dental politics, the College of Dental Surgeons of Saskatchewan never accepted the SDP; however, under an NDP government, they received little sympathy for their arguments. This changed when the government changed. After the 1982 election, the dental profession found that it had the ear of a government that was sympathetic to their dislike of the SDP.

The view that the CDSS and the government conspired to end the SDP was upheld in court. A suit was filed by the Saskatchewan Government Employees Union (SGEU) alleging that there had been a conspiracy between the Provincial Government and the College of Dental Surgeons. The court ruled in favour of the employees.

Finally, it is worth considering the character of the two different work forces, the SDP and private practice. The approximately 200 dental therapists and 200 dental assistants who lost their jobs were virtually all females and they were from all parts of the province. The therapists were some of Saskatchewan's brightest young people. They were all potential university material but, upon leaving high school, chose to make a career of dental therapy. Many had returned to work in their home communities and hoped to have a lifetime career there. The dentists of Saskatchewan, on the other hand are predominantly male. For economic and personal reasons, dentists are less likely than dental therapists to end up living and working in a small rural community. So, how can a smaller group of people that are less representative of the province displace a larger more grassroots group? Perhaps this question will never be answered, but one has to wonder had the gender of these two groups been reversed, if the government would have had the political will to put 400 men out of work.

Conclusion

There are many opinions about the SDP and many unanswered questions. One of the most important outstanding issues is determining the impact dismantling the program had on the dental health of the province's children. One may hope that this question and others will be investigated impartially by the subsequent NDP Government.

Even when the scientific questions are answered, there will always be differences of opinion about whether or not there should have been or should again be a school-based dental therapist program in Saskatchewan. One thing that nearly everyone can agree on is that the approach taken by the SDP was an innovative one. It was the answer to a problem that had been recognized since at least the 1930s. It had been seen by some in the provincial government as the solution to the problem since 1952. It was popular with children and their parents. It was a program that drew interest from around the world. It was also an innovation that the dental profession in Saskatchewan and in Canada would not accept. When the profession and the government both agreed for their own reasons that it was an unacceptable innovation, it died.

Governments that are considering taking innovative approaches to solving problems should consider the SDP experience. The benefits of the proposed innovation should be weighed against the costs of mounting a program that is at high risk of being swept away by political change. If the benefit is seen to be worth the risk, program planners should develop preventive strategies to lessen the possibility of abolition by a new government.

REFERENCES

Ambrose, E.R., A.B. Hord and W.J. Simpson. 1976. *A Quality Evaluation of Specific Dental Services Provided by the Saskatchewan Dental Plan.* Regina: Department of Health, Government of Saskatchewan.

Barker, Paul F. 1985. "The Formulation and Implementation of the Saskatchewan Dental Plan." University of Toronto, School of Graduate Studies, PhD Thesis.

Department of Health. 1987. *Saskatchewan Health Dental Plan, Annual Report, 1986–87.* Regina: Government of Saskatchewan.

Department of Public Health. 1972. "Proposal for a Children's Dental Plan." Unpublished document. Regina: Government of Saskatchewan.

Lewis D.W. 1981. *An Evaluation of the First Six Years of Operation of the Saskatchewan Dental Plan.* Regina: Department of Health, Government of Saskatchewan.

8

Social Justice for Workers

by Gordon T. Snyder

My appointment as Minister of Labour in 1971 provided me with the opportunity to shape, enhance and protect the rights of the working people of Saskatchewan. I believe this was accomplished in a very major way. Morale among department employees was excellent. We were known to declare that we were not only the best Department of Labour in Canada — but that we were the ONLY Department of Labour.

This chapter describes the large number of changes and innovations which saw Saskatchewan lead all other provinces in measures which made life more secure, safe and rewarding for the working men and women of our province.

The Context

The preceding seven years of Liberal administration were described as the "seven long, lean, gaunt years" by Allan Blakeney. Nowhere was this more true than for labour. The relationship between the Saskatchewan Federation of Labour (SFL)[1] and the Liberal government of Ross Thatcher got off to a combative beginning at the first SFL convention following the 1964 provincial election. The newly appointed Labour Minister, Lionel Coderre, received a cool reception. In the course of his remarks, he asked the members of the SFL for the opportunity to demonstrate his good will and impartiality. The SFL was unforgiving and as he left the podium in a chilling atmosphere of silence, a motion was proposed from the convention floor which called for the SFL to "take whatever action is necessary to bring about the defeat of the new Liberal government."

In the following seven years, the distrust and concern that the SFL felt for the Thatcher government seemed justified. Amendments to The Trade Union Act made it more difficult for unions to organize workers. Labour Standards, which established hours of work, minimum wages, annual vacations and statutory holidays, enjoyed virtually no improvement during

---

[1] The SFL was an umbrella group for unions in the province.

the Thatcher years. Industrial relations, a vital function of the Department of Labour in the resolution of labour-management disputes, was largely non-existent in 1971, with a single officer on staff to help extinguish the labour-management brush fires over the entire province.

Only token support was offered on the question of women's issues at a time when increasing numbers of women were entering the workforce and demanding recognition. A single employee in the Women's Bureau had a mandate which did not extend far beyond public relations and speaking engagements.

The problems associated with the Workers' Compensation Board had become monumental. The Board had been directed to keep levies assessed upon employers as low as possible. Accordingly, the Board was seen as the agent for denied claims, tardy rulings and petty adjudication of injury and disability awards. Aggrieved workers who were convinced that they had been unjustly treated could appeal to the full Board, but invariably felt they were appealing to the same body which had already rejected their claim.

Against this backdrop, the Injured Workers' Association sprang up to represent those who felt wronged and neglected. As their members increased and became more vocal, a clear public awareness of the plight of injured workers emerged.

By 1971, the Thatcher government had given clear notice of a declaration of war on the trade union movement with the passage of *The Essential Services Emergency Act*. This statute gave absolute authority to the provincial Cabinet to declare any work stoppage an emergency, without recall of the Legislature. The statute also provided stringent penalties for violations of the edict. To organized labour, this was the last straw which rendered the process of collective bargaining impotent.

It had become increasingly obvious that the government of the day had scant regard for Saskatchewan's working men and women — and had relegated the Department of Labour to a lowly position as the poorest of Cabinet relatives, starved for funds and personnel to perform its role.

An Occupational Health Unit, located in the Department of Health, performed a limited function in providing for the enforcement and regulation of health matters in the workplace. It was regarded as less than enthusiastic in pursuing a health program which affected workers on the job.

It was in this atmosphere that the NDP government was ushered into power in 1971. The Department of Labour emerged with an understood mandate to preserve and enhance the circumstances under which Saskatchewan's working men and women earned their livelihood. The new government provided a reasonably free hand to the Department in formulating a strategy to overcome the damage and neglect of previous years despite the fact that only three members of the NDP Caucus had any real ties with the trade union movement. Although very many changes were made affecting working people, only North American innovations will be reviewed here.

Labour Standards

The Labour Standards Act was the basic legislation which spelled out a full range of provisions affecting the working conditions of practically every wage earner in the province. In 1971, the labour standards provisions had slipped close to the bottom of the scale as compared to other provincial jurisdictions.

In an attempt to stop the erosion, in August 1971 an amendment was passed establishing a universal 40 hour week, with time and one-half for overtime, the first province in Canada to do so. The amendment provided for a reduction from 44 hours per week to 40 hours in urban areas and from 48 hours a week to 40 hours in the rural areas, thus eliminating the urban-rural disparity. Saskatchewan was the first province in Canada to introduce the universal 40-hour week.

In May of 1972, the right of an employee to obtain a leave of absence to run as a candidate and serve a term in any public office was enshrined in law. This was a first in Canada. In 1973 equal pay for similar work provisions was adopted to protect the rights of working women. The statute was also amended to provide four weeks' annual vacation after 20 years of service and three weeks' annual vacation after one year of service. This was, again, a first in Canada.

In 1974, legislation was provided to protect employees from loss of wages when an employer fails financially. In 1975, "Saskatchewan Day" became the 9th Statutory Holiday, to be celebrated on the first Monday in August. Only the Government of Canada, British Columbia, the Northwest Territories and the Yukon had nine designated statutory holidays. In addition, 18 weeks' unpaid maternity leave was provided, and somewhat later six weeks' paternity and adoption leave was provided in *The Labour Standards Act* to allow an opportunity for adjustment following the arrival of a new child in a worker's home. Saskatchewan was the first jurisdiction in Canada to provide for paternity leave. Saskatchewan also became the first province to legislate bereavement leave.

In 1980, an amendment was enacted which provided for a period of notice of termination or layoff of an employee which lengthens with length of service and allows for regular pay in lieu of notice. The notice period extended progressively from one week for employees with more than three months but less than one year of service, up to eight weeks after more than 10 years of service.

During the late 1970s, increasing demands by retail workers and their respective unions in particular centred on the question of "two consecutive days off." In many cases, a worker would have a work arrangement with Sunday and another day of the week off, other than Saturday or Monday. Accordingly, *The Labour Standards Act* was amended to ensure two consecutive days off, subject to a more mutually acceptable arrangement to be agreed to by the employee and employer. This, again, was a first in the country.

Instead of emerging as a conquering hero for retail workers, numerous workers in the retail industry descended on me with the wrath of God. They invited me to stay out of their lives. A number of them maintained that they were older employees who needed to split the week with their usual Wednesday off. Others told me in plain language that Wednesday was the day they played bridge with the girls, that they had done so for years, and would I kindly mind my own business.

This was the only labour measure which was less of a success than had been forecast by those who promoted it, and hounded me until I succumbed. The legislation remained in place, but employees were given an exemption on request. Accordingly, I do not look back on this particular legislative amendment as my greatest accomplishment.

Still another amendment provided that an employee could not be discharged solely because he or she had been served with a garnishee proceeding.

Finally, one of the fundamental cornerstones of labour standards, the minimum wage provisions, received continuing attention. It is important to remember that the lowest-paid workers, almost always unorganized and without union protection or significant voice, are solely dependent upon the actions of government to provide a degree of financial protection for them.

The Minimum Wage Board was reactivated in 1971 and progressive adjustments made in order to reflect rising costs as they affected those low-paid workers. When the NDP was elected in 1971, the minimum wage was raised to $2.00 per hour, with regular adjustments to the level of $4.25 on January 1, 1982, which was the highest rate in Canada at that time. Provision was made for an increase to $4.50 to be effective January 1, 1983, an adjustment which did not take place when the Progressive Conservative government was elected in April 1982.

This does not represent a complete summary of all the labour standards changes during the 1971–1982 period. It does, however, outline the major revisions during that 11-year period.

Occupational Health and Safety

The Saskatchewan approach to occupational health and safety represented one of the major initiatives by the Department of Labour following the 1971 provincial general election. At that time, the functions of the Occupational Health Branch resided in the Department of Health which relegated that agency to a rather minor role in the total scheme of its mandate. The government decided that both Occupational Health and Safety Services (electrical and gas inspection, the fire commissioner's office, etc.) should be located under one umbrella organization. Dr. Robert Sass, who subsequently

143

became the Director of the new Occupational Health and Safety Division, provided exemplary leadership to the program.

The 1972 legislation was developed in recognition of the health and safety concerns which were causing increasing anxiety in the Saskatchewan workforce; however, these worries were not limited to the workers. Many employers were uneasy about the effects of technological change and the introduction of new and dangerous chemicals into the workplace (e.g. the rising incidence of chronic bronchitis, occupational dermatitis, allergies and a host of complex medical problems). A new set of ailments were manifesting themselves, including neuro-muscular weakness caused by vibration, deafness produced by the noise of machines, and beryllium poisoning. The government felt a clear-cut obligation to take steps designed to safeguard the welfare of employees on the job in an attempt to eliminate dangerous and unhealthy working conditions.

The original Bill provided for the transfer of the responsibility for occupational health from the Department of Health to the Department of Labour and permitted the setting-up of an Occupational Health Council of between 9 and 12 persons representing management, labour and agriculture who had expertise in the field of health and safety. Additionally, the Minister was given the authority, where there was seen to be a dangerous work environment, to require arrangements to be made for medical supervision of the workers in that environment. Additionally, doctors and hospitals were required to provide, without charge to the Chief Occupational Medical Officer of the Department, reports concerning people who became ill or were injured while engaged in an occupation.

An important part of the legislation required that Occupational Health and Safety Committees be established in all places of employment with ten or more employees. This Occupational Health and Safety Committee, with representatives of management and labour, could convene a meeting to deal with matters of concern. The intention was to resolve occupational health and safety problems at the local level. Failing a resolution of the problem, provincial Occupational Health and Safety Officers were available to intervene. In the vast majority of cases, committees solved their problems without intervention.

In the early stages, some employers resisted the committee concept, believing it to be an intrusion upon their rights to manage without interference. Most employers complied willingly, however, believing that a mutual benefit was to be expected. Nevertheless, it was considered prudent to provide that a worker could not be discharged for activities or involvement as a member of an Occupational Health and Safety Committee, another first in Canada.

The requirement in *The Occupational Health and Safety Act* providing for worker involvement in the occupational health and safety committees was a slow and halting step in the direction of Industrial Democracy as it is widely known in the Scandinavian countries, the former West Germany and other European countries. It was a concept endorsed by the International Labour Organization and given credit for a cooperative arrangement between labour and management which had reduced conflict in labour-management relations to an impressive degree.

From 1971–82 the Saskatchewan Department of Labour explored the policy with a view to a modified form of worker participation on management boards. It was greeted with scepticism by organized labour: in some quarters it was feared that in sharing management responsibilities workers might be co-opted and begin to see management's point of view with greater clarity than the union's.

An effort was made to interest the Energy and Chemical Workers at the Crown-owned Sodium Sulphate Plant at Chaplin (100 miles west of Regina), in a pilot project. Workers were ambivalent and the union unenthusiastic. The program did not get off the ground.

Another attempt at worker participation was somewhat more successful. The SFL nominated a trade unionist to serve on the board of a number of Crown Corporations (e.g. a member of the Communication Workers would serve on the Board of the Saskatchewan Power Corporation). It was felt that the worker should not be from the union that bargained for that particular Crown Corporation: a conflict of interest was seen with a union member on the board which was negotiating a contract with his or her union. The concept of worker participation or Industrial Democracy had not advanced beyond that stage in 1982.

Legislation also provided that a worker could refuse to perform what that worker believed to be "unusually dangerous" work until it was determined that the workplace was safe. If the problem was not resolved, an Occupational Health Officer of the department was to be called in to make that determination. Workers were protected from disciplinary action in the exercise of this right, and while some employers feared that this right might be used irresponsibly, this fear proved to be unfounded as workers acknowledged the value of the "right to refuse" clause and chose not to abuse it and run the risk of losing this basic protection. The "right to refuse" was not available in any other jurisdiction in Canada at that time.

The occupational health and safety legislation also provided for stringent fines for violations of the Act and an educational program was devised to provide information to employers and employees in order that the rights and obligations of both parties were understood. In select cases, employees were provided with monitoring equipment to measure levels of carbon monoxide and other toxic substances in the workplace.

The plan was successful and received widespread attention from other jurisdictions. While some employers resisted the provisions of *The Occupational Health and Safety Act* in the early stages, the program developed widespread support when the reduction of accidents and injuries in the workplace had the effect of lowering the assessments paid by employers to the Workers' Compensation Board in a number of occupational classifications. In the main, employers acknowledged that a safe, secure and healthy working environment provided for a happier and more productive workforce.

Workers' Compensation

Embodied in the workers' compensation legislation is a requirement for a review committee to be activated every four years which must report and recommend legislative changes to the government. Judge Alistair Muir of Moose Jaw, who had chaired the review committee on previous occasions since 1971, was chosen to again head the 1978 review. The review committee was composed of a chairman, a workers' representative named by the SFL, and an employer representative appointed by various employer groups. The report of the 1978 Review Committee, endorsed by both employer and employee representatives, recommended a significant change in direction in the administration of workers' compensation. The report noted that there was a genuine unfairness in the system at that time. Two workers might suffer identical injuries with an identical degree of impairment; however, because of the nature of the work each performed, one could return to work at his or her former occupation and, in effect, be better off financially because of the lifetime workers' compensation disability pension. The other worker, unable to return to her same job because of the disability, could be forced to take a lower-paying position and suffer a major financial loss.

From this emerged the concept of an "income replacement system," which was translated into legislation in 1979. It involved an entirely new "two-part" concept, which would protect an injured worker against income loss as a result of the injury and also provide a recognition of permanent impairment caused by the injury. Provision was made for maintenance of income to 75% of a worker's wages at the time of the injury, even if the worker had to accept a lower-paying job. As the second component, the worker was provided with a lump-sum payment which recognized a permanent impairment as a result of the injury.

The 1979 legislation provided full income support for surviving spouses for five years, or until the youngest child reached 16 years of age. For example, if the youngest child was six years of age, benefits would continue for 10 years and the benefits would be reviewed each year after the fifth year and adjusted in relation to the Consumer Price Index. In the event a spouse remarried, the benefits continued for two years.

In summary, the worker's wages were protected until age 65. At 65, compensation was based on lost retirement income. Real wages were protected against inflation by a cost of living feature and any physical impairment caused by an injury was compensated for by way of a lump-sum payment.

Much credit was due to the chairpersons of the Workers' Compensation Board (Dick Fowler, Alex Taylor and Brian King) and the Commissioners representing labour and management during the 1971–82 period. They approached the job with empathy and understanding of the problems of injured workers.

To their everlasting credit also, their financial management was outstanding. While other provincial jurisdictions were piling up mountains of unfunded liabilities, the Saskatchewan Workers' Compensation Board, via employer contributions, developed a fully funded plan and in the early 1980s was prepared to contribute $7 million towards the construction of a new rehabilitation centre which was on the drawing board. The rehabilitation program was a vital component of the compensation system in rehabilitating injured workers in order that they might return to gainful employment.

Judge Alistair Muir also deserves to be singled out for special mention for the consecutive reviews he chaired and the leadership he provided in his reports and his recommendations to government. His work, and that of the committee members, pointed the way for the changes mentioned above.

Women

In 1971 the Department of Labour had a single employee who filled the role of the Women's Bureau, providing token recognition of the greater numbers of women who were entering the workforce and demanding recognition. Women rarely found their place in positions of authority in private industry and governments at all levels were slow to respond to the fundamental changes that had taken place. Women were traditionally paid less than their male counterparts with no reason or justification offered.

The Women's Bureau attempted to educate and inform women's organizations and the public of the problems of women in the workforce, but was limited in its mandate by a lack of resources and the impossible task to be undertaken by a lone person in the Bureau. Speaking engagements and production of pertinent pieces of literature did not meet the expectations of large numbers of women.

In 1973, an amendment to *The Labour Standards Act* provided for "equal pay for similar work" which gave recognition to the fact that the injustices and discrimination against women in the workplace were to be addressed.

By 1982, the Women's Bureau had been expanded to the status of a bona fide division in the department, with a full-time director and assistant director, and a complement of coordinators, investigators, affirmative action officers and an expanded office staff. Staff had increased from one in 1971 to around a dozen employees in 1982.

With the enactment of the equal pay for similar work provision, the Women's Division was charged with the responsibility of investigating violations of the "equal pay" provisions. When violations were identified and

147

a solution was not found, the Women's Division could refer the matter to the Saskatchewan Human Rights Commission for final adjudication.

The division also investigated complaints when maternity, paternity and adoption leave provisions were seen to be violated and when an employee was unjustly dismissed because of pregnancy. Education was one of the important roles of the Division with employer and employee groups taking advantage of the services of the Division. Additionally, cases of sexual harassment in the workplace were investigated as part of the mandate of this unit. Affirmative Action Officers provided assistance to women by facilitating contacts with employers, helping in the preparation of resumes, and providing counselling services.

During the late 1970s and early 1980s an emerging awareness of women's rights began to manifest itself, with women in limited numbers being appointed to positions of greater authority. Several women became Deputy Ministers in the Blakeney government and the Crown Corporations began to recognize the realities of the 1980s. This may now be seen as modest progress.

When the NDP left office in 1982, women's organizations and the trade union movement were actively pressing the government for an extension of "equal pay for similar work" to a full-blown adoption of the concept of "equal pay for work of equal value." The concept made eminently good sense, but no one at that point was able to identify in a practical administrative way how to evaluate and measure "work of equal value," particularly when market conditions often dictated remuneration when an employee with a particular set of skills was in short supply. It was believed that remuneration did not necessarily reflect the value of work performed. The concept, while legislated by the federal government, was largely dormant as they, too, were in a quandary concerning the practical application of the law. The concept of equal pay for work of equal value was still a very live issue, not yet resolved, when the NDP left office.

The Women's Division was abolished by the Conservative government of Grant Devine in April 1983.

Construction Industry Labour Relations Act

An attempt was made to reduce the friction and animosity in the bargaining process in the construction industry. In 1979, *The Construction Industry Labour Relations Act* was passed after lengthy consultation with the construction industry and the affected trades. The *Act* provided for province-wide trade-by-trade bargaining to replace the fragmented process which had engendered a multitude of labour-management problems over many years.

The *Act* prohibited the practice of "double-breasting," a practice undertaken by many construction firms. In practical terms, a "non-union company" formed another "union company" with the same board of directors, and the same corporate management, allowing the company to bid on both union and non-union jobs with impunity. This legislation was short-lived, being repealed by the new Conservative government following the 1982 general election.

Proposed Sickness and Accident Plan

When the NDP government left office in 1982, the Department of Labour was actively exploring an important program for the purpose of protecting the income of a worker who fell ill or was injured in a non-industrial accident. In the case of an industrial accident, income protection was provided by the workers' compensation program, and when a worker's income was interrupted by an injury related to a traffic accident, Saskatchewan Automobile Insurance offered some limited benefits.

About two hundred Saskatchewan wage earners were permanently disabled yearly as a result of sickness or an accident which occurred away from the job. If a worker was stricken with multiple sclerosis, or disabled from an accident which happened at home, that worker's income ceased, often with catastrophic results.

The Sickness and Accident Plan under consideration was intended to provide income replacement. Funding had not been finalized. The government considered it reasonable to expect the plan would be financed by contributions from workers, employers and the government. Both workers and employers contended that the program, if introduced, should be funded solely by the government from general revenue. No final judgement had been made and the matter of sickness and accident insurance was one which could be listed under the heading of "unfinished business" when the NDP government left office.

The accomplishments and initiatives in the labour sphere were made possible through the patient, though forceful, leadership of the four Deputy Ministers of Labour during the 1971–82 period, Donald Ching, Robert Mitchell, Donald McMillan and Gary Simons. The dedication of these people and their talents for interacting with organized labour and management groups made many innovative changes possible with a minimum of conflict. Additionally, their relationship with directors and staff provided for a degree of enthusiasm and loyalty which made the department the very best.

A number of people have suggested that the eleven years of the Blakeney administration produced the best and the most progressive labour legislation on record in Canada. Other provincial jurisdictions followed the lead of many labour initiatives introduced by the Government of Saskatchewan from 1971 to 1982.

9

Self-Enforcement of a Rights-Based Approach to Workplace Health and Safety

by Robert Sass

Introduction

In 1972, the New Democratic Government in Saskatchewan introduced into the legislature an *Occupational Health and Safety Act* which was based on affording workers' rights to participate in work environment matters. This was a legislative first for North America. More specifically, the Act required the establishment of joint occupational health and safety committees in every place of work with ten or more employees. The following year, an amendment was introduced in the *Labour Standards Act* which gave workers a right to refuse work they *believed* "unusually" dangerous to their well-being. Both these rights represented a departure from public policy throughout North America, although they were more developed in Scandinavian countries.

This rights-based approach which complemented the traditional technical approach had its origins in the Department of Health under its Minister Walter Smishek, who was, at the time of his election, a representative for the Retail, Wholesale and Department Store Union in the province. Mr. Smishek was familiar with workplace health and safety developments in both Sweden and the United States, and with the passage of the *Occupational Health and Safety Act* (OSHA) in the United States in 1970. He was also aware of the resolutions put forth by the Saskatchewan Federation of Labour (SFL) calling for similar legislation in Saskatchewan. Shortly after the election of the NDP in June 1971, Mr. Smishek established various "probes" or committees to examine health issues for the establishment of short-term and long-term policies. One such "probe" dealt with occupational health. It was initially chaired by John Richards, an elected Member of the Legislative Assembly from Saskatoon, who served as Mr. Smishek's Legislative Secretary. Out of this administrative process came the recommendation for an occupational health and safety act modeled on the *Occupational*

Safety and Health Act (OSHA) in the United States (1970). The members of the committee, however, added the inclusion of joint health and safety committees giving workers direct involvement in occupational health and safety. This particular point of view was promoted by the labour members on the "probe", especially Mr. Bill Gilbey, a representative of the Saskatch-ewan Grain Services Union.

The proposal was then sent to the Minister of Labour, Gordon T. Sny-der. It was Mr. Smishek's understanding that the SFL wished to have all relevant labour legislation under "one roof," within the Department of Labour, so "labour" would have one place to go regarding all matters pertaining to collective bargaining and working conditions. The Minister of Labour, who was a member of the United Transportation Union, worked for CP Rail in Moose Jaw. Since both Ministers had labour backgrounds, there was no conflict between them regarding the idea of all occupational health and safety matters being located within the Department of Labour. Thus, the Department of Health turned over to a new administrative structure their radiation unit, and an occupational health physician. Afterwards, the Depart-ment of Mineral Resources sent over their mines inspectors. The adminis-trative establishment of a single "home" went smoothly, and the passage of an *Occupational Health and Safety Act* in 1972 also met with little political resistance.

The Opposition (Liberal Party) did not object to the establishment of the innovative joint health and safety committees, primarily because "health" was seen not as a trade union demand, but as an extension of medicare, in the province which first introduced universal medical insurance.[1] Only the Province of British Columbia had mandated safety committees prior to the passage of the Saskatchewan legislation which was more specific and elaborated on the role of the committee members.

Seventeen new amendments were introduced in the Legislative Assembly in 1977, and in 1982 far-reaching regulations were enacted. The *Occupational Health and Safety Act, 1977*, embodied no change in the coverage, legislative intent or general approach of the 1972 Act, which was essentially an enabling Act, and brand new legislation without precedent anywhere. The 1977 legislation corrected some omissions, and spelt out for the guidance of employers, workers and the courts some of the specifics which the drafters of the original legislation did not have the experience to anticipate. It clarified the authority of occupational health officers to issue orders, including stop-work orders. It provided for substantially increased penalties

---

[1] This observation regarding the political sociology of Saskatchewan became evident to me as Executive Director of the occupational health and safety program from early 1976 to 1982. For instance, in 1976 when the federal and provincial governments established wage and price controls, they specifically excluded restrictions pertaining to occupational health and safety regulations.

for violations of regulations or orders. These penalties, for the first time, included the possibility of two-year jail sentences for individuals convicted of offenses under the Act. It extended liability to directors and officials of corporations who knowingly participated in offenses committed by corporations.

Probably more important than any one of these, however, was the legislative recognition of a new stage in the development of occupational health committees. The original Act provided simply for the creation of committees and gave them certain duties and responsibilities. Once they had created the committees, employers had fully discharged their statutory duties. Under the 1977 Act, they were as well required to consult and co-operate with the committees in the resolution of problems of health and safety.

Beyond this, the committees were built into the inspection and enforcement process. For example, copies of all occupational health officers' inspection reports and notices of contravention had be provided to the committees. Where there were no committees, they were required to be posted in the workplace. Promptly upon the expiry of the time specified in a notice of contravention, employers were required to report to the committees what progress they had made towards remedying the contravention. Only in the case of a risk of serious personal injury were the employers required to report their corrective measures to the officer who issued the notice. Again, where no committees existed, employers were required to post a notice of progress for the information of workers. This provided a mechanism for insuring compliance with orders without the necessity of a large number of routine, and in many cases unnecessary, follow-up visits by division officers. In the section specifying the purposes for which regulations might be made by the Lieutenant Governor in Council, specific reference was made to the participation of committees in inspection and related matters without loss of pay.

A number of committees had already become involved in environmental monitoring of noise, heat stress, dusts and fumes — matters normally reserved for industrial hygienists. The division had prepared and distributed guidelines on these subjects — it had made up test kits and made loans of equipment needed to conduct the measurements. Occupational health officers were provided with kits to be left in workplaces, and they conducted the training of committee members in the use of the equipment. Many of these problems were worked out without further reference to the professional personnel, and industrial hygienists' time was able to be spent where committees had not reached this stage of development. A new training program for committee members and supervisory personnel was initiated in 1977, which introduced to employers and employees the range of monitoring services available and which they could learn to carry out for themselves. This program also dealt with new worker orientation and training, counselling of workers who refused to use protective equipment, supervisors' responsibilities in the safety area,

accident investigations and similar matters. A number of audio-visual materials were developed for use in this course and were available for committees to use in their own workplaces independently of the course. In early
1981, committee members participated in this and other training programs
offered by the Branch.

Finally, the 1977 Act extended the individual worker's "right to refuse"
to include work believed unusually dangerous to any other persons at the
place of employment, and prohibited *any form* of discriminatory action (not
limited to wage and job protection, as formerly) against such worker for
exercising this right.

Efforts to reform workplace health and safety in other Canadian provinces met with much greater resistance by employers. In Saskatchewan, on
the other hand, the "joint" occupational health and safety committees were
not perceived as a threat to management prerogatives. In 1973, however,
the introduction of the "right to refuse" clause did prompt outspoken employers in the province to criticize this particular amendment as unnecessary.
The labour movement was united on the introduction of this clause in order
to strengthen the functioning of the joint occupational health and safety
committees. Obviously, the right to refuse was seen as analogous to the
right to strike in collective bargaining. Further, this new innovation was not
seen by the NDP members in the legislature as "dividing" the urban population from rural. On the contrary, many in the rural areas worked full-time
or part-time in urban or industrial settings, such as potash mines, steel
fabrication or farm machinery manufacture and saw the benefits of the
legislation. Since health was seen as a "good" in itself, the far-reaching
innovations for the time were not viewed as particularly "radical."

One example of the worker's right to refuse dangerous work, and how
it functioned on a day-to-day basis, illustrates that if workers did not have
such a right, they would suffer adverse health effects or bodily damage far
more often than they did. An incident occurred in a large plant which
utilized high-pressure steam. The first refusal of workers to perform acts
which they believed could be dangerous was made by instrument mechanics,
whose tasks included repairing control lines. Also called steam-sensing lines,
these three-eighth and half-inch steam lines seldom failed during normal
operation. Over a four-week period prior to their refusal to work, however,
over 10 of these lines had ruptured. The instrument mechanics foresaw the
possibility of a control line bursting while they were working on an adjacent
one — which could cause severe scalding of the worker.

The unusual problem with breaking steam lines originated when a steam
turbine was taken out of service for repairs. The system was designed to
function only for short periods under these conditions, which caused increased
pressure, noise and vibration. At one point, noise levels as high as 126 dBA
were measured. As one worker put it, "the noise was deafening and the
vibration felt like it would shake the fillings out of your teeth."

153

But the boiler and high-pressure steam system, constructed in accordance with the Boiler Code, had been declared safe by a Saskatchewan Labour Boiler Inspector. Consequently, the Plant Safety Director maintained that the workers did not have the right to refuse to work under Section 26. Section 26 of the Act states, in part, that a worker "may refuse to do any particular ... acts at work which he has reasonable grounds to believe are unusually dangerous to his health and safety ... until sufficient steps have been taken to satisfy him otherwise, or the Occupational Health Committee or Occupational Health Officer has investigated the matter and advised him otherwise." Although one of the boiler inspectors regarded the boiler as safe, the employee co-chairperson of the Committee and the Occupational Health Officer on the scene supported the workers' refusal.

By this time other workers, besides the instrument mechanics, were becoming seriously concerned about the noise, vibration and possibility of a steam-line blow-out. Two operators refused to go into the header system to work on pressure-reduction valves, and received the support of the OHC employee co-chairman.

Then two days later it happened! An eight-inch steam line, under 600 p.s.i. pressure, blew. Scalding, high-pressure steam was suddenly released into the surrounding area. If anyone had been standing close to it, they could not have survived.

As it was, the tremendous heat touched off the sprinkler system and water from the sprinklers disabled four 14,000-volt power distribution transformers, causing a power failure in the plant. Ironically, it was a steam line and pressure-reduction valve modification, added into the steam system by management to alleviate the problem of excess noise and vibration, which blew. The plant was out of production for five days.

This case illustrates a basic principle of occupational health and safety — workers are the best instruments of detection of occupational hazards. If they say something is wrong, more often than not they are right in their judgment.

In this case management people, including professional engineers, as well as one of the labour department boiler inspectors, said it was safe for the workers to go back on the job. These were the experts. But in this case the workers were right and the experts were wrong. This incident demonstrated that the basic occupational health and safety philosophy of trusting the workers' assessment of a potentially hazardous situation was a sound one.

This example also demonstrated the value of centralization at the top and decentralization at the grass roots of the Saskatchewan occupational health regulatory system. Because of decentralization at the grass roots level, the workers' right to refuse was recognized — with the preventive value hoped for by the regulators. Because of centralization of authority at the Branch Director level, he was able to make a decision when called upon to do so. A boiler inspector said that the boiler and steam lines appeared to be safe according to the Boiler Code. An OHC employee co-chairman and an occupational health officer said the workers were justified in their refusal to work under possibly dangerous conditions. If the boiler inspector and occupational health officer had been under the authority of two different branch directors in two different government departments (e.g., Labour and Health), then no single person would have had the authority to make a decision to support the workers.

Background

The following is a description of the legislation and the underlying assumptions behind the regulations and Branch policies. The program emphasized three worker rights which may be expressed as: workers must have the "right to know" about dangers in the work environment; workers must have the "right to participate" in the day-to-day detection, evaluation, and reduction of workplace hazards; and workers must have, without fear of reprisal, the "right to refuse" to work in conditions known or believed to be unusually dangerous.

These rights encompass a vital area of labour relations and are interdependent. It would be ineffectual to provide workers with the right to refuse and the right to participate, while excluding their right to know about workplace hazards.[2] On the other hand, the right to participate and the right to know must be supplemented by the right to refuse, if a holistic preventive approach is to exist. All three rights act like different gears in a complex mechanism: remove one and the machinery breaks down, becoming immobile and useless.

Directly related to the worker's right to participate is the worker's right to have access to information concerning workplace health and safety hazards. If worker, and indeed management, representatives are to be fully effective occupational health and safety committee members, they must be knowledgeable about various dangers created in the work environment by different products, processes, equipment, and toxic substances. Section 67 of the *Saskatchewan Occupational Health and Safety Regulations* required every employer, in cooperation with the committee, to list "all chemical substances regularly used, handled or produced in the course of the work processes, and of any other chemicals that are present at the place of employment which may be a hazard to the health and safety of workers, or are suspect of the workers."[3]

---

[2] Section 28(2) of the *Saskatchewan Occupational Health and Safety Regulations* states that: "Every employer shall ensure that the worker representatives on the committee or, where there is no committee, the workers, are kept fully informed of any information in the employer's possession concerning the *work environment* and the occupational health and safety of workers in that place of employment...." (emphasis added)

[3] These policies were enacted into law by Order-in-Council 437/81 on March 17, 1981,

Further, the employer shall record: the chemical formulation, expressed in generic or chemical names, of the substance; the hazards which might arise from the handling or use of the substance; and the precautions that need to be taken with respect to the substance to ensure the health and safety of workers.

Another aspect of joint participation in the control of health and safety hazards in Saskatchewan workplaces is workplace monitoring of health hazards. Since 1972 and the merging of safety and health inspection functions, occupational health officers have furthered their expertise in recognizing and monitoring health hazards as well as safety hazards. A crucial step in this process was the development by the Hygiene Unit of a basic hygiene monitoring kit in 1975, for the use of the occupational health officers.

Each kit consisted of 11 instruments neatly packaged in a carrying case. Use of the instruments was quite straightforward; a novice could be taught how to use any one of them in about 10–15 minutes. They measured such workplace health factors as temperature, air flow, air contaminants, noise, humidity, and light intensity. Joint participation in workplace monitoring was a natural development. When the occupational health officers had mastered the use of the instruments in the kit, they were able to instruct committee members in their use.

A major wave of "do-it-yourself" monitoring began in 1976. Besides introducing the hygiene monitoring kits, the Hygiene Unit made up 35 Wet Bulb Globe Thermometer Kits (WBGT Kits), which were used to measure exposure to heat. Heat stress had been identified by the Branch as a widespread problem. Guidelines for rest periods required for different conditions were drawn up and copies were sent out, along with the WBGT Kits, to commercial kitchens and laundries, meat-packing plants, bakeries, and mines.

Most workplaces took readings and applied the guidelines without Branch intervention and also introduced rest breaks where necessary. And there were the many improvements made to the physical environment including air conditioning, better ventilation, and heat shielding — all of which effectively eliminated sources of heat stress. In most cases, the committees handled the situation themselves by arranging rest periods or making suggestions for the removal of heat stress sources.

During 1977, 1978 and 1979, the demand for our WBGT Kits diminished. This was a positive sign: many workplaces had by then installed their own permanent heat stress monitoring equipment. It was also evident that the kits were no longer required in many workplaces because heat stress problems had been eliminated. The WBGT experience and others had

---

effective sixty days later, May 17, 1981. These statutory provisions simply gave recognition to what had already in practice developed in Saskatchewan.

indicated that putting monitoring instruments in the hands of workers was not only "good sense" but also "good science".

But how did the committee system really work? Computer print-outs, the use of monitoring kits, and other such statistical indicators are all rather abstract. Perhaps the best way to get a real feeling for the workings of joint participation in Saskatchewan is to look at some examples.

One example of the committee system at work involved a recently constructed meat-packing plant. Workers in the cooling room complained to management about the noise there and were informed that the design specifications ensured that noise levels would be no more than 85 dBA. The Committee then borrowed a noise meter from the Branch and, after one month of testing, discovered that the noise levels were reaching as high as 96 dBA. Upon hearing this, management brought in their own tester who confirmed the results of the Committee's tests.

Management responded by holding back payments to the building contractor until the original design specifications were met. The fan blades in the cooling area were identified as the culprits and the contractor found a place in the U.S. that indicated it could design and manufacture a set of "low-decibel" blades. The first batch of blades were manufactured and set up, but all of them fractured from vibration one-half hour to two days after installation.

They were sent back, the stress points were analyzed, and a new set was made. The new blades stood up and noise levels in the cooler boxes were all down below 85 dBA. As a result of the initial measurements and activities of the Committee, the hearing of workers in the cooling rooms was more adequately protected and a new technological advance was made in the area of low-noise fans.

Another early example experienced by the administrators in the Occupational Health and Safety Branch occurred when two converted vans used by a mobile dental unit were found to be contaminated by carbon monoxide. The 110-volt AC generators which provided power for the vans was producing carbon monoxide, which was being blown back into the vans on windy days. There had been complaints about the fumes, and on one occasion two women working in one van became ill. Both vans were shut down. The Branch was notified and made an investigation. Upon being told what the problem was, the Occupational Health Committee took both vans down to a local muffler shop and set about trying to design a workable exhaust system.

An exhaust system was designed by the Committee and was installed in one of the vans. The van was run and tested for carbon monoxide with assistance from the Branch. The carbon monoxide level was still too high, so the Committee went back to the muffler shop to discuss the problem. It was finally decided that the only effective way to handle the problem was to use a 40-foot long flexible pipe and to clamp it to the existing exhaust system. This pipe could then be positioned to compensate for any wind conditions. This system was tested and found to be workable and the vans were put back into operation.

Of course, not every occupational health and safety problem encountered by committees was as complicated as these, and solutions to them were more often than not fairly routine — the installation of light fixtures to improve lighting, the repairing of an air conditioner to relieve minor heat discomfort, and so on.

In 1972–73, some said with justification that committees and joint participation were nothing new. They had been tried before at different times and places and were found to be of only limited value because workers had found out that participation on health and safety committees was often just another way of appeasing workers without giving them any real power to change things. Without the right to know and the right to refuse, the joint committee system was seen by workers as, at best, a well-meaning but paternalistic form of co-optation.

Since 1974, most provincial federations of labour have lobbied their respective provincial governments for legislation incorporating worker involvement in workplace health and safety; more specifically, the three rights adopted by the Province of Saskatchewan.

The Occupational Health Committees

An indication of the scope of worker participation in Saskatchewan is, first of all, the number of joint worker/management committees — as of 1981, there were over 2,800 of these, covering some 80 percent of the Saskatchewan non-agricultural workforce. Computer printouts indicated that 29,723 committee meetings were held in Saskatchewan between 1972 and the end of 1981. Eighty-four percent of these meetings considered specific health and safety concerns — only 16 percent showed "no concerns". The meetings which *identified* specific problems also saw a large percentage of them being solved; some 168,834 specific problems were identified at these meetings, and 151,193 solutions were agreed upon and wholly or partially implemented.

Naturally, not all problems were settled immediately. Thus, in the period analyzed, 45,951 discussions were held on "old concerns" — those not settled when first considered by the committee and appearing on subsequent agendas. When the 124,745 new problems and the 45,951 old concerns are taken together for a total of 170,696 old and new concerns dealt with by the committees, we find that 106,202 — 62.2 percent of these concerns — related to physical safety hazards as opposed to health problems.

The 64,494 health related and other problems were somewhat fewer in number than the safety concerns. Some of the health categories include: 24,626 related to physical agents or environmental conditions (noise, lighting, heat or cold, sanitation, crowding, ventilation); 14,690 related to work processes or procedures (working alone, adequacy of training or supervision, heavy lifting); 7,061 related to hazardous materials.

The role of the occupational health committees was promoted by legislation, regulations and policies of the Occupational Health and Safety Branch of the Saskatchewan Department of Labour, and their occupational health and safety inspectors as of 1974. The worker's right to participate can further be illustrated by reference to the Branch's inspection record for the 10 month period of April 1, 1979 to January 31, 1980. Of 2,219 written reports in the Branch's files (including notices of contravention and occupational health officers' inspection reports), 532 — or about 24 percent — directly involved occupational health committees. They would have involved infractions such as safety hazards, physical agents and hazardous materials.

Underlying Assumptions

The Saskatchewan approach was based upon the notion that occupational health and safety is an integral part of working conditions generally, and not a matter solely for physicians, industrial hygienists, industrial engineers, safety specialists, inspectors, or other "experts". Rather, workplace health and safety is part of the industrial relations system structured by the relationship between labour, management, and government. Further, it is primarily the power relationship between these "actors" which produces the rules regulating working conditions.

Secondly, so-called "technical" questions pertaining to workplace health and safety are, in reality, "social" in their origin. This refers to the power relations in production — who tells whom to do what and how fast! After all, a machine does not go faster by itself; someone designed the machinery, organized the work, designed the job. And officials in the Saskatchewan program asked: just how congenial are our workplaces to the needs of workers? If reforms were to come about in working conditions in Saskatchewan, it was believed that the regulatory agency had to be an equalizer in the power relations. It is, of course, evident that those who have the power to hire and fire are more than equal to those who sell or rent their labour power. The social relations in production are unequal and asymmetrical. From the passage of the *Occupational Health and Safety Act* in 1972 until the change of government on April 26, 1982, the Occupational Health and Safety Branch attempted to balance the "social" and the "technical" by promoting the rights of workers. Post-1982 occupational health and safety matters were confined to physical hazards such as open machinery, chemicals, pollutants, and other contaminants and did not address the issue of "worker rights" whatsoever.

Over time, the Saskatchewan program extended and expanded the legitimate items for occupational health and safety committees to deal with. It was the intention of the Branch to stretch or expand the concept of "risk" to other matters which concern workers: monotony, pace of work, the job cycle, planning, new machinery, sexual harassment, scheduling of work. In other words, the necessity of strengthening the link among occupational health and safety, work organization, and psycho-social issues was recognized.

Such an expansion or "stretch" more directly confronts management prerogatives. Employers have demonstrated greater resistance to this expansion than to expenditures relating to lowering noise, better ventilation, machine guarding, chemical substitution, and provision of safety equipment of all sorts. This stretch of the concept of risk is seen as an unwarranted intrusion upon management's legitimate right to manage (for example, to pursue greater productivity and efficiency) through absolute control over the human factor of production. This resistance was evident in Saskatchewan, as elsewhere.

Attempts to deal with psycho-social matters are often undertaken within the context of various humanization programs. However, even where humanization techniques do not threaten management power or control and require only a limited dose of shared power, diffusion of power has been inordinately slow. Although there is a growing consensus about humanization, this disappears when it is stretched to democratization. Worker participation in regulating work organization has not been widely accepted amongst government regulators or public and private employers in Canada. Thus, technological innovations generally continue to deskill the workforce.

The Saskatchewan approach included the formation of joint occupational health and safety committees with a mandate to participate in the inspection and enforcement process. This approach was viewed by labour as an alternative path to the "conventional wisdom" pertaining to the way we thought, talked, and regulated occupational health and safety in Canada in the early 1970s. Worker rights as an integral part of workplace health and safety became the basis of labour's public policy position in the 1970s, better reflecting the workers' experience and perspective.

Critique of Joint Occupational Health and Safety Committees

Certain problems arose in the implementation of the Saskatchewan program. First, the joint committees became involved with occupational health and safety concerns only on the shop floor, but it was clear that the working conditions were a direct result of a long series of decisions, clearly limiting the efficacy of the role of the joint committees in relation to the work environment.

Nonetheless, there is no reason to discredit the Saskatchewan model of committee procedures in workplace health and safety entirely. The involvement of workers on joint health and safety committees was an important precondition for the betterment of working conditions, the reduction of accidents, and the minimization of industrial disease. This involvement presented us with an opportunity to widen and deepen the rights of workers on these joint committees and broaden the legal parameters pertaining to

160

these committees in provincial jurisdictions. And by these means, workers had some opportunity to deal with broader work environment questions such as the pace of work, monotony, job cycle, planning, new machinery, scheduling of work and other work environment matters dealing with qualitative aspects of work, and not just the measurable quantitative aspects of work (for example, heat, cold, dust concentrations, noise levels).

Another criticism of the Saskatchewan program concerned the supposed beneficial effects of providing workers with occupational health and safety information. Many of the most active worker committee members complained that the research articles pertaining to specific problems in their workplace could only be interpreted by professionals employed by management. Often, worker members of the committees felt incompetent and inadequate to criticize these "scientific" studies. Dr. Mauk Mulder has found in his studies of "power" that joint consultative committees can be used to the advantage of the party with greater knowledge (so that knowledge *is* power), enabling that party to influence the other. Since managers tend to have professional staff (medical or engineering), they can more readily control the direction of the committees (Mulder, 1971, 1975).

Dr. Mulder also states that "when there are relatively large differences in expertise (expert power) between members of a social system, an increase in participation of the less expert members will not lead to a smaller power distance between members, but to its opposite."

Further, Dr. Mulder indicates:

> This great expertise (expert power) of managers and specialists represents potential power. Those with the expertise must communicate with the less powerful to influence them effectively and to realize their power. Thus, when there are large differences in expert power, the introduction of greater participation provides the more powerful with an opportunity to exercise their influence over the less powerful, and thereby makes their greater power a reality. (Mulder, 1975)

Nonetheless, although disparities in power did exist in the committees, the *1981 Occupational Health and Safety Regulations* pertaining to committees did extend the rights of workers on committees in regard to their right to know. Employers thus had a clear legal obligation to provide information to workers on matters pertaining to "*work environment* and occupational health and safety". Work environment concerns preceded occupational health and safety, indicating a desire to extend the legitimate items for occupational health and safety committees to deal with.

Consequently, the Branch promoted the notion of Work Environment Boards which would establish parity between labour and management in dealing with all matters pertaining to the work environment. Prior to the change in government, there was an agreement by the former Minister of Labour and the former chairman of the Worker's Compensation Board to transform the "joint occupational health and safety committees" in the

Occupational Health and Safety Act into Work Environment Boards with the power to negotiate monies from the employers as well as receiving monies from the Worker's Compensation Board for a work environment fund. This money was to be negotiated *outside* of the normal bargaining process, and not be a trade-off for wages and benefits. In this manner, workers would have money to do their own occupational health research, bring in their own experts, and visit other plants to see varied and alternative technical solutions to the problems they faced. This money would also better insure that the committees would become more activated, and not be just "paper" committees.

This approach was accepted by the Potash Corporation of Saskatchewan (PCS) as an experiment. Unfortunately, developments were only beginning in this area when an election was called, and a new government with different values and a different notion of economy gained office. The PCS Board has not officially met since that date.[4]

Background to Work Environment Board Agreement

On February 29, 1980, the President of the Potash Corporation of Saskatchewan (PCS) and other senior management met with representatives of their three certified bargaining units in the four PCS mines. The union representatives were from the Energy, Chemical Workers' Union, United Steelworkers of America, and the Rocanville Potash Employees' Association — an unaffiliated independent local union. Present also was the Executive Director of the Provincial Occupational Health and Safety Branch within the Saskatchewan Department of Labour.

The President of PCS indicated concern pertaining to the unacceptably high accident rates within PCS, a provincial Crown corporation, as compared to rates in the private sector of the industry. PCS was composed of four potash mines whose general managers were appointed by the President of the Corporation who reported to a Minister of the Crown.

As a result of the President's initiative, a Work Environment Board (WEB) was established. It was composed of 12 representatives — six from labour and six from management. Also, a smaller Executive Committee was formed composed of three representatives from the certified bargaining agents, the President of the Mining Division of PCS, an engineer and a mine manager. The Chair of both the WEB and the Executive Committee was the Executive Director of the Provincial Occupational Health and Safety Branch.

The Board agreed that there was no need for confidentiality regarding any PCS research, and that the Board and its Executive Committee would determine what research needed doing, and who should do the research. The Executive Committee undertook this responsibility, and during the first

---

[4] For a positive account of the Work Environment Board of the Potash Corporation of Saskatchewan, see Bobiash (1984).

year, contracted out $80,000 worth of research regarding occupational health concerns of the unions and potash miners. The Joint Committee also interviewed prospective researchers, and all the contracts regarding research were granted without any problems between the labour and management representatives of the Executive Committee and the Work Environment Board. The employee co-chairpersons in each of the four mines within PCS listed the kinds of information they wanted and the Executive Committee formulated the research to be done.

This co-operative and harmonious relationship started to break down when the worker members of the Board began to consider matters relating to Article 1, Section 3 of the Agreement, which stated that one of the functions of the Work Environment Board was "to consider possible improvements to the *psycho-social* and physical aspects of the work environment ...." (emphasis mine) "Psycho-social" factors were defined as matters of technology, production methods, types of supervision, work organization, work rhythms, machine control of work methods, and monotonous-repetitive work activating only a limited part of total human capability. Also included in the definition was lack of possibilities of contact with other workers, piece rate and related payment systems, and authoritarian and detailed control of the potash worker. The union and worker representatives on the Work Environment Board also indicated that they wanted to explore opportunities and possibilities for increased worker participation regarding all work environment matters.

After a year of operation by the WEB, the corporation hired a President of the Mining Division. The new President of the Mining Division joined both the Board and Executive Committee. Thereafter, representatives of the union complained that the activities of the Board were becoming increasingly frustrated, and brought this matter to the attention of the President of the Potash Corporation of Saskatchewan. On December 17, 1981 a letter was sent to the President of PCS stating that:

> There are those on the Work Environment Board who believe that PCS as a Crown corporation represents a regime different from that of private capital. If so, then it ought to have policies different from those of the private potash corporations regarding its workers. One important distinction, we believe, is affording PCS workers a measure of involvement in issues which matter to them. If this is not possible or encouraged, what then is the difference between working for PCS and working for privately-owned businesses? In the mere substitution of public entrepreneurs for a private bureaucracy, I could see no cause for rejoicing.[5]

On January 12th, the President of PCS responded to this letter, stating that the matters raised in the letter of December 17th "should be reviewed

---

[5] Letter from Robert Sass to the President of PCS dated December 17, 1981.

by the new President of PCS Mining". Since the labour members on the Board believed the "new" President of Mining was the reason for their frustration in the first instance, matters worsened and labour-management relations on the Board became increasingly fractious. The Executive Committee of WEB put forth a motion to hire a consultant to review the activities of the Board, and to make recommendations regarding increased worker participation. The Executive Committee hired Professor Gerry Hunnius for this assignment. Hunnius was a social scientist at York University, Toronto and a theoretician on worker participation in industry.

Mr. Hunnius toured the PCS Mines and interviewed workers, managers and union officials. His report was presented to the Executive Committee of the Work Environment Board on September 20, 1982, after the government turnover in April of that year (Hunnius, 1982). With a new Progressive Conservative Government, the recommendations of the report were ignored, and the Acting President for PCS Mining notified the unions that the company would no longer participate on the Work Environment Board. The *Canadian Occupational Health and Safety News* (1983) also reported that

> At first, PCS claimed that the dispute was simply about who would be the Board's chairman. There was no question that it was the status of Sass at issue, the Acting President at PCS said in an interview. But he later confirmed that the issue was in fact a much broader one.
>
> Sass represents a philosophical approach based upon increasing workers' control over the production process. PCS, while favouring more input from workers, wants to retain what it considers to be its traditional managerial rights over health and safety.

The union members on the Board considered taking legal action against the PCS for its termination of the Work Environment Board agreement. Unfortunately, the termination of WEB coincided with a major downturn in the potash industry, and at the same time they suspected that there would be no cooperation with WEB by the government's newly appointed president of the Potash Corporation of Saskatchewan.

The Work Environment Board began as an experiment to deal with the many problems and frustrations encountered by the mandatory Joint Occupational Health and Safety Committees in the province. It was established as an experiment which gave the worker representatives on the four Joint Occupational Health and Safety Committees within each of the PCS mines wider authority to deal with workplace health and safety problems. Also, the establishment of a Work Environment Fund (WEF) enabled the worker representatives on committees to be more effective since they could initiate their own research or bring in their own experts regarding work environment matters — which was deemed to be wider than the legally defined occupational health and safety concerns. Administrators of the Occupational Health and Safety Branch and representatives of the mining unions hoped appropriate statutory changes to both the *Workers' Compensation Act* and the *Occupational Health and Safety Act* would transform all the provincial Joint Occupational Health and Safety Committees into Work Environment Boards. A Work Environment Fund with monies from the *Workers' Compensation Act* would enable the committees to initiate their own research, visit enterprises in similar industries to see how health and safety practices were carried out, and bring in their own experts to assess their working environments. While the NDP Minister of Labour was in agreement with this approach prior to the April 1982 election, the NDP was defeated and this supposed next step or stage in the development of the Occupational Health and Safety Program never became public policy.

Conclusion

During the 1970s, the NDP in Saskatchewan pioneered three rights as an integral part of workplace health and safety reforms: the right to know, to participate and to refuse work believed (not known) to be dangerous. Throughout the decade of the 1970s, the administrators of the Saskatchewan Occupational Health and Safety Branch promoted regulations and policies to strengthen these worker rights.

In 1977, the government passed 17 amendments to the Saskatchewan *Occupational Health and Safety Act* intended to give workers on Joint Occupational Health and Safety Committees a wider range of control of work environment matters. The 1981 Regulations ensured a worker role in the monitoring, surveillance and inspection of items that committees could deal with under the legislation.

These regulations evolved out of the observation that employers generally had professionals and experts on staff who were in a much better position to interpret empirical research pertaining to workplace health and safety. On the other hand, the workers' right to refuse what they believed to be harmful to their well-being was further frustrated by the unequal power relations between owners and their managers, and workers on the shop floor level, although this was less so when workers were organized in trade unions or where there was a high degree of solidarity among the workers in the enterprise. It thus became evident that worker refusals were frustrated because of their understandable belief that managers viewed such refusals as insubordination, and would in time, be in a position to penalize the worker for using their legal right.

Consequently, the administrators of the Occupational Health and Safety Branch sought to develop policies aimed at strengthening the rights afforded workers in legislation, and more specifically, to move from "weak" rights to "strong" rights. This was to be done by amendment to the *Occupational Health and Safety Act* which would transform Joint Occupational Health and Safety Committees into Work Environment Boards. These Boards would deal with all matters pertaining to the work environment, such as pace of work, job cycle, the organization of work and job design. At the same time, a proposed amendment to the *Workers' Compensation Act* would allow funding for these Work Environment Boards so they could operate more effectively. The Work Environment Fund would allow worker representatives on the Boards to visit other plants, initiate their own research, and enable workers to get information and data pertaining to the risks and hazards in their workplaces.

In the late 1970s, a single experiment along these lines was set up in the Potash Corporation of Saskatchewan (PCS). Unfortunately, while the Corporation generously allocated $80,000 for research during the first year of the operation of the Work Environment Board, it was reluctant to move from "weak" worker rights to "strong" worker rights. The leadership of the Potash Corporation of Saskatchewan viewed this move as an unwarranted infringement on management prerogatives. Consequently, the WEB experiment within the Potash Corporation of Saskatchewan was frustrated at an early stage and never, thereafter, provided an adequate "beacon" for further reforms within the Saskatchewan occupational health and safety program.

While there was agreement among the Minister of Labour, the Chairperson of Workers' Compensation Board, and the Executive Director of the Occupational Health and Safety Branch to propose such legislative changes which would transform the Joint Occupational Health and Safety Committees into Work Environment Boards, and the establishment of a Work Environment Fund, this never occurred because of the defeat of the NDP government in 1982 by the Progressive Conservatives. The first act of the Progressive Conservative Minister of Labour, Lorne McClaren, was to disband the Work Environment Board in the Potash Corporation of Saskatchewan.

Since the formation of an NDP government in Saskatchewan in late 1991, there has been no move by present policy-makers to revive the proposals of the former administrators of the program prior to 1982. Trade unions continue to support the initial NDP philosophy of 1971 which promoted worker rights as a technical matter in minimizing worker harm in workplaces.

REFERENCES

Bobiash, D. 1984. "Attempts to Promote Industrial Democracy in the Potash Corporation of Saskatchewan." A paper presented as part of the degree requirements for the M.Sc. in Industrial Relations and Personnel Management at the London School of Economics and Political Science, August 31.

Canadian Occupational Health and Safety News, Vol. 6, No. 5, February 7, 1983.

Hunnius, G. 1982. "Reports to the Executive Committee of the Work Environment Board." Potash Corporation of Saskatchewan, Mining Division, July.

Mulder, Mauk. 1971. "Power Equalization Through Participation?" *Administrative Science Quarterly* 16, 1(March): 31–38.

———. 1975. "Reduction and Power Differences in Practices." Paper read at the seminar "European Contributions to Organizational Theory," Fontainbleau, France, May 13–15.

10 Saskatchewan Community Colleges: An Innovation without Walls... or without Resources?

by Allan Walker

INTRODUCTION

The community college system introduced by the recently elected New Democratic (NDP) Government in the early 1970s, has been pointed to as a unique and successful innovation in adult education, social democracy and community development. The colleges were established as institutions "without walls" (Dennison and Gallagher, 1986, p. 57), somewhat similar to the British experience with the Open University concept (International Commission, 1972, p. 135). This chapter examines not only this concept of a learning institution without walls but also the impact of introducing a learning institution without other traditional forms of resources, including permanent facilities, staffing and programs. Did this innovation really work or was it a grand experiment that did not pass the test of time?

The introduction, development, evolution and essentially the demise, of the Saskatchewan community college system are examined. The analysis is based on a review of initial documents that captured the development of the system, a few critical analyses written by other authors and this author's personal experience working with the college system during its formative years.

The 1960s was the golden era of education, and included tremendous interest in adult learning opportunities. As a result of public demand for more learning/training opportunities, jurisdictions responded in different ways. The federal government, through its various training agreements and transfer payments strongly influenced training strategies. However, the structure of post-secondary and adult education was, and is, up to each province's Legislature.

Every province considered its response to the growing demand for adult education as appropriate, based on its unique political, social and economic factors. All provinces, with the possible exceptions of Alberta and British Columbia, emphasized a provincial planning approach to introducing new adult education opportunities (Dennison and Gallagher, 1986, p. 186). Unlike Saskatchewan, other provinces tended to take the more traditional route of establishing junior colleges or technical institutes, including the development of physical campuses in major centres.

In many ways, what the Saskatchewan community college system purported to do would be considered "extension" programming in other jurisdictions. However, Saskatchewan community colleges were not initiated as an extension *per se* of the technical institutes and universities, but as institutions in their own right which would "buy" services as needed from the established learning centres and offer local programs as well. While the Saskatchewan system emphasized autonomy from the existing adult education institutions, the new college system offered no degrees, certificates or diplomas of its own but rather brokered them from established institutions.

The label "unique" can be best applied to the "brokerage" component of the Saskatchewan community college response (Dennison and Gallagher, 1986, p. 55). In structural terms this differentiated the Saskatchewan system considerably from other provincial systems. "Brokering" meant that facilities were rented, there was minimal staff, and there was an emphasis on responsiveness to individual and community needs.

BACKGROUND

Saskatchewan took a different course than most other provinces in responding to adult education demands, due to its social, economic and political background. Saskatchewan had a proud history of innovation with education, health and social issues. It required a response that would reflect its rural-based population and accommodate its need for further postsecondary and adult education opportunities but not aggravate out-migration trends. Throughout Saskatchewan there were limited postsecondary opportunities; an education system was needed to provide opportunities for people to learn and continue to work in their home communities. In addition to these social and economic forces, the election of a new government fuelled change — a desire to chart a new course and to address long standing problems. Many supporters of the new government felt that the province had not been very responsive to adult education needs.

The "modern" development of adult education opportunities in Saskatchewan can be traced to the landmark 1956 Royal Commission on Agriculture and Rural Life (Saskatchewan Royal Commission, 1956). The Commission emphasized the need for more opportunities in rural areas and, where possible, the use of existing resources. Reliance on collective action and self-help was stressed. An example often referred to in initial community college development, was the "lighted schools" program, which encouraged adults to use their children's schools at night (Faris, 1972, p. 5).

The postwar economic boom resulted in the development of training institutions in the major centres in Saskatchewan. In the late 1950s, a technical institute was built in Moose Jaw followed by one in Saskatoon. In 1969, a community college was initiated in Prince Albert and finally, in 1972, a training institution focusing on health sciences was opened in Regina. These institutions were primarily provincial technical institutes and significantly expanded the training opportunities previously available through the school boards, adult vocational centres and university. The Prince Albert situation was different as the local college was initiated under the auspices of the local school board. With an elected board, it was a forerunner in many ways of the community college system (Dennison and Gallagher, 1986).

During the Liberal regime of the 1960s there was expansion of technical institutes, primarily in the four major urban centres, but little was done to serve the rest of the mostly rural province. Some consideration was given in the late 1960s to the introduction of a regional college system similar to the one in Alberta which would be tied to the technical institutes and universities (Dennison and Gallagher, 1986, p. 54). The universities were under considerable pressure to expand. The Regina Campus of the University of Saskatchewan was undergoing major expansion and would, by 1974, become a separate institution. By 1971, when the NDP government was elected, there had already been considerable debate and some initiatives to enhance technical and postsecondary opportunities.

A NEW INITIATIVE

The newly elected government wanted to give priority to education. Based on community consultations, a 1972 Minister's Advisory Committee Report outlined the need for a community college system, including the nature and form that it should take (Faris, 1972). The Committee was chaired by a prominent adult educator, Dr. Ron Faris, who was seconded by the government from his position as Head of General Studies, Department of Extension, University of Saskatchewan, Regina Campus (Pepper, 1973, p. 207).

The Faris report, similar to other Canadian adult education planning exercises at the time, was influenced by lifelong learning concepts (Dennison and Gallagher, 1986, p. 173). A timely UNESCO report (International Commission, 1972) contained many of the community college philosophical underpinnings including the promotion of and access to lifelong learning and the idea that all adults had not only the right but the ability to choose how and what they would learn.

Community action was prevalent in the late 1960s and early 1970s, complementing long-held traditions of the NDP of emphasizing collective or community action. The combination of lifelong learning and community development concepts evolved into the seven principles outlined in the Minister's Advisory Committee Report (Faris, 1972).

The seven principles were broadly disseminated and discussed at the over fifty community college public meetings held during the committee's deliberations and became the basic community college goals:

1. promote formal and informal learning;
2. respond to community needs;
3. help individuals and communities identify needs;
4. promote community development (enhance rural life);
5. coordinate delivery (broker, not duplicate);
6. be governed through a representative council from the region; and
7. operate under the Minister of Continuing Education. (Faris, 1972, p. 59)

The following analysis of the impact of the community colleges is structured as a review of these seven principles or goals.

OPPORTUNITIES FOR FORMAL AND INFORMAL TRAINING

Profile of College Participation

Starting with four pilot regions in 1973 and expanding province-wide by 1975, college enrolment peaked in 1977–78 with nearly 100,000 participants (Saskatchewan Continuing Education, 1978). Participation statistics, as measured in participant numbers, started to decline after this year. As a consequence, the Department of Continuing Education began to publish the number of participant hours as well as the number of participants. In the Annual Reports this was indicated as a more valid indicator of participation. By the late 1970s, however, the number of participant hours started to decline as well (Saskatchewan Continuing Education, 1979a).

One explanation for the declining participation numbers and hours rests with a change in the type of programming. In their first year of operation, nearly 90% of college participation was in the personal development non-credit area (Saskatchewan Continuing Education, 1974). By 1980–81 this had dropped to 72%; furthermore, only 24% of the participation hours[1] were in the non-credit personal development areas (Saskatchewan Continuing Education, 1981b). Over the 1970s the percentage of participant hours in adult basic education

During the 1970s, college enrolment continued to be primarily rural. Indeed, most of the colleges were centred in small urban centres serving surrounding rural areas. In the first year of province-wide operation, 1975–76,

---

[1] College participation refers to the number of people enroled in courses; participation hours (or contact hours) are the total hours of courses taken (some participants took many hours, others few).

69% of college programming was in rural areas (Saskatchewan Continuing Education, 1976). While this had dropped to 60% by 1980–81, participation rates in the rural areas were still higher than in the urban areas — 14% versus 7% of the adult population (Saskatchewan Continuing Education, 1981b).

As well, the shift in college programming to provide ABE programs came at the same time that the average education level of college participants was rising. For instance, in 1975–76, 45% of all college participants had less than grade 12 education (Saskatchewan Continuing Education, 1976). By 1980–81 only 35% of participants had less than grade 12 education (Saskatchewan Continuing Education, 1981b). As the colleges stabilized, some programs focused on clients needing more basic literacy skills while others served those needing more advanced credit and technical programming. The colleges had begun to specialize.

Due to changes in the way provincial statistics were kept and programs delivered, it is difficult to compare in a comprehensive way total enrolment or participation in adult education activities from one year to the next. Participation rates were influenced by various provincial and federal incentives for training programs as well as how records were kept. With these limitations in mind, however, it would appear that the colleges were successful in helping increase participation in adult education in Saskatchewan during the 1970s. Three main types of programming were offered.

Before there were community colleges (1972–73), the school boards were the prime deliverer of non-credit programming throughout the province of Saskatchewan, offering programs to about 10,000 adults (Saskatchewan Continuing Education, 1973). By 1980–81, the community colleges had largely taken over this role from the schools and about 66,000 participants were registered in non-credit community college activities, the most popular being courses such as macrame and Chinese cooking (Saskatchewan Continuing Education, 1981b). This six-fold increase can be largely attributed to the active role of the community colleges and their local contact committees.

A second type of programming offered by the community colleges was the various short-term employment-oriented, adult basic education and special needs programs, university transfer programs, employment upgrading programs, etc. In 1972–73, under programs administered by the provincial Department of Continuing Education, about 9,000 participants were served (Saskatchewan Continuing Education, 1973). Some 20,000 participants were in similar kinds of programs by 1980–81 (Saskatchewan Continuing Education, 1981b). Again, the colleges played a major role in increasing participation.

A third area was technical institute extension programming. In 1972–73, participants in extension programs through the province's technical institutes totalled around 4,300. By 1980–81, this had increased to over 11,000. According to the Department annual report, about 6,000 of the 11,000 students participated through contracts with the community colleges. Again the colleges played a major role in more than doubling participation in this kind of program. However, during this same period the number of full-time students in the institute programs increased by only about 1,000, to some 7,600 students (Saskatchewan Continuing Education, 1973, 1981b).

Opportunities for credit and non-credit programming improved throughout the province. The colleges played a major role in delivery. It must be acknowledged, however, that technical institute extension, university extension and other agencies also played significant roles in bringing more programming to more communities through the community colleges. And especially in the urban areas, much of the college growth was the result of an administrative transfer of ABE programs from the vocational centres.

Expenditures

Expenditures on education in all jurisdictions and at all levels continued to increase into the 1970s. Between 1975–76 and 1980–81, after the community colleges were established province-wide, there was an increase of approximately 78% in postsecondary and trades training expenditures in Saskatchewan. This increase compares favourably to the 24% increase in Manitoba and parallels the 76% growth of expenditures in Alberta. Looking only at expenditures on community colleges and excluding universities and trades training, Saskatchewan experienced an increase of 80% during this five year period, compared to only 34% in Manitoba, but pales compared to the more dramatic growth in Alberta of 111%. Part of the greater increase in expenditures in Saskatchewan, compared to Manitoba, is due to the fact that, going into this period, Saskatchewan had been spending less per capita than Manitoba (Statistics Canada, 1982, p. 190).

Although there was an increase from $4M expended in 1976–77 to $6M in 1980–81, overall the college grants represented only about 4% of the $154M total Continuing Education expenditures for colleges, institutes and universities in 1980–81 (Saskatchewan Continuing Education, 1981b).[2] When the Department's and other agencies' contractual expenditures on training are considered, however, the relative magnitude of the colleges is significantly larger. The Department spent about $9M in 1980–81 (up from $4M in 1976–77) through contracts with other centres — largely urban colleges — to deliver ABE and other adult training (Saskatchewan Continuing Education, 1981). For instance, the 1980–81 Regina Plains Community College budget showed the Department operating grant represented about 25% of revenues, tuition fees 10% and the remainder was from contractual training (Regina Plains Community College, 1981). The rural-based colleges

---

[2] It should also be noted that these expenditures only relate to the twelve southern colleges not the three small northern colleges or the Saskatchewan Indian Community College developed to serve reserve and status populations and funded through the federal government.

relied more on the annual operating grant than the urban colleges. All in all, despite their small piece of the education pie, the low cost colleges received considerable political and social attention throughout the 1970s.

Criticisms

The adult education programming conducted by the colleges was largely dictated by provincial funding arrangements. The colleges had no local tax base of their own, unlike school boards. The colleges' sources of revenue were primarily the provincial grants, revenues from tuition fees as well as specific arrangements to deliver employment related or other programs for other provincial or federal agencies.

Initially, most of the college activities were focused on informal or non-credit programming. Extensive programming for personal development activities generated mixed publicity for the colleges. On the one hand, they gave instant visibility to the colleges as institutions reaching tens of thousands of adults. On the other hand, these activities tended to discredit colleges as being unable or unwilling to provide "serious" academic or vocational programming. The emphasis on providing non-credit programs also may have undermined some of the colleges' initial role of facilitating rather than duplicating other programs. With a focus on producing "results," there may have been undue emphasis on providing short-term courses. Initially, most of the funding for these programs was through the annual provincial college grants. These grants were determined using a per capita formula which also incorporated past participation levels (Saskatchewan Continuing Education, 1978).

By 1982, due to increasing demands on college budgets for other kinds of programming, and with Department support, all colleges adopted a policy of direct cost recovery on personal development or non-credit, non-vocational programs (SCCTA, 1986, p. 35). This move represented a major shift from the programming and orientation of the first decade. Since the "social demand" programs now had to pay their own way except for infrastructure costs, demand for these programs dropped. This could be seen as a positive development. In some colleges, citizens developed their own programs without using the college (SCCTA, 1986, p. 35). Although it is unclear how extensive this practice was, and it hurt college participation, it did fit the goal of empowering people to decide and initiate their own learning. It also was cheaper for the government.

In the mid-1970s the Department directed the colleges to be the delivery agent for ABE on a full-time and part-time basis, as well as to be the major deliverer of the Non-Registered Indian and Metis (NRIM) upgrading programs (SCCTA, 1986). These were contractual programs whereby the colleges delivered services and received direct funding from the Department, Canada Employment and Immigration, or other funding sources. Through these initiatives the colleges began to be deliverers of more traditional programming, but could also be seen as addressing their goal of responding to the needs of disadvantaged groups.

During a decade of development, the colleges shifted dramatically from focusing on the delivery of short-term non-credit programs or facilitating new groups to develop community programs to the delivery of full-time employment or academic provincial programs. By 1983, 60% of the participant contact hours were in these contracted programs (SCCTA, 1986, p. 44). Although 75% of the participants still enroled in personal development programs, these represented only about 15% of the contact hours (SCCTA, 1986, p. 48). Furthermore, the number of participants in community college activities, peaking at about 100,000 when the primary emphasis was on short programs, dropped to about 90,000 with the shift to more intensive literacy and employment programs (Saskatchewan Continuing Education, 1980).

A further indication of how provincial funding directed the role of the colleges is in the area of career development. Prior to special funding being designated in 1980 to career development programs, few colleges offered such initiatives. With the implementation of special programming earmarked for this service, within a couple of years 15,000 people had participated in career planning activities (SCCTA, 1986, p. 49).

Another outcome of continual underfunding, as viewed by the colleges, was that, with the increasing emphasis on the delivery of technical modules, employment and literacy programs, there was little money left for community development activities. For instance, very few colleges after the first ten years retained a full-time information officer (SCCTA, 1986, p. 16). Information campaigns were a major component of the colleges in their early days (e.g. promoting lifelong learning and variety of opportunities). In later years, colleges directed information resources to the more traditional purposes of promoting particular course offerings.

Another funding concern experienced by colleges, as the more affluent 1970s moved into the less affluent 1980s, was that there was little money for program development. Increasingly there were requests to the Department to provide a developmental service in the areas of adult basic education, literacy, etc. Without this additional development effort, the colleges became more traditional deliverers of high school completion programs, technical institute programs, etc. (SCCTA, 1986).

NEEDS IDENTIFICATION:
THE COLLEGE COMMITTEES

Throughout the Department's Annual Report and the community college promotional literature (e.g. annual reports) much credit was given to the over 600 community college contact committees established throughout the province (Saskatchewan Continuing Education, 1978, p. 7). These committees played a vital role in needs identification, co-ordination, promotion and delivery (Harper, 1975).

Although extensive in numbers, the 600 committees could not be considered to be demographically representative of the communities. Surveys of community college committees conducted in the mid-1970s and in 1980 indicate that they were primarily female (69–84%), homemakers and had university or other post-secondary training (Biss, 1975; Walker, 1982). In other words, they tended to be middle class housewives with above average education. Participation rates for females was twice that of males and was highest in the 30–39 age group. Younger adults and older adults were under-represented. Moreover, only about 3% of college participants were unemployed (Saskatchewan Continuing Education, 1981).

Comparing participation rates, survey rates and the population at large indicates that certain groups were under-represented. For instance, 15% of the population was over 65 years of age; however, the interest surveys done in the rural areas included only 4% senior citizens and participation statistics included 3%. The population was 50% male; however, the survey respondents included 40% males and the program participation rate by males was 32%. Looking at education levels, 44% of the adult population had less than grade 9, but 13% of those surveyed and 14% of those who participated had less than grade 9 in the rural areas surveyed (Saskatchewan Continuing Education, 1977).

During the 1970s, the type of programming did indeed seem to reflect what survey data indicated people wanted. The community colleges conducted nearly 40 interest surveys, primarily in rural communities, using a question-naire listing a variety of vocational and avocational learning opportunities (Saskatchewan Continuing Education, 1977). But again it could be that the image of the college was such that people saw adult education or asked for adult education in terms that the colleges were prepared to offer. In the interest surveys, home-making skills, personal development courses and arts and crafts constituted about 60% of the specific requests wanted. Vo-cational improvement or occupational training accounted for about 20% (Saskatchewan Continuing Education, 1977).

The hundreds of college committees were active, provided a great deal of service, and generated an immense interest. There was, however, a bias toward personal development programs that tended to reflect the backgrounds and interests of the college committees more than those of the general community. It could be argued that "interests" rather than "needs" were being served. While overall participation statistics did increase dramatically, the under-representation of participants with lower education levels and low numbers of literacy programs lead to initiatives by many college boards and the Department to push for more basic education programs (SCCTA, 1986).

CONSULTATIVE PROCESSES

The 1972 Report of the Minister's Advisory Committee on Community Colleges provided the blueprint for the development of the new system. The Advisory Committee, similar to previous consultative attempts, met with

175

other interested agencies (the universities, technical institutes, Women's Institute, the Canadian Adult Education Association — Saskatchewan Branch, etc.) to compile its fifty-four recommendations (Pepper, 1973). The Minister responsible, Gordon MacMurchy, representing a rural riding, immediately began implementing the college system on a pilot basis (Saskatchewan Continuing Education, 1973, p. 8).

Four rural pilot regions were selected, including an area around the Minister's riding. In 1975, a review committee was established, chaired by a member of the 1972 Faris committee, Rev. Bud Harper, to examine how well the pilots were going (Harper, 1975). This quick review recommended some fine tuning, but indicated that the model seemed to work and should be implemented province-wide. No extensive external or objective review was held at this time. Another nine colleges were added in the 1975 election year, including the four urban colleges, to blanket the province. The Saskatchewan Indian Community College, covering reserve lands, and two more northern college regions were added to bring the total to 16 by the end of the decade (SCCTA, 1986). The model for the urban colleges was similar to that developed through the rural experiments. For years afterwards, there was continual debate as to which model would best fit the urban centres which already had access to a variety of university, technical and library programs (SCCTA, 1986, p. 27).

The rapid implementation of a province-wide community college system was probably hastened to meet provincial political needs rather than educational needs. The colleges continued a consultative process to direct their activities. Response to the growing concern for expanded vocational and technical training, an issue since the 1960s interest in establishing regional colleges, culminated in a Department report *Vo-Tech '90* (Saskatchewan Continuing Education, 1979). This report, released in 1979 after extensive consultation, indicated that there was a strong need for development of modules of technical programs to facilitate delivery throughout the province via the community college system. Further consultation in 1981, at a Ministers' Invitational Conference with college trustees, looked at clarifying the mandate of community colleges (Saskatchewan Continuing Education, 1981a). Emphasis was placed on being facilitators and not trying to replace other agencies. However, the need for college visibility was also acknowledged. There were further calls for looking at filling new gaps or newly discovered gaps such as literacy, women's, natives', and vocational programs.

Following the election of a Progressive Conservative government in 1982, there were further reviews of the postsecondary mandate (SCCTA, 1986, pp. 75–76). The emphasis shifted away from a grassroots community college focus and more towards employment-oriented programming, including the development of a technical school in Prince Albert (Dennison and Gallagher, 1986, p. 111). The Saskatchewan Community College Trustees

Association, with funding and encouragement from the new provincial government, released a report called *A Better Tomorrow* which concluded that the basic principles and structure of the Community College system were sound, but there was a need for more employment and literacy programming (SCCTA, 1986).

COMMUNITY DEVELOPMENT

As discussed above, much of the community college programming tended to be "interest" programming for the middle class, and middle aged. Yet many of the colleges developed programs relevant for the more difficult to reach groups. Special note should be made of the Saskatchewan Indian Community College headquartered in Saskatoon and developed to meet the specific needs of Status Indians. The 1979–80 profile of the 2500 Indian clients reached through this unique community college was significantly different from that of the other southern, non-native colleges. For instance, 99% of the Indian college clients were sponsored through Canada Employment Centres or other agencies versus 4% through the regular community colleges. Almost all (88%) of those served lived in rural areas. Most interesting, 76% were under 30 years of age and 66% had less than grade 9 education. This profile is further reflected in the type of programming taken. About one in six were enroled in adult basic education programs, one in four in employment programs, and one in four in university credit programs. Only about 30% of the participation statistics for the Saskatchewan Indian Community College were in the personal development area (Saskatchewan Continuing Education, 1981, pp. 55–58).

The urban colleges struggled to differentiate their programming from other adult education services. For instance, the Regina Plains Community College focused on developing special programs for women, natives, and mentally handicapped people (Regina Plains Community College, 1980). This "community development" work did not usually generate large participation numbers but did attempt to achieve other goals of the community college, e.g. to assist health groups to identify needs and respond to them.

COORDINATION AND COLLABORATION WITH OTHER AGENCIES

A key principle of the college system was not to duplicate but to use — to broker from — other systems. The Faris (1972) and Harper (1975) reports emphasized using the Provincial Library system, school facilities at night, the university extension programs, technical institute modules, etc. The difficulty was that many of these systems were already taxed to the limit and, without additional funding, could not meet further demands placed on them by the colleges. For instance, the provincial library received no additional funds for the thousands of community college participants who required library services (SCCTA, 1986, p. 53). Furthermore, agreements were difficult to reach with the universities, which were also strapped for funds, to deliver programs at anything less than total cost-recovery (SCCTA, 1986).

There were often difficulties in cost-effectively delivering programs from the urban technical institutes to rural areas because technical programs were not usually designed for decentralized delivery. This problem was partially addressed in the 1980s with the introduction of the Saskatchewan Skill Extension Program which facilitated rural delivery of institute programs, but continual underfunding of program development and delivery remained a major concern of college trustees (SCCTA, 1986).

Nevertheless, the college system did assist in increasing delivery of agriculture programs, technical programs and university programs throughout the province. From an economic viewpoint, however, it is difficult to say to what extent these additional services could have been delivered by directly enhancing funding for extension programs at the existing institutions.

In the cities, the role of the community colleges was actively debated (SCCTA, 1986, p. 55). In both Saskatoon and Regina university, university extension, technical institute and technical institute extension programming were already available. In addition there were active public libraries. The colleges tried to work out distinct roles for themselves. In part, this was based on the above programming thrusts by the Department in terms of the delivery of full-time literacy and employment-related programs (SCCTA, 1986). In addition, the urban colleges, in keeping with the initial college development principles, emphasized work with community groups to empower them to develop their own learning programs. This included work with immigrant groups, women, natives, and other disenfranchised groups. Interagency co-operation resulted in the development of comprehensive learning opportunity calendars, publications which the colleges were instrumental in coordinating (Regina Plains Community College, 1980). Nevertheless, the uneasiness and perceived duplication of efforts, especially in difficult economic times, contributed to the 1987 amalgamation of the provincial technical institutes with the urban community colleges (Danielson, 1988).

REPRESENTATIVENESS: COLLEGE TRUSTEESHIP AND ADMINISTRATION

The Community College Trustees were provincially appointed. This was recommended in the Faris Report (1972) and supported by the Harper Report (1975). However, the Harper report also recommended that at such time as the community college philosophy was fully understood, a more democratic approach could be used. However these reports contended, and it was never fully challenged by the trustees at least, that an elected college trustee system would be more representative (SCCTA, 1986). Appointments accentuated the influence of the Department and provincial policies since it was the Minister of Continuing Education who appointed the trustees on the

178

basis of recommendations of the Departmental representatives, other trustees, or political interests.

The autonomy issue surfaced occasionally. It was particularly hot in the Prince Albert region, where local groups had already elected and established a community college prior to creation of the community college system. With the new provincial system, a compromise was reached whereby the local people could select four out of the seven trustees and these would be automatically appointed by the Minister (SCCTA, 1986, p. 11).

Unionization in the 1970s encouraged the development of provincial policies as well as provincial negotiating committees of trustees and administrators. By the early 1980s, ten out of the sixteen colleges had unionized with the Saskatchewan Government Employees Union, one with Alberta-based unions (in the joint Alberta-Saskatchewan Region of Lakeland), and five colleges had chosen not to unionize (SCCTA, 1986, p. 18).

College governance and administration evolved. At first, the Department called meetings of the provincial trustees to discuss common areas of policy and programs. By the late 1970s, the college trustees developed their own association, conducted annual conferences and formed sub-committees. The Department established these agencies and then through training and organizational maturing allowed them to take more and more responsibility; however, the Act still governed all major decisions. Although there was some evolution to local decision making, the continued strong role of the Department, emergence of province-wide issues and the co-operative work among trustees and administrators, led to very similar staffing and programming situations across the province.

AN INSTRUMENT OF PROVINCIAL POLICY

It is important to recognize that the college system could be considered unique and innovative from a provincial point of view. The emphasis was on implementing a provincial system not in developing unique community-based approaches. This meant that although the system had unique features relative to community college approaches in other jurisdictions, the implementation of the system was fairly standard throughout the province.

As an instrument of provincial government policy, changes that occurred in the system can largely be traced to changing provincial priorities. This is not to say that the process used was strictly unilateral. Throughout the development of the colleges, considerable efforts were made to have ongoing regional and provincial consultation with various stakeholders (SCCTA, 1986). But major changes in direction were governed at the provincial level which appointed the trustees and directly funded the large majority of activities.

The community colleges were established to fill the gaps identified between what adult learners require and what existing institutions were willing, or able, to provide. As social, economic and political factors changed, these needs, or at least the perception of these needs, changed. Therefore it should not be surprising that the community college system, by its very nature, tended to evolve rapidly in order to respond to real or perceived community needs.

The creation of the new Department of Continuing Education in 1972 could be seen as primarily to facilitate the implementation of the new college system. The *Community College Act* (1973) provided extensive provincial powers to the Department. A college needed Department approval for all major aspects of its operations (SCCTA, 1986), including leasing of facilities, staffing levels, program directions, etc. This double approval approach, whereby college trustees had to check with the Department on all major decisions, often lead to disputes over "autonomy". It was noted, as in the 1986 SCCTA report, that this could be an inefficient way of making decisions; however, the Act did ensure that the college system operated in a fairly consistent manner throughout the province.

Although the Department of Continuing Education itself could be seen as being initiated to implement the community college system, the senior provincial administrator of the college system never achieved higher status than director level (SCCTA, 1986, p. 30). The Director reported to an Associate Deputy Minister, also responsible for technical institutes and related operations. Although the colleges did not have direct access at the deputy minister level, the Department had considerable influence on the colleges through its local Field Representatives and other officers. Many in the college system would have preferred less "hands on" supervisory functions and more direct access to senior government officials in order to resolve policy or program issues (SCCTA, 1986, p. 33).

The Department of Continuing Education played a major top-down role in expeditiously implementing and monitoring the community college system across the province. The regional boundaries were not coterminous with any existing education, health, social or other regions, but were loosely based on trade areas with a major centre. It is not surprising that some issues of autonomy and insensitivity to local needs surfaced.

CONCLUSIONS

In 1972, the provincial government established seven principles to guide the introduction of the new community colleges. Examining these principles as goals, it can be concluded that the innovative adult education system was largely, but not completely, successfully implemented. The success of the community colleges is also assessed by reviewing process, outcome and impact.

The first goal of the community college system was to promote formal and informal learning. The system both increased participation in and resources for adult educational programming in Saskatchewan. Starting with four pilot regions in 1973, in a few years the system had expanded to a total of sixteen colleges covering the entire province. This included rural, urban and northern regions. By the end of the 1970s, up to 100,000 participants (14% of the adult population) were using College resources annually. Participation certainly increased in the non-credit area and it would appear also in the university credit and technical areas. Some of this participation could have been achieved through other means, for instance satellites of existing institutions, but the level of participation could not have been achieved without the new community college system. This increased participation was supported through an infusion of funds for the community colleges themselves and for the university and technical institutes which offered programs to the colleges.

The colleges were a qualified success at achieving their second goal of responding to community needs. During the 1970s, the colleges initially delivered what the majority of the rural population seemed to expect from the community colleges. Activities were largely in the non-credit social demand area, the need identified by the community college contact committees. However, the voluntary advisory committees were not fully representative of their communities, and may have failed to identify more occupationally-oriented educational needs. As government policy changed (and possibly public interests), there was a movement toward more credit, technical, employment-related and literacy programming. The colleges were sufficiently flexible to deliver different kinds of programming for different groups and to change as needs changed. As well, the introduction of northern colleges and the Saskatchewan Indian Community Colleges were innovative initiatives to help special groups identify and address their adult education needs.

The third goal of helping individuals and groups identify educational needs was partially met. Particularly when funds were designated to deliver career counselling programs within the colleges, individual counselling occurred. The emphasis on working with groups and establishing contact committees provided needs identification on a collective, not just an individual basis. Although provincially appointed, Boards were quickly established throughout the province in sixteen different regions. Over 600 volunteer college contact committees were established which had direct input into needs identification and delivery of programs.

The fourth goal, to promote community development and in particular improve the rural way of life, was successfully achieved in many regards. Dennison and Gallagher (1986, p. 113) concluded that "In terms of the original goal of improving the quality of life, particularly in rural communities, the colleges had proved to be an unqualified success". Started initially in rural areas, the colleges continued to focus on the delivery of rural programs. College budgets were spent largely in the rural areas. The colleges provided a range of learning opportunities there and provided rural persons with opportunities to transfer their skills and receive income for doing so. The college system also enabled greater utilization of existing facilities in

181

rural as well as in urban areas. Although the colleges could be considered a success in this regard, it is debatable whether there was sufficient emphasis on the delivery of university credit and technical programs in the rural areas. This was one of the shortcomings addressed through the *Vo-Tech '90* Report (1979) which called for more modularized development and delivery of institute programs in rural areas. Of the two parts of the goal, the colleges were less successful in the "community development" aspect. The emphasis on more immediate program delivery reduced resources for longer term development.

For the most part, the college system was a success in achieving its fifth principle of facilitating not duplicating activities. Its most distinctive feature was probably its brokerage approach. There were some difficulties in the urban areas where colleges were more likely to be considered in conflict with the institutes, universities and libraries. The failure to establish a clear separate mandate contributed to the 1987 amalgamation of urban colleges with urban technical institutes. However, for the most part, the colleges facilitated the delivery of institute and university programs throughout the province. In the urban areas, there was a deliberate attempt to work with new groups who were not participating in mainstream programs. Therefore, the colleges could be considered a success in brokering and facilitating rather than replacing or duplicating services.

A sixth goal of the colleges was to be representative. The college boards continued to be provincially appointed, except in the case of Prince Albert area. The 1975 Harper Report and the 1986 Trustees (SCCTA) Report indicated that representation was not a major issue. The hundreds of college committees, however, were not very representative of the age, sex, education level, vocations, etc., of the population. To some extent, the Department rectified this by having separate colleges for native peoples. So, overall, it was a mixed success regarding representation of the college system.

The final principle of the community college system was to be its operation under the Department of Continuing Education. This was done except in the 1970s when the northern colleges were placed under the Department of Northern Saskatchewan (Saskatchewan Continuing Education, 1974). This helped the northern colleges to be more in tune with the rest of the socio-economic milieu in the north. It would also seem that this goal implied that the college system should be a major player within the Department of Continuing Education. In this regard, the colleges were partially successful. The colleges and the technical institutes both reported to the same associate deputy minister. Yet, although the operating grants and service contracts to the colleges grew considerably during the 1970s, their total share of the adult education budget paled in comparison to the technical institutes and universities.

Education initiatives can also be evaluated in terms of process, outcome and impact. In terms of process, the community colleges should be considered a success as they did generate a great deal of interest in the governance and direction of adult education. The 16 colleges, 600 contact committees, and up to 100,000 participants per year, attest to tremendous involvement in the educational process. In terms of outcome, the colleges did achieve considerable success in reaching more adults throughout Saskatchewan and in adapting to changing programming needs.

In terms of impact, however, the college experiment must be further evaluated by considering the issues of resources, programming and governance. Although the emphasis on brokering was innovative and pragmatic, the colleges' lack of long-term investments in technical facilities and faculty, particularly in the rural areas, likely restricted the province's ability to provide the advanced vocational training required for the 1980s and beyond. The initial emphasis on avocational personal enrichment programming rather than basic literacy and employment programs likely limited the colleges' ability, and their public image, of meeting the most pressing or "real" needs of the community. And lastly, locally determined (e.g. elected) trustees would have given the colleges a stronger community-based governance structure that might have been able to withstand the major changes to the system in the 1980s when the government changed. The colleges, as discussed, were very much an instrument of government policy. As governments or government policy changed, so did the direction of the community colleges. Was that a good or a bad thing?

AFTERMATH

The above issues can be seen as shaping the evolution of the community college and technical institute systems in Saskatchewan. By the late 1980s, the system had undergone considerable change, which in part can be attributed to the election of a new government with a new focus in 1982. The Progressive Conservative government, similar to the Liberal government of the 1960s, placed more emphasis on technical and employment related programming and centralized planning. The shifts reflected political differences as well as changing social and economic times.

The manifestations of the evolution were clear. In 1987, the four urban colleges were combined with the four urban technical institutes into one mega-institute, the Saskatchewan Institute of Applied Science and Technology (SIAST). Instead of local boards there was one provincial board to govern the four consolidated campuses. In part this was a response to perceived duplication of services within the urban areas and among the province's technical institutes (Saskatchewan Education, 1987). In the rural areas, the eight southern colleges were realigned and renamed "Regional" Colleges. The three northern colleges, largely serving Aboriginal communities, were combined into one region. In many ways the college role as broker was emphasized but narrowed to the delivering of more employment-oriented and technical programs.

183

The colleges' innovative approach, emphasizing brokering services and grassroots community involvement, was widely applauded as a progressive, cost-effective way to increase adult learning opportunities. Dennison and Gallagher (1986, p. 57) commented that "the early success of the Saskatchewan colleges was, in large part, a credit to the perseverance of ordinary citizens"; however, the government of the 1970s could have capitalized more on the colleges' attractive concept by providing the development and delivery resources so often requested. Without a more substantial investment in local resources and decision making, the fledgling system proved extremely vulnerable to changing political priorities and processes. Consequently, with a new provincial government, the symbolic term "community" was replaced with "regional" in the rural areas and the urban colleges soon ceased to exist as separate entities.

The college system was implemented to meet provincial priorities, whether they were the "community development" focus of the 1970s NDP government or the employment focus of the 1980s PC government. In terms of innovation, the college system experiment, despite its many changes or "evolution" within two decades, leaves at least two legacies for Saskatchewan and other jurisdictions. First, the emphasis on brokering has been increasingly emphasized by Saskatchewan planners and is a preferred model to cost-effectively and rapidly meet changing learning needs of special or diverse populations. For instance, Nova Scotia (1988) largely adopted a brokering model when it introduced a new college network in the late 1980s. A second innovation, not unrelated to brokering, that continues to unfold is the establishment of aboriginal-run institutions. The Saskatchewan Indian Community College continues and has been joined by similar institutes for Metis peoples. These initiatives are grounded in the early community college principles of helping communities identify and address their own learning needs.

REFERENCES

Biss, J. 1975. "Report on Local Committee Questionnaire." Working Paper. Regina: Saskatchewan Continuing Education.

Danielson, D. R. 1988. "The Reorganization of the Saskatchewan Community College System: A Case Study in Educational Policy Making." M.Ed. Thesis. Saskatoon: University of Saskatchewan.

Dennison, J. and P. Gallagher. 1986. *Canada's Community Colleges: A Critical Analysis*. Vancouver: University of British Columbia Press.

Faris, R. 1972. *Report of the Minister's Advisory Committee on Community Colleges*. Regina: Saskatchewan Continuing Education.

Harper, R. 1975. *Harper Committee Report on Community College Development*. Regina: Saskatchewan Continuing Education.

International Commission on the Development of Education. 1972. *Learning to Be: The World of Education Today and Tomorrow*. Paris: UNESCO.

Nova Scotia Advanced Education and Job Training, 1988. *Foundation for the Future: A White Paper on a Community College System for Nova Scotians.* Halifax: Government of Nova Scotia.

Pepper, E. 1973. "A Case Study of Citizen Participation: The Involvement of Adult Educators with Provincial Governments in Developing a Community College System for Saskatchewan." Master of Continuing Education Thesis. Saskatoon: University of Saskatchewan.

Regina Plains Community College, 1980. *Annual Report, 1979–80.* Regina.

Regina Plains Community College, 1981. *Annual Report, 1980–81.* Regina.

Saskatchewan Community College Trustees Association (SCCTA). 1986. *A Better Tomorrow.* Muenster, Saskatchewan: St. Peters Press.

Saskatchewan Continuing Education. 1973. *Annual Report, 1972–73.* Regina: Government of Saskatchewan.

———. 1974. *Annual Report, 1973–74.* Regina: Government of Saskatchewan.

———. 1975. *Annual Report, 1974–75.* Regina: Government of Saskatchewan.

———. 1976. *Annual Report, 1975–76.* Regina: Government of Saskatchewan.

———. 1977. *Community Colleges: Community Interest Surveys.* Regina: Government of Saskatchewan.

———. 1977a. *Annual Report, 1976–77.* Regina: Government of Saskatchewan.

———. 1978. *Annual Report, 1977–78.* Regina: Government of Saskatchewan.

———. 1978a. "Community Development Submissions from Saskatchewan Community Colleges: Prepared for the Colleges, Institutes, University Extension Committee." Working Paper. Regina: Government of Saskatchewan.

———. 1979. *Vo-Tech '90: Report of the Department of Continuing Education Task Force on Future Technical/Vocational Training in Saskatchewan.* Regina: Government of Saskatchewan.

———. 1979a. *Annual Report, 1978–79.* Regina. Government of Saskatchewan.

———. 1980. *Annual Report, 1979–80.* Regina: Government of Saskatchewan.

———. 1981. *Community Colleges: 1979–80 Participation Statistics.* Regina: Government of Saskatchewan.

———. 1981a. *Minister's Invitational Conference with Community College Trustees: Proceedings.* Regina: Government of Saskatchewan.

———. 1981b. *Annual Report, 1980–81.* Regina: Government of Saskatchewan.

Saskatchewan Education. 1987. *Preparing for the Year 2000. Adult Education in Saskatchewan.* Regina: Government of Saskatchewan.

Saskatchewan Royal Commission on Agriculture and Rural Life. 1956. *Report #6: Rural Education.* Regina: Queen's Printer.

Statistics Canada. 1982. *Education in Canada. A Statistical Review for 1981–82.* Cat. 81-229. Annual. Ottawa: Information Canada.

Walker, A. 1982. "An Examination of the Relationship between Attitudes toward Local Autonomy and Citizen Participation: A Rural Saskatchewan Case Study." M.A. Thesis. Regina: University of Regina.

Section IV

Innovations with Cost-Containment Strategies

11 Getting People off Welfare: The Employment Support Program — Innovative Grassroots Community Economic and Social Development

by R.N. (Toby) Stewart and Larry Flynn

For Saskatchewan Social Services and central agency financial planners, in the early 1970s, the central social welfare challenge was expanding caseloads of Social Assistance recipients, despite an increasingly buoyant provincial economy. Many unemployed were considered "employable" by the welfare system, but they had no immediate prospects for regular employment, in some instances because of race, age, minor physical handicaps, or lack of appropriate certified training. Many academics and a few practitioners recognized that change was necessary.[1] The solution chosen was to create short-term projects which would "employ" such people, build up their Unemployment Insurance (UI) credits, and thereby shift the income transfer burden to the federal government. From this simple analysis the Employment Support Program (ESP) was conceived in 1972 and launched as a pilot project in April of 1973.

ESP began as a short term, application-driven summer job creation program. Projects of a maximum of 22 weeks were to employ exclusively social assistance recipients. The Department of Social Services (DSS) was authorized to hire temporary staff to deliver the program in its first year.

---

[1] "The social scientists who have studied it, the bureaucrats who have administered it, and the poor who have experienced it are of one mind that in today's swiftly changing world, the welfare system is a hopeless failure. The matter is not even controversial; everybody's against it." (Special Senate Committee on Poverty, p. xii)

In the succeeding years, the program both extended the duration of its projects, and expanded the scope of their activities beyond the initial restrictive parameters. In 1977, staff positions were finally converted from temporary to permanent and projects were permitted to be funded for up to 52 weeks duration.

THE PROGRAM

What was ESP? In the early 1970s, many a bureaucrat, politician, municipal administrator and average Saskatchewan citizen was puzzled on their first exposure to the Employment Support Program. Within DSS, there was debate over whether ESP was an economic or social development program. In fact, ESP was neither fish nor fowl; it was certainly not a pure economic development activity for expectations of self-sufficient viability were never uppermost in our minds as projects were being developed or approved; nor was it a purely social "soft" sheltered activity where what a person did as a project member had no bearing on anything else inside or outside the project. Rather each project was a combination of the two elements, flexible enough to emphasize either social or economic ends and means, but never exclusive of one or the other.

Economically-focused ESP projects emphasized production of a good or service to generate revenue. But, they also made extra allowances for the social needs of most of their employees in such areas as day care support (some of these spinning off into viable enterprises on their own), transportation to/from the workplace, time off for training, or the provision of other support services such as budget counselling as part of the working routine. Such "caring" on the part of the employer to ensure "workers" were able to function more effectively on the job presaged some of the employment benefits negotiated in collective agreements of the 1980s and 1990s.

Similarly, projects which focused on rehabilitation and training attempted to emulate market-place production values, by searching for revenue-generating sources to supplement supervisory, training, and other overhead costs and to extend the employment period beyond the 20 to 26 weeks funded through ESP.

We used a takeoff on a TV commercial of the day ("Certs is a breath mint. No, Certs is a candy mint.") to humorously acknowledge our inability to fully and absolutely define ESP either as a social or as an economic development program, even to ourselves. However, once the program had been approved and staffed in 1973, the concept which had been used to "sell" ESP, shifting the income transfer responsibility to Canada, was no longer a part of the program staff's mission or consciousness, except to respond to our federal colleagues' occasional aspersions regarding "off-loading."

In truth ESP was many things. Seen by central agency planners as a positive income and activity alternative to non-productive welfare subsistence, it was also a means to move individual assistance recipients to some other government level of transfer payment, principally UI. As the program evolved, and as its projects "succeeded," ESP was perceived from different quarters variously as an economic, social and/or community development vehicle.

Such views permitted many to support the expansion of the resources of the program later, albeit for different reasons. A series of budget expansions permitted ESP to undertake a more proactive role. It became a significant and credible social program for community self-help groups, and not infrequently the established community, in preference to many other government programs.

THE INNOVATIONS

Innovative aspects to the program included its developmental approach, working with the "unemployable," developing of community-based organizations, and building economically-based operations which employed the unemployable to produce saleable goods and services. For smaller rural communities it also represented an innovative means to support initiatives for which they did not have sufficient initial seed or investment capital.

The program took a planned, conscious, proactive developmental approach to its projects, its clients and the community contexts within which they functioned. ESP's formal developmental approach was initiated by staff with a search for potential participants, although there was generally no shortage of interested individuals and groups in subsequent years. Staff then assisted them to come together as a group, and to identify project ideas relevant to their own and their community's needs. ESP staff and the group then developed a detailed business plan which became their application for funding. Once approved, ongoing staff assistance was provided to assist the project in areas as diverse as budgeting, payroll, remittances; community-media relations; bid-bonding, insurance, and staff relations and counselling. Following completion of their project, staff provided some post-project job-finding assistance to individual ESP participants, although this was more often undertaken by the client's former social worker, when caseloads allowed.

ESP staff also provided other "above & beyond the call of duty" support for both projects and individual participants, occasionally co-signing loans, providing paraprofessional alcohol and family counselling, transportation, babysitting, etc. in order to support "their" people and to maintain the viability of "their" projects. Such formal and informal commitment on the part of the staff and the province-wide political support for the ESP program contributed to unique government-supported developmental projects, especially for the time.

Another significant innovation undertaken by the program was to work with people who had been categorized by the Social Services system as "unemployable." These codings were assigned by social workers to people who may have simply been older than 45 years of age, female single parents, those with minor physically disabling conditions and other "misfits." The decision to work with "unemployables" was based on two alternative theories. From the broader social perspective, having non-productive people working, ie. producing goods and services which they otherwise would not, was a more positive alternative than non-productive welfare assistance, and only marginally more expensive for the state, over the short term.[2] From the individual's perspective, even subsidized employment, as an alternative to subsidized unemployment, gave a greater sense of self-worth within one's family, and increased one's status within family and the local community.

However, probably the most significant innovation with a lasting impact, was ESP's support for the development of community-based organizations[3] which could, and did, articulate the needs of their respective disadvantaged members or constituencies to the politicians and senior bureaucrats to whom such access by single individuals would have been denied or ineffective. These ongoing organizations also successfully lobbied local and provincial authorities for improvements in government programming and, on occasion, engaged in political actions which forced or embarrassed the government(s) to bring about changes to the benefit of their members and communities. It would be vain to suggest that ESP was uniquely causal in the emergence in the 1970s of this community-based infrastructure and the networks which subsequently evolved, but without funding and ESP staff assistance and support, the process would have been significantly delayed, and/or the results might not have been achieved at all.

Finally, in smaller rural communities, by targeting local people who had been "written off" as unemployable, ESP developed economically-based, often sheltered and supported, operations which employed people to produce saleable goods and services. ESP projects were viewed by communities as another means of contributing to their growth and stability. Many of these smaller rural communities saw the projects as an innovative means of supporting initiatives and ventures they wished to carry out, but for which they did not have sufficient initial seed or investment capital of their own.

---

[2] "A well designed employment strategy is probably of equal or greater importance (than the income maintenance approach) in addressing the goal of 'encouraging people to improve their ... position,' or further, of assisting people to achieve self-dependence. The strategy of seeking to provide adequate income through employment remains the primary strategy in the pursuit of this major goal." (Federal-Provincial Conference of Ministers of Welfare, 1975, p. 5)

[3] "Local Employment Development Committees (LEDCs) will be a type of formal inter-agency body at a regional office level. The LEDC will initially bring together local agencies with program resources committed to serving the DSS client population's employment, rehabilitation or training needs. The purpose is to more effectively coordinate the use of these local resources (staff and fiscal) in achieving employment for our clients. A further purpose is to ensure that other departmental/governmental resources are expended to compliment our own employment programming." (Employment Policy Committee, October, 1977a, p. 16)

PROGRAM HISTORY AND PROJECTS ASSESSMENT

Having described some of the significant innovative features which characterized ESP, we now wish to present a chronology and a matrix of project types which evolved over the life of the program. There were probably six stages of program development, most of these demarcated by significant cabinet and central agency decisions, usually to expand either the program's scope and/or its resources. Overlapping ESP's chronological stages were the approximately seven evolutionary program "streams" which emerged when projects of a similar type were initiated, refined and replicated in other communities (sometimes with different sponsoring groups).

The Beginnings

During the spring and summer of 1972, discussions between officials of Social Services and Continuing Education on the feasibility of providing social and economic development resources for communities and for disadvantaged persons in the province led to a trial short-term summer employment program for students (STEP), a Human Resources Development Agency (HRDA) for the disadvantaged, and an employment program for social assistance clients. The last two programs would be linked, with HRDA providing developmental aid to communities and DSS supplying grants for related employment activity.

Plans stagnated until November, when the federal government announced an expanded Opportunities for Youth (OFY) initiative to provide student employment. This announcement was perceived as an opportunity to direct some OFY resources to employable social assistance clients. Alex Taylor, Social Services Minister, sent a letter to his federal counterpart, Robert Andras, requesting inclusion of social assistance recipients within the employment initiative. The request fell upon unresponsive ears, and Taylor turned to his own department for a provincial initiative. The plans for the employment program for welfare clients were dusted off, recosted, reformatted into a Treasury Board submission, and within two weeks of the rejection by Ottawa, Treasury Board and Cabinet approval were granted. Key to the approval were projections of offset Saskatchewan Assistance Plan (SAP) savings from the initiative.[4] This projected that the combination of assistance dollars saved during the employment period plus an equal amount for a period of UI eligibility would entail no incremental costs to the province.[5]

---

[4] Memo from W. Charabin, Director Administration, DSS, to M. Wallace, Director of Budget Bureau, Dec. 19, 1972.

[5] "The purpose is to more effectively coordinate the use of these local resources (staff and fiscal) in achieving employment for our clients. A further purpose is to ensure that other departmental/governmental resources are expended to compliment our own employment programming."

The 1973 employment initiative was divided into three parts. The first was an in-house provincial survey of housing conditions of assistance recipients, conducted by clients and controlled by the department's Research and Planning Branch. The second was a parks tree planting and improvement project, again using the labour talents of about 100 clients to carry out the enhancements. The third was a 22-week, 250-person summer employment program targeted towards self-help groups, local governments and anybody else in the community willing to apply.[6] This latter component was viewed with significant scepticism, but the economic arguments for offset savings prevailed.

The first year of programming exceeded its objectives in every aspect. Planning settled in for a winter of analyzing the masses of numbers produced by the housing survey, and parks staff were pleased with the improvements. Interest was sufficient to generate 273 ESP jobs, including community improvements and cemetery cleanup, start-up of day cares, furniture repair ventures, market gardens, community newspapers and home improvements and repair services. Sponsoring groups included many self-help and community groups, local governments, and various entrepreneurs.[7]

In addition to the actual work carried out, communities — and very soon politicians — identified their satisfaction with the jobs created and the quality of work produced by the clients. Responses ranged from such comments as "I never thought those bums could work so hard!" to "We were so pleased by what they did we are now hiring them into vacant positions." It was too soon to track any offset savings, but the other benefits and the obvious enthusiasm with which clients volunteered to work seemed sufficient to justify another year of programming. HRDA was involved in this first year, but as it began to take on more of a public role in lobbying for changes to government programs, it worked less and less with ESP groups.

Conceptual Constructions

During 1974 and 1975, ESP solidified as a valuable rehabilitative resource for clients. Successful projects throughout the province gradually converted social work field staff and the active opposition experienced in the first year began to dissipate. The newly announced day care division of the department not only hired one of the temporary ESP staff workers, but also encouraged ESP to assist in developing groups and assisting in the start-up of new day care centres. Community Services Division similarly

---

[6] "providing authority under Section 8, parts (1) and (2) of the Department of Social Services Act, 1972; with authority to the Minister for grants less than $5,000, and amounts greater subject to the authority of the Lieutenant-Governor-in-Council." (Saskatchewan Treasury Board, 1973)

[7] Staff did identify and shut down one market garden enterprise whose main personal use crop was and is considered illegal to grow and market. Rumour had it that it was later refunded by the OFY program.

identified ESP as a developer and frequently as a tester of new resources and services and encouraged funding of groups involved with welfare rights counselling, women's crisis intervention and other client services.

Co-operative ventures were developed with other Departments. By 1976, over $12 million dollars in new housing stock was built, using resources from ESP, Saskatchewan Coops and the Saskatchewan Housing Corporation (SHC). Ventures such as this both improved the image of welfare recipients and the profile of the ESP. Preserved for one of the authors is the magnificent memory from the Coronach Housing Co-operative of six middle-aged women and an 84 year old man busily constructing eight houses. Supervising them was a retired carpenter who had abandoned his crutches and was perched on a roof showing the crew how to shingle.

Consolidation

The trends of the first three years were continued, with gradual modifications to make the program more responsive to community needs. Provision was made for overhead costs, particularly for projects with few other resources. Exemptions were permitted to enable hiring of skilled supervisory or trades staff where expertise was not available from the ranks of the client population. This provision tended to be most frequently used to exempt individuals returning from previous projects to retain their skills and experience. The employment period was lengthened to 26 weeks to maximize UI benefits and, of course, SAP savings.

Linkages were established with other provincial and federal departments and joint initiatives increased. During the Department of Health hearings prior to establishing a home care program, ESP staff made a presentation extolling the virtues of using existing self-help groups, which had been delivering many non-medical home care services for years. Municipal governments began to budget for materials and supervisory costs, and anticipate annual ESP projects to develop and improve community infrastructure. The Valley Park at Rosthern is a prime example of successive annual funding creating a large park and tourist area, and permitting the community to promote the park and the town as a wonderful place to visit.

Linkages were also made with other community organizations, the most significant with the Association of Metis and Non-Status Indians of Saskatchewan (AMNSIS). Metis self-government efforts emerged while ESP groups were demonstrating their capacities to meet multiple and diverse goals. With many of its membership receiving social assistance, not surprisingly AMNSIS began looking to ESP for assistance and help. Support from ESP staff generated a level of trust not associated with most other government programs. Staff were frequently called upon to help develop proposals and plans far beyond the boundaries of ESP.

The increased demands of AMNSIS and other organizations for more resources led to tensions with government. That ESP was viewed positively by AMNSIS was seen by many bureaucrats and a few politicians as evidence the program was out of control. The attractive features of ESP, its flexibility, its capacity to assist in identifying needs and then support community agendas, the willingness of field staff to work directly with the groups, were features not always perceived positively by others with more rigid definitions of the role of government and of civil servants.

Time to Take Over the World

In the midst of this tension, ESP staff began to develop measures to demonstrate the benefits of the program. A major study of the program in 1977 was to review, and possibly lead to putting some limits on ESP. Staff used this to demonstrate the significant cost reductions to the provincial government as a result of the ESP-subsidized employment. Going further than measuring the direct savings, estimates were obtained of the marketplace values of the goods and services produced by the clients. Projections were made of the revenues to various levels of government in the form of taxes, and of the multiplier effect of overall increased community spending. Cost-return estimates were produced varying from 200% to 750% of the grant expenditures, depending on assumptions used.

Budget analysts could usually make it through one annual review with a sceptical mind, but ESP-initiated tours of sample projects for the analysts (and successive executive directors, deputy ministers and ministers), combined with these impressive statistics, usually won over the sceptics. Initiatives were begun to include ESP under federal cost-sharing.

In 1976, negotiations began between the federal and provincial governments and native organizations for renewal of the Special ARDA Agreement. This was a funding agreement with significant capital funding specifically targeted towards non-urban natives. ESP staff had already worked with Metis groups to apply for funding support, but these applications had met with substantial resistance from the provincial Industry and Commerce Department (I&C). When DSS made a presentation to provincial Inter-Governmental Affairs (IGA) with respect to the new agreement, they were astonished to be asked to replace the Department of Agriculture as the second provincial delivery department. This decision was apparently aided by the appearance of an internal memo from I&C which castigated both ESP "radicals" and their gutless sympathizers within IGA.

Once DSS/ESP became a full partner within the Agreement, additional staff and budgetary resources were provided by Treasury Board; these funds were now cost-shared 50/50 by Ottawa. A matrix of fundable activities supporting economic and social development was identified and, in 1978, support for urban-based economic development including some limited capital was designated for both native and non-native participants. An individualized training and placement stream was officially identified, emerging from a network of small urban projects providing direct job training placement for clients. Subsidized industries employing primarily clients with mental handicaps or serving as a work experience for a rotation of clients were developed and supported across the province. These included numerous market gardens and membership in the Saskatchewan Vegetable Growers' Association. Economic initiatives ranged from housing development corporations with the six AMNSIS area associations, an individual welding entrepreneur in Reserve Siding, and a major industrial workshop in Prince Albert. This latter, Pine Industries, was also assisted in obtaining contracts with DNS to refurbish trailers, and grossed over $1 million annual revenue in its best years.

Using government as a purchaser of ESP products was a major way to establish the legitimacy of these organizations. Particularly in the area of social support services, ESP developed and supported agencies creating services which the DSS was willing to buy.

Staff roles became more diverse, with expertise required for bid-bonding procedures, log housing construction techniques and rutabaga harvesting operations. The Program continued its practice of hiring many of its staff from the ranks of social assistance clients, mostly persons who had come to their attention through working on projects. Regretfully, this too contributed to the "unprofessional" view of ESP held by its critics.

Periodic and frequent reviews of ESP continued. Support for the program was typically far stronger outside of the Department than inside. Indirect and sometimes direct contacts with significant Cabinet ministers and central agency officials ensured that the program maintained a high profile. In 1978–79, ESP was encouraged to put together a major program to retrofit houses throughout the province. This would use expertise from SHC, Coops and Sask Power, and develop insulation retrofitting units across the province. This initiative only made it to the pilot stage, but is an example of the diversity the program offered as a tool of government policy.

Community Development

Throughout its history, ESP and its staff attempted to consider individual projects from the community context within which they operated. Many projects remained localized in impact but, in a number of instances, successive funding of a range of activities created significant development within a community. A prime example was the small community of Archerwill and particularly the Metis side of the town. The first ESP support was extended to a group of women to assist in establishing a leather handcraft industry, sewing moccasins and gloves. ESP then assisted the Metis local to put together a carpentry training initiative for a number of men, with Canada Employment and Immigration Training on the Job (TOJ) funds supplying instructors and training materials and ESP paying wages during the training period. Coincidentally, the materials acquired were sufficient to complete a workshop for the handicraft group. The next phase consisted of securing agreement from CMHC and SHC for contracts to build 18 houses under the Rural and Native Social Housing Program, again with ESP to cover some of the labour costs, and more significantly to give the Metis local a capacity to bridge finance the operation. While preparing tenders and negotiating contract details, the group took time to build a community hall and office for the Metis local. Finally, to assist in developing a fully integrated industry, ESP/Special ARDA assistance was provided to an elder to establish a moose hide smoke-tanning operation in her backyard to supply the leathercraft operation.

With varying degrees of success, this scenario was repeated in a number of small communities throughout the province.

Retrenchment

By 1980, the program had successfully demonstrated the effectiveness of a wide range of program options. Initiatives such as the insulation retrofit crews were intended as activities to be started by ESP and then turned over to other departments or the private marketplace. The diversity of effort began to take its toll. Staff resources were stretched to their limits and several key individuals left as bureaucratic restrictions became more onerous. The inevitable failures of some of the high-risk ventures were highlighted by the Program's critics, particularly by some recently arrived and relatively inexperienced DSS executive managers.

Succeeding politicians and senior bureaucrats in the early 1980s were not enthused about operating at the intensity which had prevailed in earlier years and did not exercise opportunities to become more comfortable with their resident mavericks. Staff too became increasingly resentful and resistant to the constant demands for justifying their self-evident sensible recommendations, and frequently chose not to disguise these thoughts in interactions with more conservative departmental management officials.

More significantly, program resources became more and more tied to repeat funding of existing organizations and it became increasingly difficult to develop and support innovative ventures. And as intended, many of the better projects were either absorbed into established funding streams of government programming (e.g. day care centres) or naturally moved away from ESP as they became successful in the open market. Program regulations became increasingly restrictive and overly bureaucratic. DSS senior administration moved into second guessing the political thinking and held up or proposed changes for reasons of "community acceptability" rather than program criteria or pragmatic need. Increasingly the policy messages to the program shifted towards administrative details. In short, by 1982 and the end of the NDP government's era, the program's capacities were restricted to funding "safe" ventures — and the only truly safe venture was one which had already succeeded.

Program Streams

By the late 1970s, the program funded seven distinct streams: community improvements, services to individuals, service development, subsidized industries, work placement and placement subsidies, economic development, and partnerships with larger community development efforts. We have characterized "streams" in hindsight; however, at the time, we rarely formally distinguished them in this fashion. These streams were all present during the first pilot year in 1973, but later took on clearer characteristics. It was rare that a single project would fit one stream exclusively but various decision makers felt considerable relief with the categorization.

THE PROGRAM CONTEXT/ENVIRONMENT

ESP was not universally embraced by all of the interested stakeholders in its environment. A series of professional "orthodox" senior Social Services (DSS) headquarters executives and Regional Welfare Directors were sceptical: "its not conventional 'social work,' therefore it can't work." As well, a major conceptual difficulty faced by many DSS social workers was the apparent contradiction when clients (whom they had coded as "unemployable" in order to qualify them for financial assistance), were hired on ESP projects, thereby demonstrating their capacity to "work" (albeit on jobs that were tailored to their individual situations and skills). Outright vitriol and enmity was exhibited on the part of some Industry & Commerce (I&C) middle managers: "anyone who really wants a job can always find one — if they'll just put their ass on the line."

Generally, the Social Services "show me" scepticism was overcome when, over time, ESP's global results continued to speak for themselves and when certain key DSS field social workers became ESP allies and converts. On the other hand, some of the I&C people simply had neither the breadth of experience working with "disadvantaged" clients (although these people were also supposedly I&C's target constituency), nor the capacity to comprehend the ESP model as a legitimate and complementary economic development alternative to their grant/loan program assistance. Their disdain generally did not diminish, even when faced with concrete evidence of ESP's successes.

Compared to other "make work" programs, ESP was never a lavishly funded program, particularly in contrast to our "rich cousin" federal counterparts.[8] The largest single year budget of $4.04 million was approved in 1979/80 at which time the staff complement was 10. (This compared with average total annual allocations in Saskatchewan for LIP, Young Canada Works, and LEAP, of over twice that amount, and a staff complement of almost 40 person years.) However, with the 1979/80 allocation, ESP and Special ARDA created a total of 1030 employment positions, a quite significant impact from such a relatively small program allocation.

---

[8] "LIP, LEAP, FLIP, FLOP, YAHOO & WHOOPEE" — F. Bogdasavich, then Deputy Minister of Social Services.

ANALYSIS

ESP contributed to the climate of innovation which characterised the 1970s in Saskatchewan, both in its policy development processes and the roles its clients played.

Policy: To the chagrin of most of the senior DSS executives, (and initially to the new Director in 1975), ESP policy development was largely the product of program staff initiatives. Over time, and especially towards the latter part of the decade as ESP engaged in a conscious "outreach" developmental approach, changes in policy came to be increasingly influenced by initiatives from ESP client groups, and from community-based political organizations such as AMNSIS.

While this initially unplanned policy development approach was in marked contrast to the then-prevalent centralized planning model, there was support and understanding from some central agency quarters, and from DSS Planning & Evaluation staff, for the results achieved. There was, however, very limited policy development and direction provided from above. Nevertheless, with greater exposure to the program and its obvious "success stories," most senior DSS managers developed degrees of comfort with and tolerance of ESP and its unconventional style.

At the political level, the program and the governing party were philosophically consistent. This was not planned or even encouraged by the senior politicians, but it probably contributed to the acceptance of the program by the Cabinet and successive DSS Ministers. There was no visible political policy direction which came down to the program and ESP staff were definitely not "political hacks." As a result of the approval process which required an order-in-council for each project (no matter how small), ESP was regularly on the Cabinet agenda and most MLA's were keenly aware of its positive profile "back home."

Until 1981, the program was allowed to develop its own policy directions, drawing primarily from its field/community networks, which were also largely attuned philosophically to the governing party's social and economic principles.

The Key Actors: These were initially the field staff and the two office supervisors, some project (client) leaders (a few of whom were employed later as ESP staff), and later, some key DSS field workers, who saw ESP as a Saskatchewan manifestation of the emerging "small group social work" paradigm. Of course, none of the successful ESP projects could have worked without core groups of committed workers/participants who wanted to actively leave welfare dependency, despite psychological and structural barriers and limited conventional social support resources.

Later, the program's directions were influenced by community and client groups who lobbied politicians at local and cabinet levels for support and funding for successful local projects. The program was also influenced in a couple of cases by visionary elected officials who understood and supported the ESP developmental/community process as a whole. Such support was instrumental in the consolidation and expansion of the program into a "permanent" and broadly-based program.

ESP AND INNOVATION — CONCLUSIONS

The Employment Support Program (ESP) in Saskatchewan, over the years 1973 to 1983, can be viewed in hindsight as breaking new ground from a number of different perspectives.

From the clients' perspective: For clients it created opportunities to initiate/plan/manage their own jobs; to experience success in a job (albeit initially of short duration and sheltered) after being perfunctorily categorized as unemployable; to organize and work with other welfare recipients in a (supportive) group environment; and to create more positive self-images, better role models for their children and families, and higher status in their communities.

From the community's perspective: It created an alternative positive image of welfare recipients, in contrast to the "lazy welfare bum" stereotype; an alternative use of provincial tax dollars making a visibly constructive contribution to the benefit of the community at large; an opportunity to add (usually limited) local community resources (funds, equipment, buildings, etc.) to the ESP wage subsidy where "the whole became greater than the sum of the individual parts."

From some DSS (senior and field) staff perspectives (over time): ESP developed a limited but effective paraprofessional alternative to the traditional hierarchic social worker-client file/case management approach, engaging and supporting their clients in productive work activities, and offering a practical "made in Saskatchewan" application for the then-emerging "group" approach to social work theory and practice. The program also supported a slow recognition of both the "employment alternative" and the value of an integrated continuum of employment program options for employable and unemployable "clients," with ESP as one of the array of "tools." Moreover, ESP offered "work instead of welfare," in contrast to the mid-1980s politically directed "work for welfare" philosophy.

From a Central Agency perspective: ESP presented an opportunity to reduce direct social services welfare expenditures (the "numbers game"); an opportunity to move people from "dependency" into (at least marginal/temporary) "participation" in the work force; a shift of transfer payment costs (after the UI qualification period) from the provincial to the federal level.

From a political perspective: It presented an opportunity for an appealing political alternative to the increasing welfare caseload numbers; helped politicians walk a fine politically correct line between the later "work for welfare" and "work instead of welfare." However, it never quite achieved "a guaranteed job for everyone who wants to work." Also, in traditional political style, it offered opportunities for political "photo opportunities" e.g., cheque presentations, openings, speeches, etc.

AFTERMATH

By 1982, when the government changed, ESP was in a state of stagnation: the budget for 1980/81 had dropped to $1.75 million and 399 positions; for 1981/82 to $2.2 million and 338 positions. The new DSS senior management direction was to restrict program activities. Internal leadership at the field and supervisory level was under pressure to moderate the formerly innovative delivery style or to get out. Following the 1982 election, grants were approved to the employment placement agencies, subsidized industries and to some municipal improvement projects, but the remainder of the discretionary/developmental funds were virtually frozen for the rest of the year.

In early November, the federal government announced a job creation initiative and invited provincial participation. Some staff of ESP (5 of a total of 9) were seconded to assist with the initiative and in 1983, the two levels of government funded approximately $15 million in projects, creating 3,000 jobs. Jobs were targeted to persons receiving a transfer payment through SAP or Unemployment Insurance. Along with this joint venture, the province also spent another $2.5 million through a provincial JOBS program, targeted to private sector sponsors not deemed a priority for the federal government program. Not surprisingly, ESP staff brought along many proven concepts for procedures and policies with respect to program, sponsor and employment conditions. Economic and community development did not, however, survive the transfer. Responsibility for the subsidized industry projects was transferred to the Community Living portion of the Department. In 1984, when the province extended the JOBS program at a $10 million level, the Placement Agencies were once more supported.

On the surface, the changes represented a curtailment of overt support for economic development but little else. Slight vocabulary changes were required, but the notion of "subsidized employment instead of subsidized unemployment" continued to carry weight. Cost-sharing with the federal government, originally proposed in 1974, was achieved in 1984 under the Canada Jobs Strategy of CEIC. Changes in the SAP system, setting up a two tiered level of support and placing "employables" at a lower assistance rate tightened the pressures on SAP clients, but other than being used as a justification for continued DSS involvement in Job Creation, the reality in the field changed very little in the first years under the Conservative government. If anything, there was a loosening of the bureaucratic knots which had restricted ESP in the early 1980s, as the new administration emphasized results rather than process.

As the neo-conservative concept of "Work for Welfare" began to predominate, ideologically influenced shifts occurred in activities which could be supported and, more significantly, in the definition of acceptable sponsors. By 1986 the program was being used as a tool for eliminating "undeserving welfare bums" from the welfare roles and was even at times promoted as a punishment program for those on assistance, e.g. those thought by the police to be prostitutes and pimps. At the same time, the economic development spin-offs of job creation were once more recognized and program staff were directed to fund private sector employers to subsidize what were in actuality marginal business operations.

In 1989, the program name was changed to Saskatchewan WORKS and Work for Welfare became the overt politically inspired modus operandi for the program. In hindsight, ironically this too was "innovative," but certainly not progressive, and not of great benefit to the people affected.

REFERENCES

Employment Policy Committee. 1977a. *Report of the Employment Policy Committees.* Regina: Saskatchewan Department of Social Services, May.

———. 1977b. *Report of the Employment Policy Committee, Volume Two.* Regina: Saskatchewan Department of Social Services, October.

Federal-Provincial Conference of Ministers of Welfare. 1975. *Federal-Provincial Social Security Review, Background Paper on Income Support/Supplementation.* Published under the authority of the Federal-Provincial Conference of Ministers of Welfare. Ottawa: Government of Canada, February.

Letter to Hon. R. Andras from Hon A. Taylor, Dec. 15, 1972.

Memo from W. Charabin, Director Administration, Department of Social Services, to M. Wallace, Director of Budget Bureau, Dec. 19, 1972.

Saskatchewan Treasury Board. 1973. *Minute #7000/73*, March.

Special Senate Committee on Poverty. 1968. *Poverty in Canada.* Ottawa: Government of Canada.

CHAPTER # 12 Reducing Drug Prices: The Saskatchewan Prescription Drug Plan

by John Bury

By 1975, all provinces had some form of Drug Prescription Reimbursement Program. Saskatchewan's program was unique when introduced because it was universal, covering the whole population with the exception of Status Indians, members of the armed forces and R.C.M.P, whose medical services were covered by the federal government. There was no deductible that had to be paid before benefits began.

What distinguished the Saskatchewan Prescription Drug Plan from those of other provinces was the mechanism of calling for Standing Offer Contracts which introduced real competition among drug manufacturers. The contracts guaranteed the manufacturer the privilege of being the preferred supplier of a guaranteed minimum quantity of a drug for a six-month period, and were awarded on the basis of the lowest cost bid. This resulted in dramatic reductions in the price of drugs, particularly those which were manufactured under Compulsory Licensing, which permitted the manufacture of patented drugs by generic companies.

Drug purchasers, except those receiving Social Assistance, were required to pay a proportion of a fixed dispensing fee, but the plan demonstrated its universality by paying the total cost of the drugs for everybody. Those provinces having coverage beyond social welfare recipients (Alberta, British Columbia and Manitoba) required recipients to pay either a deductible or a percentage of the total prescription cost or both (Table 1).

The Background

Saskatchewan, together with Alberta, Manitoba and Prince Edward Island, had drug remuneration plans in place for welfare recipients and some special categories of people from the late 1940s and early 1950s. These were straightforward reimbursement plans with or without some patient contribution but with no mechanism to control the cost of drugs.

TABLE 1

Coverage of Provincial Government Drug Reimbursement Programs, 1983

Province	% Population Covered	Class of Population and Method of Payment Date of Origin[1]
Alberta	21	Welfare, nil; over 65, 20% of prescription; if not covered under private third party scheme or either of the above categories — $15 and 20% in excess of that amount in a year. 1950, 1973
British Columbia	100	Welfare and over 65, nil. Others $175 plus 20% of cost per individual per year above that. 1974, to "others" in 1977
Manitoba	100	Welfare, nil; over 65, $50 plus 20% over this per year per family unit; under 65, $75 plus 20% in excess of that per year per family unit. 1950s, present coverage since 1975
New Brunswick	21	Welfare under 18, $1 per prescription; welfare over 18, $2; over 65, $3 per prescription to a maximum of $30 per year. Not known, present since 1976
Newfoundland	22	Welfare, nil; over 65 and receiving Guaranteed Income Supplement, the dispensing fee. 1960s, 1970s
Nova Scotia	13	Welfare, over 65, nil. Not known. 1976
Ontario	14	Welfare, over 65; those under Family Benefit Act, Extended Care Services and Home Care, nil. 1974, 1976
Prince Edward Island	11	Welfare, special disease categories, nil. Not known, Early 1970s
Quebec	19	Welfare, over 65, nil. 1977
Saskatchewan	100	Certain welfare and special beneficiaries, nil; others pay portion of dispensing fee up to a maximum $3.75 to November 83, $3.95 from December 1983. 1948, 1975

[1] The second date is the inception date of expanded programs.

Source: Eastman, Harry C., *The Report of the Commission of Inquiry on the Pharmaceutical Industry*, 1985.

205

The report of the Committee of the U.S. Congress on Anti-Trust and Monopoly chaired by Senator Estes Kefauver in 1961 stimulated considerable public interest in the issue of profits of the drug industry and the ethics associated with the promotion of drugs. As both private and government sponsored medical care insurance became more common, increasing attention was paid to the costs of pharmaceuticals.

In Canada, a study of the industry was undertaken by the Restrictive Trade Practices Commission and reported in 1963. It concluded that "prices of drugs in Canada are amongst the highest in the world" (Harley, 1967, p. 15). Following the Commission's report the Canadian Parliament established a special committee on Drug Costs and Prices chaired by Dr. Harry Harley to review the findings and recommendations with a view to legislation. This exhaustive process examined every aspect of the Canadian drug industry. The committee reported that profits of pharmaceutical companies appeared to be twice as high as for the manufacturing industry as a whole (Harley, 1967, p. 12) and concluded that Canada had unacceptably high drug prices.

The Drug Industry

There are thirty or forty international companies which produce new drugs based on research, often derived from fundamental research originating in academic or national institutions, and develop them for the market. The principle contribution of these companies is developing the processes which allow the drugs to be manufactured on a commercial scale. This may involve significant modification of the chemical structure and process of manufacture from that used in the research laboratory. It is these changes and the processes involved that are patented by the brand name companies also known as the "innovators." In Canada, the process not the pharmaceutical is covered by Patent. Having produced what they hope is a commercially viable product, the companies are required to conduct pharmacological and clinical trials to determine the pharmaco-dynamic properties as well as the effectiveness and safety of the product in actual practice. Before the product is allowed to be placed on the market, the evidence from these trials is reviewed by a branch of Health Canada. If the evidence shows that the drug is effective and safe, then a Notice of Compliance is issued and the drug may be placed on the market. Drugs so introduced are called "New Drugs" and another company wishing to enter the market with the same drug has to proceed through all the steps outlined above before being able to market. This process takes in the region of ten years from the Patenting of the process to Notice of Compliance. It is important to remember that the drug itself is not patented. Until the enactment of the provision of Compulsory Licensing in 1969 (see below), a drug remained a "new" drug until it had been in use for sufficient time and in sufficient quantity to assure the Department that it was safe and effective. This was usually five or more years. After that time had elapsed, other manufacturers could manufacture the drug without the clinical testing required by a new drug but subject to all the other requirements. Patent protection was granted for seventeen years. Most drugs on the market were of foreign brand name manufacture (see below Prolonged Patent Protection). The active ingredients in drug products are nearly all manufactured outside Canada. Drug manufacturing in Canada means compounding and packaging.

The High Cost of Drugs

The Canadian inquiries had found that there were five main reasons for the high cost of drugs.

Prolonged Patent Protection Due to legislation peculiar to Canada, importation of drugs manufactured abroad by processes patented in Canada was prohibited (Hall, 1964, Vol. 1, p. 702), thus preventing drugs manufactured by companies other than the originator being available to Canadians. Denmark, Italy, Hungary and Israel had thriving "generic" drug industries and the availability of their products partly accounted for lower prices of prescription drugs in Europe and the U.S.A.

Costs of Promotion Hall (1964, Vol. 1, p. 661) estimated that sales promotion and marketing accounted for 30 per cent of the manufacturer's dollar as opposed to 7% devoted to research and development (Harley, 1967, p. 21).

Lack of Generic Prescribing Drugs were rarely prescribed by their generic names.

Tariffs Tariffs ranging from 15–25% were imposed on imported drugs.

Dispensing Practices The function of dispensing was inefficient due to too many pharmacists serving too few people (Harley, 1967, p. 34). The inquiries also noted certain practices such as "coding" prescription labels so that a second pharmacist filling the prescription as a repeat would not under-sell the first (Harley, 1967, p. 35).

Federal Medicare and Drug Plans

The Hall Commission on Health Services in addition to recommending a comprehensive, universal, publicly administered and tax-financed medical care program also called for Dental and Drug programs based on the same principles. It is interesting to note, particularly at a time of deficits and constraint on government spending, that it was during the period between Hall, 1964, and the federal medicare legislation of 1968 (that is, not after medicare was introduced), that the first large federal deficit made its appearance. Worsening federal-provincial relations that Premier Robarts of Ontario described as a "Machiavellian federal scheme to introduce the federal government into a field of provincial jurisdiction" (Taylor, 1978, pp. 373–75) probably was the key factor in inhibiting the Liberal government, either then or thereafter, from progressing to truly comprehensive federal medical insurance.

Some changes were made, however, to deal with the perceived high cost of drugs. In 1969, amendments were made to Section 41[4] of the *Patent Act* which allowed the importation of drugs with Canadian Patents from foreign (generic) manufacturers on the payment of a fee to the innovator company prior to the elapsing of the normal seventeen-year patents. This allowed many commonly used drugs to be manufactured by generic companies and marketed at significantly lower prices than those of the innovators. Despite the amendments, the innovators still retained long periods of market exclusivity averaging between seven and a half and ten years (Eastman, 1985, pp. 348–54).

In addition, in response to physicians' and pharmacists' concerns over the equivalency of the generic products, the federal government established the Quality Assessment of Drugs program (QUAD) under the Health Protection Branch of the Department of National Health and Welfare. This continued the task of plant inspection but introduced greatly increased product testing of pharmaceutical products, for their pharmacological properties.

After the introduction of Compulsory Licensing there was considerable expansion of government drug remuneration programs. Appearance on the market of many generic products and the consequent reductions in cost of many commonly prescribed drugs acted as a catalytic stimulus to the development of the Saskatchewan and other prescription drug plans. From 1969 to 1983, the value of the entire pharmaceutical industry grew by 400 per cent compared to all manufacturing shipments of 334 percent (Eastman, 1985, p. 349). Profits in relation to sales, capital and equity remained consistently higher than the average for all industries. Eastman attributes some of this to an aging population and to publicly-financed purchasing and reimbursement programs. Multiple source drugs, i.e. those where there are several manufacturers of the same drug and therefore significant price competition, only accounted for 14 per cent by value of drug sales in Canada in 1983.

The Saskatchewan Story

The Prescription Drug Plan started in September 1975 and was the last of a series of health programs initiated by the Blakeney government. The origin of the drug plan as part of a government program goes back to the Final Report of the Advisory Planning Committee on Medical Care (Thompson, 1962). In a dissenting view Walter Smishek,[1] representing the

---

[1] Smishek, the Secretary of the Retail Wholesale and Department Store Union, had for many years supported and campaigned for a universal comprehensive medical care system. As a member of the Advisory Committee in its interim report of September 1961, he had strongly proposed salaries rather than the fee-for-service method of payment for doctors.

Saskatchewan Federation of Labour, wrote that he "regretted the non-implementation of a comprehensive pharmacy program." The report estimated the cost of prescribed drugs to be $8 million in 1961 and that the cost was rising rapidly. By the time the plan was introduced, the cost had risen to $22 million.

By the time the Final Report of the Thompson committee was published the Medical Care Insurance Plan had been functioning for three months and the world had experienced the first organized doctors' strike. Review of reports of the annual conventions of the New Democratic Party shows that resolutions calling for a drug program begin in 1963 and are repeated in various forms through to 1969, by which time it was assumed that a drug plan had become firmly entrenched in party policy. Among fourteen N.D.P. promises devoted to health in its 1971 election platform, the second read, "Establish a prescription drug program based on a drug formulary and central purchasing to provide drugs at greatly reduced cost."

The doctors' strike had lead to the creation of a series of community clinics dedicated to providing comprehensive medical care under the government plan. These were organized on a cooperative basis and were owned and operated by patients who found the physical facilities and employed the staff, all of whom (including the physicians) were paid by salary or on a contractual basis. It was hoped to provide optimal services for minimum cost. This they successfully accomplished but the members, like other citizens, began to notice the barrier to care presented by paying for medications. The author was one of the many United Kingdom physicians who had come to Canada to work in the clinics. On my first day in practice, when I wrote a prescription for my third patient and give it to him, he told me he would not be able to pay for it. This was a new experience for me, as it was for my colleagues from the U.K., for we had been used to prescribing under the "free" National Health Service. Hall had noted "outlay on prescription drugs is ... equivalent to about 43 percent of medical expenses" (Hall, 1964, Vol. 1, p. 345).

At the request of the board of the Saskatoon Community Clinic, the physicians began to plan a drug program based on a formulary. In the latter half of 1966, the author and Dr. R.J.M. Gold surveyed carbon copies of the prescriptions written by the eight family physicians and four specialists on every fifth day over a six month period and reviewed repeat and phoned prescriptions filled by two pharmacies that dispensed the bulk of clinic prescriptions. The total number of preparations prescribed was 298 (Bury and Gold, 1969). No single physician prescribed more than 99, the average number being 66.

By eliminating duplicate brands, it was possible to construct a formulary of 200 items that would fill 95 per cent of all prescriptions. This was in marked contrast to the more than 3000 preparations listed in the then current listing of Canadian pharmaceuticals. All drugs were listed by their approved (generic) names thus avoiding multiple brands of the same drug. It also eliminated a large number of "copy-cat" drugs having similar actions. By 1967, through the assistance of Godfrey Chelsom whose small pharmacy was in the same building as the clinic, it was possible for patients to obtain their generic prescribed drugs from a source who, because he needed to stock only one brand of each drug, was able to negotiate reduced prices with drug salesmen. Although the changes to the *Patent Act* had not yet been enacted there were enough generic equivalents to make substantial savings.

In 1970, the clinic acquired its own pharmacy and the pharmacist, Stanley Rice, designed a revised formulary of 225 drugs in approximately 500 dosage forms. A repeat survey in 1971 showed that 23 items filled 50 per cent of all prescriptions and the cost to the patient was reduced by 27% (Rice, 1971) because of the use of generic drugs.

The need to improve access to prescription drugs was highlighted by the response of the public to the medicare deterrent fees introduced by the Liberal government in 1967. These were felt and subsequently proved to be a barrier to access for care (Beck, 1973; Beck and Horne, 1976). The fee for a visit to the doctor's office was $1.50, yet the average cost of a prescription at that time was in the region of $3.50. Given the increasing cynicism regarding the practices of the multinational pharmaceutical industry it is not surprising that a demand for some action to deal with prescription drug prices became stronger, particularly in Saskatchewan. By the time of the 1971 election, the population had become rather fond of their medical care system despite its traumatic origin and were hoping to improve it.

On taking office, Blakeney appointed Walter Smishek Minister of Public Health. He immediately established a mechanism to implement the election promises. In November, a committee chaired by the Associate Deputy Minister M.B. Derrick, called THRUST, was established, consisting of senior members of the staff of the department. Its mandate was to consider and plan programmes to meet the objectives outlined in the "New Deal for People." This committee, in turn, established eleven sub-committees called PROBES. These consisted primarily of members of the bureaucracy, the chairman usually a member of THRUST, but also with members drawn from outside government. Thus there were Probes on Hearing Aids, Chiropractic Services, Financing of Health (Community) Clinics, Children's Dental Care (Chapter 7), Occupational Health and Safety (Chapter 9), Abortion and Family Planning, and Prescription Drugs. THRUST set terms of reference and time frames for reporting.

The Probe on Prescription Drugs was chaired by Dr. David Penman, Executive Director, Medical Care Insurance Commission and included John Richards, M.L.A., an economist and the Minister's Legislative Assistant, Bruce Lawson from the Department, a secretary and the author. During the next year the committee reviewed the literature including the Klass Report on Prescription Drugs prepared for the Manitoba Government, and met with representatives of the Saskatchewan Medical Association, Saskatchewan Pharmaceutical Association, Pharmaceutical Manufactures Association of Canada, representatives of wholesalers and in particular with the staff of the PARCOST program of Ontario who were preparing to introduce a provincial drug program. In addition, members visited the Saskatoon Community Clinic and a generic drug manufacturing plant in Winnipeg.

Further information was needed on the actual prices of prescriptions, and the range of prices, the costs of dispensing, and whether pharmacists had taken advantage of legislation introduced by the previous government which permitted pharmacists to substitute one equivalent brand for another in the hope of reducing prescription costs. Code-named "Operation Sunrise," six young adults, working in pairs and employed through a summer work program, presented prescriptions for six drugs (five of which were among the ten most commonly prescribed drugs in Canada) in 113 out of the 334 pharmacies in the province. All prescriptions were written generically. The survey went off without many hitches. In one town my son, who was a surveyor, was apprehended by the R.C.M.P., who were tipped off by the pharmacist suspecting the surveyor to be a possible drug addict. One pharmacist abruptly changed the price when the surveyor expressed astonishment when asked $11.00 for a prescription which he knew from his findings should only cost between $4.00 and $5.00.

This example demonstrates the wide range of prices for identical prescriptions, which was one of the most significant findings of the survey (Table 2). Variations of from 20 cents to $7.02 in the dispensing fee was the principle cause of the wide variation in prices of prescriptions. There was little evidence that pharmacists chose a cheaper generic product despite the substitution legislation. In fact on aggregate more prescriptions were priced up than priced down (Department of Public Health, 1973).

The Probe concluded in late 1973: there was little use of substitution for the benefit of the patient; there was a wide range in dispensing fees having no relation to the service performed; Saskatchewan had the highest number of pharmacies per capita of any province in Canada, 1:2,896 people as opposed to the Canadian average of 1:4547; and experience from major hospitals and the government's purchasing agency confirmed that considerable reductions in price could be obtained by bulk purchasing.

The Probe's report came down in late 1973. It was a peculiar mixture of radical and conservative recommendations. The main intention was to obtain a reduction in the cost of drugs but not to proceed to an insurance program until "the market power of the drug industry has been tempered, and consumer demand had been rationalized" (Department of Public Health, 1972, p. 59). To achieve this purpose it recommended establishing a formulary consisting of a "core" of drugs representing 50 per cent of the cost of all prescriptions and a group of "life-saving" drugs such as insulin. This

211

TABLE 2
Average Price ($) of Six Prescriptions by Size of Community
— with Ranges of Price (Below)

Drug	25,000	*Size of Community* 5–24,999	1–4,999	<1,000	Average
Ampicillin	5.27	5.79	5.44	6.45	5.47
	3.89–7.35	3.75–9.10	4.45–7.50	4.70–9.15	3.75–9.15
Chlordiaze-poxide	3.09	3.34	3.53	3.16	3.31
	1.68–4.25	2.25–4.20	2.75–5.50	2.00–4.20	1.68–5.50
Diazepam	3.17	3.52	3.56	3.25	3.31
	2.18–4.40	2.95–4.15	2.80–4.70	2.50–4.15	2.18–4.70
Penicillin G	3.39	3.50	3.39	3.27	3.40
	1.68–6.50	2.50–5.90	2.55–4.95	1.75–7.00	1.68–7.00
Propoxyphene	2.60	2.87	2.76	2.59	2.68
	1.46–3.50	2.50–3.00	2.25–3.00	1.60–3.05	1.46–3.50
Tetracyline	3.06	4.41	3.63	3.42	3.37
	1.30–5.50	3.15–8.00	3.10–4.90	2.60–4.50	1.30–8.00

Source: Adapted from Department of Public Health, *Report of "Operation Sunrise,"* 1973.

was based on the "Mancore" program of Manitoba. Substitution of cheaper equivalents from the formulary would be made mandatory unless the physician wrote "No Substitution," in his own handwriting. An enforced policy of dispensing fees would be negotiated with pharmacists. The numbers of pharmacists trained by the University of Saskatchewan should be critically reviewed and a two-year dispensing program should be developed to equip a dispenser to perform the dispensing functions performed by the retail pharmacist.

To obtain the benefit of bulk purchasing, it was proposed the government should purchase all the drugs for the Prescription Drug Program and should seriously consider undertaking the wholesaling function. The most adventurous proposal was to "establish the capacity to manufacture drugs as applied to the Canadian market" (Department of Public Health, 1972, p. viii). The members of the Probe had been impressed by the capacity to manufacture large volumes of pills and capsules with a relatively small plant on their visit to Winnipeg and felt that such facilities would be able to produce pharmaceutical products inexpensively and at a substantial saving to the consumer. In addition, a market presence would be established.

The rejection of the insurance option was based on the evidence of annual studies conducted within the British National Health Service (N.H.S.

Prescribing) and of the Green Shield Plan in Windsor, Ontario (Greenlick and Darsky, 1968) among others. They showed a rapid escalation in the cost of prescription drugs when a drug insurance program was introduced, whether by a public or private enterprise compared to costs where there was no insurance benefit.

While the findings of the Probe were accepted, their recommendations were rejected almost completely. From the political point of view, they would fulfil the election promise in the narrowest sense. The patient would be paying for the cost of the drugs and even with a fixed and reasonable fee for dispensing, universality would not be achieved. Some would be denied benefit as they couldn't afford the prescriptions. As only drugs representing fifty per cent of the total cost would be covered, it was not comprehensive enough. From an administrative point of view the prospect of entering manufacturing and wholesaling conjured up a new, different and little understood area which was resisted by certain senior officials in the Department. The problem was therefore passed to the Research and Planning Branch where the director, Duane Adams, directed one of his senior staff, Jack McPhee, to come up with an acceptable plan.[2]

On the 17th of April 1974, Walter Smishek rose in the Legislature to speak on the second reading of the Prescription Drugs Act. After acknowledging the role of his predecessors Tommy Douglas, Woodrow Lloyd and Alan Blakeney in the development of comprehensive medical care insurance, he outlined the principle features of the program.

It had become necessary for the government to intervene as the hope expressed in the Hall Commission that "the industry will itself make these drugs available at the lowest possible cost" had not been achieved. In fact, the industry "has found an increasing number of ways to sustain the cost of drugs ..." and "the Canadian consumer has to pay the price out of his own pocket for all the faults, tricks, gimmicks and unusual pricing arrangements which are in use throughout the international and national drug scene" (Saskatchewan Legislative Assembly, 1974, p. 2447).

He quoted a 1966 study (Saskatchewan Pharmaceutical Association, 1967) done in Weyburn which showed that 2 per cent of families bore almost 20 per cent of all drug expenditures and 10 per cent bore one-half of all expenditures. Therefore, to make drugs accessible to those most in need the government would absorb all the cost of drug materials.

In order to reduce the cost of drugs the plan would be organized so that the lowest-priced equivalent drug would be dispensed. This would be achieved by two mechanisms. First, competition between manufacturers would be achieved by calling for bids as sole provider approved for payment

---

[2] Unfortunately, I have been unable to find his planning document so the factors and possible strategies considered can only be adduced by personal recall of the participants and from the form of the ultimate program.

under a Standing Offer Contract (S.O.C.). This mechanism would encourage the pharmacist to dispense the S.O.C. brand or lose money and encourage the suppliers to bid low in order to obtain the contract.

Second, there would be a standardized dispensing charge paid by patients wherever they lived. This would abolish the fee plus mark-up method of charging for prescriptions that was partly responsible for the wide range in costs of dispensing revealed by Operation Sunrise. Pharmacies in large cities and small towns would be compensated the same amount so patients would be less tempted to drive into the city to get a better deal. The Minister also made it clear that the drug plan would make up the difference between the consumer charge and the negotiated dispensing fee. As the plan developed two levels of dispensing fee were defined with a lower fee for the pharmacies having a large numbers of prescriptions.

To ensure that the formulary should be comprehensive, the Minister announced that it would be designed by an independent committee with representatives of the College of Medicine, the College of Pharmacy, the Hospital Association, and the Medical and Pharmaceutical Associations. The Minister appointed as the first chairman of the Formulary Committee Dr. Graham Clarkson, previously Deputy Minister of Health under the Lloyd Government, at the time of the Medical Care Plan's introduction. The Committee also included Dr. David Penman and myself, now Director of the Regional Health Services Branch of the Department of Public Health. The Minister announced that the plan would utilize the QUAD program as well as other quality assessment agencies to ensure that only high quality drugs would be included in the formulary. Subsequently a Drug Quality Assurance Committee was established as a sub-committee of the Formulary Committee, chaired originally by Dr. Gordon Johnson, a pharmacologist in the Department of Therapeutics of the College of Medicine. His expertise and knowledge of the pharmaceutical industry was a major contributor to the high technical quality of the program.

In his speech, the Minister stated that the average cost of a prescription in Saskatchewan at the time was $4.25 and he expected the price of drugs to the consumer to decline by 50 per cent.

With the Minister's speech and passage of the Bill, the Formulary Committee got to work as did the administrative arm under the direction of Prof. Jack Summers, seconded from the College of Pharmacy of the University of Saskatchewan.

The Formulary Committee proceeded with dispatch. The original draft formulary was based on that of the PARCOST program of Ontario, which was comprehensive. It was not difficult to approve most entries and add others to bring the list up to date. The key factors for inclusion consisted of: drug products must be valid therapeutic agents with proven clinical effectiveness; clinical documentation must demonstrate that a new product is more effective or safer or has an improved dosage schedule over existing products; the cost of therapy must be relative to clinical efficiency; the cost of oral combinations must be relative to the combined costs of single entities; and oral combination products must be proven to have significant advantages over the entities taken singly.

From the perspective of the physicians and pharmacists on the committee, the most critical issue was the effectiveness and safety of products of "generic" companies. They had been subjected, as had all physicians and pharmacists, to intense propaganda by the brand name companies suggesting that the generic products were likely not to be equivalent to brand name products in their biological behaviour. In order to address this opinion, the non-governmental physician and the pharmacist members of the committee were sent on conducted tours of pharmaceutical factories in Eastern Canada — both brand and generic. They discovered that both protagonists were equally well-managed and a high degree of care for quality was common to both. Furthermore, evidence was found that several brands of a drug, both brand and generic, were manufactured in the same plant but marketed in different shapes and sizes. They also found that a drug was sometimes manufactured by a "copier" for an originator. In fact, the name on the label did not guarantee that the product was manufactured by the "high prestige" brand name company.

Equivalency of different products was the most controversial issue that faced the committee for unless the products of the generic companies were included the objective of significantly reducing the cost of drugs could not be achieved; however provision of the above information, organized in a matter of fact fashion by the Chairman, was convincing. The use of the QUAD program of Health and Welfare Canada and the Saskatchewan commitment to use independent testing laboratories and the facilities of the College of Pharmacy at the University of Saskatchewan were also reassuring. When the drugs had been approved for inclusion in the Formulary, the Quality Assessment Committee reviewed data from all the manufacturers and, if they met the standards, then all such brands were classed as equivalents.

While the Formulary Committee was deliberating, the administration committee was negotiating with the manufacturers, the wholesalers and the pharmacists. Negotiations with the Pharmaceutical Manufacturers' Association of Canada representing the brand name companies and the Canadian Drug Manufacturers' Association representing the generic companies resulted in fairly rapid agreement.

Competition was established among the drug manufacturers through awarding Standard Offer Contracts to a single supplier for each individual drug under the following terms: the contract would be for six months; there would be a guaranteed minimum and expected total quantity; there would be a limited number of package sizes — this was keyed to smaller sizes to assist smaller pharmacies; there would be a limited number of drop-off points for delivery; the pharmacists would be paid the S.O.C. price or acquisition cost whichever was lower; and there would be no sales at S.O.C. prices out-of-province, to prevent wholesalers from undercutting prices in neighbouring provinces.

Both groups could see benefits for their own interests. The brand name companies, knowing that a universal drug plan would lead to more prescriptions being written and knowing that their brands still formed the largest proportion of products, recognized that their sales and profits would be substantial. They also knew that the generic companies already were competing with them for their older products which they could release on the market equally cheaply if necessary. They presumed, I believe, that they could restrict the prescription of generics by physicians through their continuing propaganda efforts. The generic companies were pleased that their products would be given the cachet of respectability by inclusion in the formulary and therefore could also expect larger sales. Experience was to prove that both series of expectations were achieved and will be discussed below.

In those cases where S.O.C. could not be negotiated on the basis of competition a Maximal Allowable Cost was negotiated with the manufacturers. If, however, pharmacists were able to obtain a better price, reimbursement from the plan would be based on acquisition cost. This would be monitored by random audits of pharmacy records.

The use of existing wholesalers eased the bureaucratic responsibility and as pointed out by Harley (p. 32) "the wholesaler provides a service for the drug retailer and in so doing does not contribute to the cost of drugs significantly." In the final prices negotiated for inclusion in the formulary an allowance of 11% mark-up to the wholesaler was included.

Negotiations for a fee with the pharmacists were prolonged and this was specifically mentioned in the first annual report of the plan: discussions started March 22, 1974 and were not concluded until July, 1975. There was some apprehension among pharmacists that the government was considering "socialized pharmacare," doing the dispensing themselves (Rice, 1992). This fear may have arisen from the preliminary discussions with the Probe members, who were certainly impressed by the inefficiency inherent in the numerous pharmacies in the larger cities (Regina had 43 and Saskatoon 49; both had populations around 150,000). They had mused on developing approximately ten pharmacies in each city, three to be in the hospitals, which would only sell pharmaceuticals. However, this was not recommended in the report.

Far more difficult was to arrive at an appropriate fee. The evidence from "Operation Sunrise" of widely varying dispensing fees showed that there was no generally accepted method of calculating them. Some pharmacists used a standard fee and some used a standard fee plus a percentage mark up on either the listed or acquisition cost. The survey had shown that, with the six drugs surveyed, the average fee in 1973 was $2.22, being

62 per cent of the total cost. By the time negotiations got underway in 1974, the Pharmaceutic Association asked for $2.75; however they finally accepted $2.25 with the patient to pay $2.00. The fee was increased within the year to $2.50 with the patient paying $2.25. Since the inception, prescription fees have increased as has the patient share but from the start the proportion of the prescription cost attributable to dispensing was less than determined by Operation Sunrise and has continued to fall as a proportion of total cost. By 1981/82 it had fallen to 40%. Subsequent to the defeat of the Blakeney government, the proportion fell still further and by 1986/87 had fallen to 30.2%. In 1989, the plan began to reimburse the pharmacists on the basis of fee and added an extra payment by allowing an average mark-up of 11.5% on the acquisition cost of drugs (Saskatchewan Prescription Drug Plan, 1975/76–1990/91).

The plan went into effect on September 1, 1975. It had been ready to go in the Spring and a formulary was printed based on prices negotiated for the first six months of the year. However, an election was called for June and the introduction was postponed.

Success or Failure?

How successful was the plan? There are a number of questions that need to be answered: Did the plan reduce the cost to the patient? Did the plan reduce the cost of prescription drugs? Where did the plan fail? Can the plan survive as an effective curb on drug costs in view of changes in legislation?

Although the Blakeney government was defeated in 1982, there were no significant changes in the administration of the plan until the Devine government introduced large co-payments and deductibles in 1987–88. Review of the drug plan from 1976/77 to 1991/92, excluding the first seven months (Table 3), shows there was an increase in the proportion of beneficiaries using the plan from 64% to 73.1% of the provincial population. The number of prescriptions per active beneficiary rose from 6.3 to 7.9 per year. The largest increase was in the cost of drugs which rose from just over ten million dollars to just under a hundred million in the eleven years under review. The cost of dispensing as a proportion of total cost fell from 46% to 30.2%.

The drop in the share of the pharmacist is dramatic. Dispensing costs which were 46% of total costs in 1976/77 had fallen to 25% by 1991/92. The original intent had been to support the smaller pharmacies particularly in rural areas. The fixed fee and the gradually falling proportionate costs of inventory certainly helped to do this. Despite the reduction in the share of the prescription dollar obtained by pharmacists there has been no reduction in the numbers of pharmacies in the province. In fact, there has been a slight increase, with very little population change.

It is difficult to be certain how much was saved as there were no provincial statistics kept for the average price of a prescription. In 1972,

TABLE 3
Summary of the Experience of the Drug Plan (1976/77 to 1987/87)

Year	Active Beneficiaries	Number of Prescriptions	Cost of Drugs	Cost of Dispensing	Total Cost[1]	Rx/ Act. Ben.	Cost of Rx	Cost of Drugs/Rx	Annual Cost/ Act. Ben.
76–77	583,358 64.0%	3,653,506	11,856,049 54.0%	10,215,638 46.0%	22,071,687	6.30	6.04	3.25	37.84
77–78	605,326 65.6%	3,708,578	12,984,124 54.0%	11,151,476 46.0%	24,135,600	6.10	6.67	3.50	40.85
78–79	610,555 65.6%	3,931,231	15,892,165 56.0%	12,665,149 44.0%	28,557,314	6.40	7.39	4.04	47.61
79–80	617,343 66.0%	4,007,899	18,224,606 57.0%	13,510,280 43.0%	31,734,886	6.50	7.29	4.55	51.40
80–81	627,053 66.7%	4,187,621	21,972,508 59.0%	15,451,593 41.0%	37,424,101	6.70	8.94	5.25	59.68
81–82	631,183 66.6%	4,289,705	25,937,363 60.0%	17,595,301 40.0%	43,532,664	6.80	10.15	6.05	68.97
82–83	661,151 69.0%	4,683,319	33,671,597 61.0%	21,607,386 39.0%	55,278,983	7.10	11.80	7.19	83.61
83–84	675,047 69.7%	4,882,285	40,246,080 62.5%	24,243,236 37.6%	64,489,316	7.20	13.21	8.24	95.53
84–85	686,854 70.0%	5,083,278	46,754,522 64.4%	25,886,910 35.6%	72,641,432	7.40	14.29	9.20	105.75

85–86	709,944 71.70%	5,445,602	55,516,453 67.0%	27,464,483 33.0%	82,980,936	7.70	15.24	10.19	116.88
86–87	723,567 73.10%	5,714,957	67,046,484 69.8%	28,982,985 30.2%	96,029,469	7.90	16.80	11.73	132.72
87–88*									
88–89*		4,729,407	83,476,518		96,297,723				
89–90	688,237 69.70%	5,357,388	87,607,011 73.8%	31,110,715 26.2%	118,717,726	7.78	17.25	14.73	125.92
90–91	688,041 71.18%	5,562,062	102,888,187 75.3%	33,812,465 24.7%	136,700,652	8.08	24.57	16.37	198.68
91–92	677,558 71.50%	5,762,245	108,279,755 75.0%	36,104,864 25.0%	144,384,619	8.50	25.95	18.79	213.00

N.B. 1975 ~ not included as only in effect for 7 months
Includes payment by patient.
Under the column "Active Beneficiaries" the percentage is the percentage of total beneficiaries.
* Blanks for the years 1987–88 and 1988–89 indicate figures unreliable due to changes in reporting format.

the Probe estimated that the average cost was $4.25. This corresponds very closely to findings of the annual national survey of pharmacies published in the *Canadian Pharmaceutical Journal* (1966–1977). This reported the average prescription cost (drug and dispensing fee) in 1972 and 1973 as $4.14 and $4.92 respectively. In the first full year of the plan, 1976/77, the survey reported the price of an average prescription as $6.29 while the drug plan reported $6.04. As the patient only paid $2.25 as a portion of the dispensing fee there was a saving to the patient, on average, of $3.79 per prescription in 1976/77. But, there is no evidence that the total cost was lower than it would otherwise have been.

Where the plan was very successful in reducing the cost of drugs was to the high users. The Weyburn study of the Saskatchewan Pharmaceutical Association quoted by the Minister had shown that 10% of users bore 50% of the costs. The same study (Saskatchewan Pharmaceutical Association, 1967) showed that 39% purchased no prescription drugs and 10.6% of families accounted for 51.3% of the total expenditure. Unlike the plans in British Columbia, Alberta, and Manitoba, there was no deductible and no co-payment except for a proportion of the dispensing fee. In the first year of the plan when the dispensing fee was $2.25 (people on welfare excluded) there were only 19.3% of families that did not have a prescription. The 10% of heaviest users only accounted for 26% of total costs, and paid 33% of the cost. The Plan, thus reallocated, costs from high to low users.

The rate of increase of the average prescription cost in the nine years before the plan was 7.4% a year. To the end of 1981 the rise was 8.2% and from then to 1986 the rise was 13.3%. The rate of annual rise in the cost of drugs accelerated after 1981. This is generally attributed to the high introductory cost of new drugs in this period thought to be due to the more complicated nature of the bio-technical processes inherent in the production of the more recent drugs.

The number of drugs subject to S.O.C.s steadily increased. In the first formulary there were only nine drugs but, by 1978, the S.P.D.P. Executive Director Steve Petz was quoted in the *Canadian Pharmaceutical Journal* saying that "approximately 50 per cent of all drugs are purchased under this system" (Kyriakos, 1978). S.O.C.s had a dramatic effect on the cost of many of the most prescribed drugs (see Table 4). As can be seen, there are vast ranges in prices between the generic S.O.C. drug and the brand name version of many of the drugs. As the plan only paid the S.O.C. price to pharmacists, unless the physician specified "No Substitution" the cost of many prescriptions fell drastically.

The prices of S.O.C. (generic) drugs rose very little over the six year period. Indeed three show a stationary or reduced price while the brand name drugs show a steady rise in prices over the same period. This demonstrates that there is competition between the generic companies while the brand names make no effort to compete in price. It should be noted that

TABLE 4

Comparison of Drug Prices between Standing Offer Contract Products and the Highest Priced Brand Name Drug.

(Dollars per unit — tablet, capsule or liquid dose)

Drug[2]	1979	%[1]	1984	%[1]
Ampicillin 250 mg	0.0414	50	0.0513	41.5
Penbritin 250 mg	0.0819		0.1236	
Ampicillin suspension 50 mg	0.0166	48.1	0.0183	33.2
Penbritin suspension 50 mg	0.0345		0.0552	
Amitryptilline 25 mg	0.0066	9.6	0.0067	6.4
Elavil 25 mg	0.0690		0.1045	
Cloxacillin 250 mg	0.0653	60.7	0.0660	37.0
Orbenin 250 mg	0.1076		0.1785	
Diazepam 5 mg	0.0025	3.4	0.0020	2.1
Valium 5 mg	0.0731		0.0950	
Dimenhydrinate 50 mg	0.0091	14.7	0.0082	9.2
Gravol 50 mg	0.0618		0.0896	
Flurosomide 40 mg	0.0085	10.9	0.0085	11.8
Lasix 40 mg	0.0781		0.0720	
Hydrochlorthiazide 25 mg	0.0052	16.6	0.0072	13.0
Hydrodiuril 25 mg	0.0313		0.0552	
Methyldopa 250 mg	0.0395	44.1	0.0533	36.4
Aldomet 250 mg	0.0896		0.1465	
Penicillin V. Potassium 300 mg	0.0364	33.6	0.0366	22.1
Penicillin (Brand Name) 300 mg[3]	0.1082		0.1655	
Prednisone 5 mg	0.0088	22.6	0.0099	14.0
Colisone 5 mg	0.0389		0.0708	
Tolbutamicle 500 mg	0.0084	12.5	0.0172	19.2
Mobenol 500 mg	0.0670		0.0898	
Cimetadine 300 mg	—	—	0.0715	25.2
Tagamet 300 mg	0.2621	—	0.2819	

[1] The percentage that the S.O.C. price is of the brand name price.
[2] The S.O.C. drug appears first in each listing.
[3] The highest price varied between several brand name companies from the July 1979 and 1984 editions of the Formulary of the Prescription Drug Plan.

TABLE 5
Average Market Share of Seven Licensed Drugs

Province	Percentage Share of Licensed Drugs by Quantity	Percentage Share of Licensed Drugs by Sales
British Columbia	30.58	19.89
Saskatchewan	58.01	36.42
Ontario	83.34	77.40
Quebec	54.71	47.17
New Brunswick	4.00	3.73
Nova Scotia	10.44	8.26
Newfoundland	47.59	43.65

Source: Modified from Table 10.6, p. 406 in Eastman, 1985.

several brand name companies have established "generic" companies as subsidiaries.

Eastman, in his enquiry into the pharmaceutical industry, assessed the savings that had been obtained by the use of generic drugs in the various drug reimbursement plans in Canada (Eastman, 1985, Chapter 10). He compared the effect of interchangeability of drugs, and determined the proportion of market share held by licensed (i.e. low-cost generic) drugs (Table 5). Using seven drugs, all interchangeable and all included in the formularies of the seven provinces, and using data submitted by the plans, he compared the aggregate share of the market.

The share results from a combination of the effects of listing and selection rules. British Columbia has no rules commanding the use of any specific interchangeable drug and this accounts for the low level of interchangeables. Saskatchewan, on the other hand, makes it mandatory that the pharmacist substitute and, as only the price of the S.O.C. drug is paid, the pharmacist chooses to dispense that out of self-interest. The rules therefore satisfactorily control the pharmacist but have been much less effective in having a similar effect on physicians. Eastman explains that "the surprisingly low market share of licensees products ... (is due) to the exceptionally high proportion of prescriptions issued by physicians with the 'no substitution' notation" (Eastman, 1985, pp. 309, 404). He goes on to report that in 1983/84 about 40 per cent of prescriptions where substitutes were available were noted "no substitution" accounting for an increase in cost to the plan of $4.4 million or about 10% of the cost of drugs. This practice had increased during the life of the plan. In 1977/78, 7.8%; in 1980/81, 9.5% and in 1983/84, 16.6% of all prescriptions were written "no substitution."

TABLE 6

Potential, Actual and Unrealised Savings Due to Compulsory Licensing

Province	POTSAV	ACTSAV	UNSAV
British Columbia	0.6538	0.5447	0.4553
Saskatchewan	0.6538	0.5213	0.4787
Ontario	0.6538	0.4053	0.5947
Quebec	0.6538	0.4405	0.5595

Source: Adapted from Eastman (1985) p. 407.

Eastman notes that "no substitution" occurs less than 3% of the time in other provinces.

Eastman proceeded to estimate the saving resulting from the use of interchangeable drugs. For the same seven drugs he estimated the potential saving by comparing the licensed drug price with the price at which patented drugs were dispensed guarded by the "no substitution" price in Saskatchewan. From this he estimated the potential saving (POTSAV) ranging from 1 for no savings to 0 as the licensees' price falls. Then he calculated an index of the actual saving (ACTSAV) realised in each province.

British Columbia and Saskatchewan did best (Table 6), but even so only achieved about half of the potential savings. In British Columbia this was due to the lack of mandatory substitution which offset the gains from the reimbursement of actual acquisition costs. In Saskatchewan the poor performance was due to physicians' use of the "no substitution" provision. In Ontario the saving of 40% despite licensee sales of about 80% of total sales was due to the excess of reimbursement prices over pharmacist's acquisition costs.

The Ontario plan asked manufacturers to quote a price which the plan would pay but, unlike Saskatchewan, this was not a competitive bid and so the manufacturers frequently negotiated lower prices with pharmacists who benefitted from this profit as well as their professional fee. This mechanism was known to the officials in Saskatchewan when planning the program and led to the Standing Offer Contract system.

It seemed that this would ensure the use of the S.O.C. product. The "No Substitution" provision was provided at the insistence of the physicians who, using information provided by the Pharmaceutical Manufacturers Association of Canada, said that, despite pharmaceutical testing, some apparently identical products could have different bio-availability once ingested. They might have slower absorption times and this might prove critical particularly for anti-convulsives used for epilepsy. This was certainly a possibility. Another not so critical factor therapeutically was the changing of contracts at

223

six month intervals with the result that the appearance of the pills or capsules would change and cause confusion and anxiety among older patients.

Problems of bio-availability are rare and confusion and anxiety about the appearance of pills can usually be overcome by a few reassuring words by the pharmacist. Nevertheless, the physicians of the province hold the unenviable record of preventing the maximal benefit to accrue from the plan. There is no doubt that the S.O.C. is the most effective way to ensure price competition, but this resulted in loss to the innovator companies. Through their representatives they carried out an intense propaganda war against "the copiers." Their words may have been particularly effective because they were falling on the ears of physicians who had or had inherited a tradition of opposition to interference into their preserves by the government, dating from the doctors' strike of 1962.

The plan funded a roving pharmacological professorship which enabled physicians and pharmacologists to travel round the province and give talks to district medical societies. In addition, the plan issued periodic bulletins to all physicians pointing out inappropriate prescribing patterns, considered both from a therapeutic and a cost point of view. These efforts did have significant successes in curbing some of the inappropriate patterns, but never made any significant inroads into the "no substitution" behaviour.

So a major failure of the plan was its inability to prevent the use of brand names despite mandatory substitution; however there was a significant drop in this practice when co-payments were introduced by the Devine government (see below).

Subsequent Developments

By 1987, as the costs of the plan continued to rise steeply, the Conservative government introduced a deductible of $125 and a co-payment of 20% of the cost of a prescription after the deductible was paid up to age 65, $75 and 20% over 65 years but with neither for those on Social Assistance. The average number of prescriptions fell to 7.78 in 1989–90. There was some reduction of the use of no substitution prescriptions. "No substitutions" fell drastically in the fiscal year 1991/92, when the rules were changed once more. If "no substitution" was specified the patient had to pay the full difference in cost between 80 per cent of the generic price and the price of the brand name drug. The injection of price as a significant determinant in choice by the patient has had a significant effect in reducing "no substitution" according to officials in the plan.

The policy choice between a minimal or no charge at the time of purchase is a serious issue for any government or private reimbursement plan. In Saskatchewan from the start, some element of payment was built into the plan. The $2.00 to $2.25 dispensing fee, which was in effect at the beginning of the plan, was designed to represent about half of the cost of an average prescription. In fact, $2.25 turned out to be only 37.25% in 1976/77. By 1980/81 the fee of $3.50 was only 34.5% of the average prescription price. Since the number of prescriptions per active beneficiary increased as did the number of total beneficiaries using the plan, it is impossible to demonstrate if the fee had a significant "deterrent" effect. However, the studies by Beck and Horne (1976) and the extensive reviews by Barer, Evans and Stoddart (1979) and Badgley and Smith (1979) demonstrate and argue cogently that fees at the time of service do deter and do so in direct proportion to income. Having to pay $125 or $75 for the first prescriptions of the year may be an insurmountable barrier to some. It may make a nasty gap in the post-Christmas budget, cause postponement of treatment, require credit with the pharmacist or mean non-purchase.

With the election of the NDP government in October 1991, many citizens hoped that it would be possible to restore the original concept of universality to the plan by abolishing the deductible and co-payment. Inheriting a provincial deficit of over $13 billion, the government focused on correcting this and, rather than abolishing the deductible and co-payment, they increased them to $380 per family to age 65; $150 over 65 and increased the co-payment to 35%. This has meant that only approximately 120,000 beneficiaries of a potential 766,000 will receive financial support from the plan. All others except those covered by social assistance programs will pay the full cost of their prescriptions.

The deductible is a blunt instrument and the co-payment can also be a significant barrier to access to service for those who probably need it most. These instruments have been associated with a fall in prescription demand. In the last year before the imposition of the deductible and the increased co-payment (1986/7), the number of prescriptions per annum per active beneficiary had risen to 7.9. Owing to a change in reporting, figures for 1987/88 and 1988/89 are not available. In the years 89/90 and 91/92, the number had fallen to 7.3 and 7.6 respectively. Furthermore, the proportion of active beneficiaries to potential beneficiaries fell from 73.1% in 1986/87 to 70% and 71% for the years 89/90 and 90/91 respectively. Since the recent (1992) changes which increased the co-payment to 35% from 25% over the family or personal deductible, the proportion of active beneficiaries has fallen to 69.6%. The government of Saskatchewan has introduced a number of mechanisms to soften the blow. The deductible is split into two for the first and second six months of the year, so that, for example, if a family's costs exceed $190 within the first six months, then no further deductible is payable until the commencement of the second six months. If a family's payments exceed $270, then the co-payment is reduced to 10%. Once a year a pharmacist may not charge a patient, if the patient says she or he cannot afford it and the plan will recompense the pharmacist fully. Any patient may make application in writing (using the prescribed forms available in drug stores) or by using a hot-line number, and make a case for increased benefits. The case will be judged in what the Minister of Health describes as a flexible way but will be determined by the relation between the family income and the actual cost of the prescriptions. How flexible this will remain, once in the hands of the bureaucrats, remains to be seen.

The introduction of what is in effect a "means test," by a social democratic government that still publicly espouses a universal and accessible medical insurance program, reflects dramatically the current fiscal crisis that the province faces. Saskatchewan has the highest per capita provincial debt in Canadian history. This is not a crisis of the escalating cost of medical care, which in fact has risen more slowly than predicted by Hall in 1965. Nevertheless, the cost of medical care is large and the cost of drugs has risen disproportionately.

The cost of drugs has risen faster than either the number of beneficiaries or the rate of prescribing. The rate of increase in the average cost of drugs per prescription has varied between 1.4% and 28% with the majority of years increasing between 7.8% and 18.8% per annum. In nearly every case, the rise has exceeded the C.P.I. The change in price of generic drugs has been small, so the rise in drug costs must be mainly attributed to the brand names (Table 4).

Similar results have been reported by Green Shield Prepaid Services of Ontario, a non-profit corporation that offers insurance for extended health benefits including pharmaceuticals. The report (Green Shield, 1992, p. iii), shows that the average drug cost per claim has increased at an annual rate of 11.4% for patented new drugs between 1987 and 1991. Non-patented drugs increased by an annual rate of 9.2%, but these rises were very small in dollar terms. This is 4–5 times the rate of rise in the C.P.I. They note that 41.8% of the rise in the cost of existing patented drugs occurred in 1988, which was the base year for the Patent Medicine Prices Review Board (P.M.P.R.P.). This Board, which was established in 1987 when patent protection of brand name drugs was extended to 17 years, monitors prices of new drugs compared to prices of similar products by the same or other companies and with international prices. It seems possible that the sudden rise in prices of existing patented drugs was to elevate the base line.

In the last report of the P.M.P.R.B. (Patent Medicine Prices Review Board, 1992, p. 1), the Chairman, Dr. H. Eastman reports that about 40% representing 29% of sales, appeared to exceed the guidelines, with much the same proportion in 1991. He further suggests that some patentees follow a strategy of setting high introductory prices so as to benefit from a temporary (non-recoverable) gain or that they resist the guidelines especially those limiting the prices of new drugs that "bring moderate, little or no therapeutical improvements to the range of products already existing" (P.M.P.R.B., 1992, p. 1).

The current proposed legislation (Bill C91) will further extend patent protection to twenty years, thus terminating compulsory licensing, and it can be safely predicted to increase the cost of drugs as old drugs exit the system and there is no availability of generics to maintain lower prices, as generics have accounted for 50% of the prescriptions in the S.P.D.P. Green Shield suggests (Green Shield, 1992, p. iv) that the extension will result in continued high levels of increases of drug costs.

It is hoped that the current situation will stimulate governments and the health professions to come together to determine more rational methods of controlling costs and that any controls of Canada's Health System can be reformed by clinical rather than administrative measures such as are being practised in the United Kingdom.

In summary, the Saskatchewan Prescription Drug Plan was innovative because of its universality, its eschewing, during the Blakeney years, of deductibles and large co-payments, and in particular in its success in controlling costs by obtaining competitive prices from drug manufacturers through the unique use of Standing Offer Contracts. It's failure to reach its full potential, was largely due to physicians' use of "no substitution" scripts. The subsequent imposition of deductibles and co-payments has significantly curbed this practice. However, another reason for its failure to reach its full cost-control potential is the high entry cost of new pharmaceuticals and the continuing high price of brand name products, upon which the S.P.D.P. and other drug reimbursement programs have had little effect. The apparent ineffectiveness of the Patent Medicine Price Review Board, together with the extension of patent protection to twenty years, almost guarantees that drug costs will continue to rise at a rate out of all proportion to the rises in cost of living.

REFERENCES

Annual Survey of Pharmacies. 1966–77. *Canadian Pharmaceutical Journal.* Published annually between the September–November issues.

Badgley, R. and David R. Smith. 1979. *User Charges for Health Services.* Toronto: The Ontario Council of Health.

Barer, M.L., R.G. Evans and G.L. Stoddart. 1979. *Controlling Health Care Costs by Direct Charges to Patients: Snare or Delusion.* Occasional Paper No. 10. Toronto: Ontario Economic Council.

Beck, R.G. 1973. "Economic Class and Access to Physician Services under Public Medical Care Insurance." *International Journal of Health Services* 3: 341–55.

Beck, R.G. and J.M. Horne. 1976. "Economic Class and Risk Avoidance." *Journal of Risk Insurance* 43: 73–8.

Bury, J.D. and R.J.M. Gold. 1969. "Costs and Organisation of Medical Care." *Symposium*, 37. Saskatoon: Saskatoon Community Health Foundation. Also quoted in: Wolfe, S., R.F. Badgley. 1972. *Millbank Memorial Fund Quarterly*, Vol. L. No. 2. pp. 60–7.

Department of Public Health. Released in 1972 (undated). *Probe on Prescription Drugs. Second Interim Report.* Internal Document. Regina: Government of Saskatchewan. In possession of author.

————. 1973. *Report of "Operation Sunrise."* Internal Document. Regina: Government of Saskatchewan. In possession of the author.

Eastman, H.C. 1985. *The Report of the Commission of Inquiry on the Pharmaceutical Industry.* Ottawa: Minister of Supply and Services.

Galbraith, J.K. 1992. *The Culture of Contentment.* Boston: Houghton Mifflin.

Greenlick, M.R. and J.B. Darsky. 1968. "A Comparison of General Drug Utilization in a Hospital Community with Utilization under a Drug Payment Plan." *American Journal of Public Health* 11: 58.

Green Shield Prepaid Services. 1992. *A Report on Drug Costs.* Toronto: Green Shield Prepaid Services, 705 — 195 Dufferin, London, ON.

Hall, E. 1964. *Royal Commission of Health Services.* Ottawa: Queen's Printer.

Harley, H. 1967. *Second [Final] Report of the Special Committee of the House of Commons on Drug Costs and Prices* (Chairman H. Harley). Ottawa: Queen's Printer.

Kyriakos, T. 1978. *Canadian Pharmaceutical Journal* 111: 350.

"National Health Service Prescribing." *Annual Statistical Reports Services*, Vol. 1, p. 19. London: Ministry of National Health.

Patent Medicine Prices Review Board. 1992. *Fourth Annual Report.* Ottawa: Minister of Supply and Services.

Rice, S.R. 1971. "A Formulary in Community Practice." *Proceedings of the Canadian Pharmaceutical Association*, 17 August.

Rice, Stanley. 1992. "First Pharmacist at Saskatoon Community Clinic." Personal Communication.

Saskatchewan Legislative Assembly. 1974. *Hansard: Proceedings of the Legislature of Saskatchewan*, Vol. XIV, p. 2447. Regina: Government of Saskatchewan.

Saskatchewan Pharmaceutical Association. 1967. "A Survey of Prescription Drug Expenditures by Family," *Canadian Pharmaceutical Journal* 100, 10 (October): 58–60.

Saskatchewan Prescription Drug Plan (S.P.D.P.) 1975/76–1990/91. *Annual Reports.* Regina: Government of Saskatchewan.

Taylor, M.G. 1978. *Health Insurance and Public Policy.* Montreal: McGill-Queen's University Press.

Thompson, W.P. 1962. *Final Report of the Advisory Committee on Medical Care.* Regina: Queen's Printer.

Assessing Innovation

by Eleanor D. Glor

While this book has described a number of the innovations introduced by the Saskatchewan government of 1971–82, this chapter will consider the innovations in their entirety and form conclusions about an innovative government as a whole. How did the Saskatchewan government come to introduce so many innovations — what factors made this possible? Did the Saskatchewan government achieve its objectives? Which innovations failed; which opportunities were foregone? Was Saskatchewan an innovative government from 1971–82? How important were the innovations? What are their broader implications for public sector innovation? And finally, can and should innovation be sustained?

HOW DID THE SASKATCHEWAN GOVERNMENT INNOVATE?

Certain elements and processes came together to enable Saskatchewan to innovate successfully. Several were at least partially beyond the control of the politicians and civil servants involved, but all were influenced by them. Five factors were essential to the capacity of the Blakeney government to produce and implement innovative policies: public acceptance, readiness, commitment, excellent management, and a focus on results.

Public acceptance was a necessary condition for innovation in the Saskatchewan public sector. Combining traditions of innovation, pragmatism and activism, Saskatchewan adopted new creative, generally low-cost solutions to very difficult problems. The government actively pilot tested new approaches: major new programs were often demonstrated, providing opportunity for them to evolve, grow conceptually, achieve administrative sophistication, and develop widespread popular and political support, before their introduction as government programs. Coupled with openness to new approaches was anticipation of pragmatic solutions. The Saskatchewan population was largely agricultural and would only accept solutions related to real, experienced needs. While it is important to understand the openness to new approaches and the pragmatism of the population, it is also essential to realize its expectations. Groups such as aboriginal people and farmers

229

expected the government to be active. However, high expectations also had disadvantages. Sometimes the government moved too fast, and was consequently less innovative than it might have been, for example with the Department of Northern Saskatchewan.

Readiness to take advantage of opportunity was another necessary condition for innovation, which the government facilitated in three ways. One of the key ways in which Saskatchewan politicians and bureaucrats took advantage of opportunity was by being ready with a **package of good ideas**. Ideas originated primarily from the guidance provided by the party platform; some were also generated within the processes of the government itself. The government's platform, which sustained it through three terms in office, was conceived through a party-based policy development and renewal process, and represented a consensus among the members of the NDP, and to some extent through them the people of the province. The *New Deal for People* was the most comprehensive election platform which had ever been introduced by any political party in Canada, and had no equivalent until the federal Liberal "Red Book" platform of 1993. This platform became the policy and program basis for the government. It was regularly reviewed for progress and referred to for guidance. In turn, the *New Deal '75*, was developed for the 1975 election. It was based largely on the 1971 platform, with the addition of some new items presented as resolutions at the intervening (yearly) party conventions.

Other groups which had credibility with the government also came forward with their ideas, including unions, aboriginal groups, family farm organizations, and educators and educational institutions.

Besides a large, researched list of ideas for innovations, a second component of readiness was a quick response capacity, **a capacity to implement programs quickly**. Some could be put in place immediately because they had already been piloted or partially implemented. The first few components of a province-wide library system had been put in place, for example, and the dental plan had been pilot tested. In other cases the key was the capacity to do very quick research and implementation. The Department of Health, for example, set up a number of Thrust Groups to plan initiatives, which reported within a few months, and upon whose proposals, in most cases, the initiatives were based.

A third component of opportunity and readiness was the **sound financial situation** which the Saskatchewan government inherited, and which then improved further within two years of taking office through increases in commodity prices, higher taxes, and sound financial management. With an improving economy and the lowest government revenue per capita in Canada, Saskatchewan had tax room. Following on the heels of a non-activist government, in 1971–72 Saskatchewan also had the lowest per capita spending among provinces in Canada. This programming shortfall offered the reformist NDP government an opportunity to implement many new programs.

A third key aspect of Saskatchewan's capacity to innovate was **commitment**. **Political will** was one crucial type of commitment. Saskatchewan politics were polarized, but included a spirit of reform dating back to the farmer, farmer-labour, teacher,[1] cooperative and social gospel movements of the 1910s through the 1940s. In later years, the political representation of this radical approach was the CCF, whose reputation for innovative programming started with the CCF government of Tommy Douglas, elected in 1944. During the Blakeney NDP government, political will was rooted in the strength of its election platform and the determination of the government; the Premier and the Cabinet were strong in their commitment to the *New Deal for People*.

Successful innovation also required **bureaucratic will**. The central agencies in the Saskatchewan government were powerful, and one was predominant — the Budget Bureau performed both a policy and budget analysis and control function. Line agencies and staff were sometimes dissatisfied with this strong central control, but they had their own opportunity to present their opinions both to their ministers and directly at Treasury Board, and they accepted the system. The processes of government served implementation of the government's will effectively.

An indication of commitment was the willingness to create and allocate **adequate resources** to the innovations proposed. The government's capacity to generate revenues also made it easier. Although the Blakeney government came into power in a recession, within a few years the economy improved. Increased economic activity, combined with higher taxes, meant more jobs, a buoyant economy, and growing government revenues. While retaining a balanced budget, Saskatchewan moved from having the lowest per capita expenditures to the fourth highest, by maintaining the third highest rate of growth in expenditures among the Government of Canada and the 10 provinces (the territories are excluded because they are so small) (Table 1). This made available substantially more expenditure resources than the government had started out with, in a recession bound 1971–72.

This sense of having adequate resources did not last throughout the government, however. As its growth rate in revenues declined steeply after 1975, the government tried to control expectations for program expansion within the public at large and the civil service. Also, new programs began to mature; for example, the school-based dental program enroled more students, the Hearing Aid Plan opened additional clinics as qualified staff was recruited and/or trained, the Department of Northern Saskatchewan expanded, and community college programs grew. A few new programs were added, such as home care. Both maturing and new programs meant added costs.

---

[1] M.J. Coldwell, C.M. Fines and W.S. Lloyd, who helped to build the CCF, were prime movers in organizing teachers. Lloyd was President of the teachers' federation when first elected M.L.A.

TABLE 1
Increase in Government Expenditures, 1971–72 to 1981–82

Government	1971–72 Expenditures ($M)	1981–82 Expenditures ($M)	% Increase
Canada	18,375	79,381	332.0
Nfld.	551	1,701	208.7
P.E.I.	99	368	271.7
N.S.	566	2,598	359.0
N.B.	515	1,959	280.4
Que.	5,027	21,482	327.3
Ont.	6,404	21,175	230.7
Man.	714	2,938	311.5
Sask.	614	3,017	391.4
Alta.	1,516	8,933	489.2
B.C.	1,520	8,015	427.3
Yukon	26	145	457.7
N.W.T.	91	375	312.1
Prov. Total	17,638	72,707	312.2

Source: Statistics Canada, Catalogue no. 68-512

As a result, the Saskatchewan government experienced a painful turn-around in expectations after 1975.

With such an increase in revenues and expenditures, it is possible to argue that the government was innovative because it had plenty of resources. Although Saskatchewan expenditures grew more than most, all provinces experienced substantial growth in expenditures during this period (Table 1), and of a similar magnitude. Outside the Yukon, those with oil and gas resources increased the most; none stands out among them, as the Saskatchewan government does, for its innovative policies. So, while increasing resources may have been a necessary condition for innovation in Saskatchewan during the 1970s (we cannot demonstrate otherwise), it was certainly not a sufficient condition. Nor perhaps was it a necessary condition. I am personally convinced that if the boom had not developed, the Saskatchewan government would have introduced much of its political agenda anyways, albeit in even more modest versions and perhaps more slowly.

An excellent administration or culture of excellence was a fourth key factor in the Saskatchewan government's capacity to be innovative. This culture had several aspects — **a professional organizational culture** was one. The Douglas government had created one of the first modern civil services in Canada, one in which people were recruited on the basis of the merit principle, not political connections (McLeod and McLeod, 1987, pp. 121, 129–30).[2] The Blakeney government inherited this reputation for excellent public administration (Blakeney and Borins, 1992, chapter 12). Both politicians and bureaucrats encouraged a professional approach to public administration.

Good leadership was another component of excellence. The government had excellent leadership from the Premier himself, who had been a senior bureaucrat in both the Crown corporation and the government sectors, and so understood the government and how it worked. His approach to government was non-partisan, he had a good mind and a desire to innovate. In turn, the senior bureaucrats chosen were competent, enthusiastic administrators who encouraged and rewarded innovation. Especially in the early years, rewards were available in the form of senior positions for young bureaucrats.[3]

A culture of excellence was also supported by recruiting and training **capable people**. The government was able to attract staff of high calibre, because it made recruiting a priority and because it offered civil servants the opportunity to believe in what they were doing: they wanted to participate in this government.

Central agencies were key staffing agents. The Budget Bureau, especially, did active national recruiting and was able, like the Douglas government, to attract bright innovative, occasionally (but not always) left-leaning bureaucrats and students from Saskatchewan, the rest of Canada, North America and Europe, who were willing to move to Saskatchewan. They brought with them their desire to try new things, and used their knowledge of innovation elsewhere.[4] Especially during the early years, many people recruited into the central agencies soon moved on to senior positions throughout the bureaucracy, so the Budget Bureau in particular was used as a feeder and training agency for the entire government.[5]

---

[2] It included many talented people, such as George Cadbury, Drs. Cecil and Mindel Sheps, and Dr. Fred Mott, who had been recruited from Britain and the U.S.; a number who became well known later as senior federal civil servants, such as Al Johnson, Tommy Shoyama, Tommy McLeod, Donald Tansley and Arthur Wakabyashi; and others who went on to academic careers, like Meyer Brownstone.

[3] For example, Murray Wallace was 29 years old when he became Deputy Minister of Finance. Garry Beatty, Ken Fyke, Doug McArthur, Gerry Gartner, Don Moroz, Bob Moncur, Frank Bogdasavich, Lynne Pearson and Arlene Hynd were all in their 30's when they became deputy ministers.

[4] The priority given to recruiting and the field from which they had to choose is demonstrated by the 1976 recruiting campaign, where the Budget Bureau received 1,200 applications, and interviewed over 800 people for eight jobs.

[5] This recruiting outside the province did not seem to generate much resentment within the established bureaucracy, although some might have been expected. This was probably due to the tradition of using the Budget Bureau this way, in place since the Douglas government, and the fact that the number of government positions was growing.

A supportive working environment also contributed to a culture of excellence. Employees of the government thought of themselves as being in the forefront of issues. There was a real sense of being heirs to the legacy of the superior civil servants recruited by the Douglas government. Many employees sympathized with the government: this government provided its civil service with an opportunity to contribute to society through an activist role, so it felt valued and needed. The public service, in turn, felt loyal to the government which provided it with this opportunity.

Support for people also implied giving people the freedom to be creative. Although in Saskatchewan, as in other governments, people sometimes chafed at the constraints of working in government, there was tremendous commitment, among both the line and central agency staff, to meeting the government's objectives creatively. Especially in the central agencies and in line agency leadership, there was also a conscious desire to do it professionally and with excellence. Creativity grew too from the fact that so much was being done for the first time — nobody knew how to do it, so there were few self-imposed constraints. The leadership provided and the will to succeed with excellence combined to create an organizational culture supportive to innovation.

As a civil servant who has worked for three levels of government and four different governments, what seemed different to me about working for the Saskatchewan government was the sense of support — that the government felt we were doing good work, that our suggestions were worth considering and were considered, that our advice was valued and valuable, that our opinions mattered. This government supported its civil servants in a way I have never experienced again. We had to take care what advice we offered in this environment, but it encouraged us to think freely and creatively.

Effective planning, management, program development, implementation and evaluation — doing public administration well — was also part of the culture of excellence. Saskatchewan CCF and NDP governments had developed innovative planning and financial structures and plans to support the implementation of innovations; the Blakeney government also had effective planning, financial and general management, coordination, consultation and evaluation mechanisms. While economic planning was provided by the Planning and Research Office and the Department of Finance, program planning was done by central agencies (the Planning and Research Office and special secretariats of the Executive Council, and sometimes the Budget Bureau of the Department of Finance) and by line department ministers, their deputies and planning and research units. Financial and management leadership was provided by the Deputy Minister of Finance and the other Deputy Ministers.[6] The Department of Finance played an important role in

---

[6] Two deputy ministers of finance of crucial importance were Gary Beatty from 1971 to 1976

policy discussions but its key role was in implementation. Line departments played the key role here, of course. Evaluation was incorporated into the budget process very early on and by 1980 all new programs were required to conduct program evaluations.

The Blakeney government innovations were introduced within a balanced budget. The Canadian economy, in contrast, was also booming during these years, and the Canadian government was growing quickly, but it was running yearly, growing deficits (Statistics Canada, 1993, p. 182). No other economy had the boom that occurred in Alberta.

A final element crucial to innovation in the Saskatchewan government was a **focus on results** — it did not get trapped in a bureaucratic straight-jacket. Creating the programs and services promised and answering the questions asked was the orientation. However, this energy eventually dissipated as program implementation rather than innovation became the locus.

These factors combined to form a population and a government more willing and more able than most to try new approaches, and made possible the implementation of innovative programs in Saskatchewan. As this choice of factors implies, in the public sector it is important to look beyond the boundaries of the organization to examine the social and political context for innovation, as well as looking within the organization for its capacity to innovate.

ASSESSING SASKATCHEWAN INNOVATIONS

Innovation should be assessed from a number of perspectives. Here we will look at major impacts of the innovations, opportunities missed, the significance of the innovations, and whether this was an innovative government.

Results of the Innovations

Although the quantity and magnitude of innovations developed and successfully introduced by the Saskatchewan government is clear, success in implementation does not speak about success in meeting objectives — about the why of innovation as opposed to the what. This is the ultimate test of success. In reviewing the balance sheet, we should bear in mind the magnitude of the problems the government addressed. In many cases it tackled the most basic and problematic issues in the province, which were not subject to easy or perhaps in some cases any government solution. They were the multifaceted, often fundamental economic and social problems of a small, land-locked, commodity-based economy with a widely distributed rural and aboriginal population.

The definition of success in such a context deserves some consideration. An innovation can be successfully implemented, and represent a part of a

---

and Murray Wallace from 1976 to 1979. They were followed by Rob Douglas and Mike Costello.

solution, without solving the total problem. An innovation can also ameliorate a problem which is not solvable by the government involved. The role of innovations in this context should perhaps be seen as elements of a solution rather than as the single tools which can achieve a total solution to major social problems. Only in their entirety are they, perhaps, capable of solving the problem. If, on the other hand, the innovation does not contribute to a solution, it is not successful. With this in mind, let us review the success of the Blakeney government objectives and innovations at a societal level (Table 2).

In the **economic development** arena, there was some diversification away from agriculture, but the economy remained largely dependent on primary industries. The government employed Crown corporations to serve economic and to some extent, social objectives, and inserted the province as an active participant in decision-making in the economy more than other jurisdictions in North America had done. Head offices were created in Saskatchewan for the potash, uranium and oil industries. The government's resource revenue policy automatically provided support to industries at the bottom of the economic cycle, but increased taxation at the top. While this cushioned the blow for industry, it also spontaneously reduced government revenues and increased deficits during slow-downs in resource industries. The government gained far greater control over its resource industries, and reduced its boom/bust cycle somewhat through creation of a Heritage Fund and control of resource development. It also created a process capable of reducing environmental degradation which, while stringent, was also predictable and comprehensible.

In agriculture, on the other hand, even a buoyant rural economy and the government's substantial and varied support to rural Saskatchewan could not countermand the historical trend: rural population and the number of farms declined during the 1970s.[7] Degradation of the soil was not solved.

Overall, however, the Saskatchewan economy did well from 1971 to 1981, the gross provincial product (GPP) increasing in constant prices one and a half times. Unemployment was low, resource and agricultural prices high. Provincially-based control of industry was increased. Some of the government's approaches were perhaps less efficient than they might have been, because of use of Crown corporations and the importance of political objectives; however, the major impediment to ongoing growth was the high

---

[7] The farm population in Saskatchewan dropped continually from 564,012 in 1931 (61% of the population) to 514,677 in 1941 to 399,473 in 1951 to 305,740 in 1961 (33% of the population) (Statistics Canada, 1973) to 233,793 in 1971 to 187,163 in 1981 (19% of the population) to 159,725 in 1991 (Statistics Canada, 1992). Unfortunately 1981 and 1971 figures are not comparable because Statistics Canada changed its definition of farm population in 1981 to exclude second households on a farm. The number of farms in Saskatchewan declined from 76,970 in 1971 to 67,318 in 1981 to 60,840 in 1991 (Statistics Canada, 1992). The pattern is one of decline.

TABLE 2
Government Objectives, Innovations and Other Inputs and Economic and Social Situation in Saskatchewan, 1971–82

Issue Areas	Objectives	Innovations	Other Inputs	Results
Economic Development	Stabilize the economy by: Maximizing the benefits of the resource boom	Inserted the province as an active decision-maker in the economy	New Crown corporations	Economy remained largely dependent on primary industries
		Province active partner in every new major hard rock mining project	Create Sask Mining and Development Corporation	Province became active participant in decision-making in Saskatchewan economy
		Province secure control of potash industry	Purchase 4 potash mines & interest in a 5th	Head offices created in Saskatchewan for potash, uranium, oil and gas industries; provincially-based control of industry increased; in-province procurement increased
		Profit-sensitive royalty	Create Potash Corporation of Sask.	Greater government control over resource industries
		Govt. secure larger % of gross value of resources	Uranium cartel failed	Resource revenues shielded from heavy federal taxation
		Create Heritage Fund	Sask. lost court cases over capacity to control resources	Boom/bust cycle reduced somewhat during course of govt.
			Canadian constitution became focal point for Sask govt; little local appeal	GPP grew by 1.5 times in constant $ over 11 years
		Fibre optics network		Manufacturing increased 5 times in 10 years
		Fibre optics production		Unemployment low
				Employment increased substantially
				Resource prices low, then high, then low again
		Environmental Assessment Act for all major developments	Dept. of Environment created	Process created for reducing environmental degradation

TABLE 2 (Continued)

Issue Areas	Objectives	Innovations	Other Inputs	Results
Economic Development (continued)	Supporting rural life	Hog and farm income stabilization	Govt. support for rural programs	Some diversification away from agriculture
		Hog price enhancement program		Rural population and number of farms declined
		Crop insurance		Agricultural prices high for part of period
		Program to facilitate start-up of new farms		Some stabilization of farm income
		Program to facilitate intergenerational transfer of land		Degradation of soil not solved
Social Justice	Public Participation	Govt. cultivated, later tolerated community activism	Community boards for local, regional, provincial programs	Public support for many innovations
	Empowerment	Day care centres run by parent boards	Community colleges, libraries, technical institutes managed by community boards	Increased empowerment of workers and aboriginal people
		Northerners participated in developing policy and making local resource use decisions	Home Care program created 45 new boards	
			Govt. supported community infrastructure	
		Support provided to the public when dealing with govt.	1 in 10 people sat on a community board	
	Strengthening the social fabric	Crown corporations served social objectives	Govt. supported labour	

Programs / Actions		Outcomes
Seniors' Income Plan	Disability payments increased under Auto Accident Insurance Act, Workers' Compensation Board; high minimum wage	Poverty declined, esp. for seniors, poor families with children, disabled workers
Family Income Program		People in need served better esp. sick, elderly, children, youth, disabled, aboriginal people
Workers Compensation changed to income replacement program		
3 social housing innovations		
Seniors Income Program		
Labour participation in the workplace		Increased empowerment of working people
Universal 40 hour week		
Comprehensive social development program for aboriginal people	Govt. supported aboriginal groups	Increased empowerment of aboriginal people
10 innovative educational programs for aboriginal people		Basis created for increased education of aboriginal people
4 innovative aboriginally controlled social service programs		Better service to aboriginal people
Step in solving Indian land claims		Economic and social position of aboriginal people did not change much.
Developmental support for those on welfare		
One province library system		
Distributed province-wide community college system	Province paid greater portion of total primary and secondary education costs	
	Second University created	
	Expansion of technical institutes	Increased (local) availability of education programs
	Govt. supported farmers	Quality of life on farms improved
Human Rights Code		Increased access to rights
Unified Family Court		

TABLE 2 (Continued)

Issue Areas	Objectives	Innovations	Other Inputs	Results
Social Justice (continued)	Strengthening the social fabric (continued)	Legal aid Fine option program Sharing of family property Comprehensive heritage program Ecological reserves Economic development subject to public scrutiny		Improved protection for environment
	Access to Health	Universal drug plan Universal dental program for school age children Free aids to independent living Free hearing testing Province-wide home care program 5 disease prevention and health promotion pilot projects		Increased life expectancy Lowest rate of heart disease in Canada Poor health among aboriginal people

interest rates (up to 21%) and inflation (over 12%) which developed in the late 1970s and early 1980s, factors which were not subject to the influence of the Saskatchewan government. Across Canada and the Western world economies ground to a halt. The Saskatchewan economy was not able to continue to thrive in this environment: the good times of the 1970s were followed by the lean 1980s. Because the major economic strategies of the Blakeney government were largely dismantled by the subsequent government, including use of Crown corporations to stimulate growth, no conclusions about their effectiveness in reducing the effects of the boom/bust cycle so common in Saskatchewan can be drawn.

In the **social justice** domain, the government involved the public in developing, implementing and running its services, but did not create an effective mechanism in its later years for receiving input about where it should focus its energies. Over time it grew less and less in tune with community activists.

In terms of strengthening the social fabric, it achieved some of its objectives, but not all of them. While it successfully created several income support programs, including the Seniors Income Program, the Family Income Program, a lifetime payment to people disabled in auto accidents and an income replacement Workers' Compensation program, it ran out of time and money for implementation of its sickness and accident and provincial pension plans. As well, because of its limited resources, it could only provide small subsidies through its government funded programs. The country-wide effort to create an integrated Guaranteed Annual Income failed on the shoals of financing as well, so each of the Saskatchewan programs remained separate too. Nonetheless, poverty declined in Saskatchewan during these years, due to good economic times, and federal and provincial programming.

In terms of long-term problems, Saskatchewan made some progress in empowering working people in their workplaces, but the full measure of its ideas for participation in decision-making was not achieved. A good start was made in empowering aboriginal people through creation of what turned out to be the first successful model for delivering post-secondary education to them; namely separate, aboriginally-run and -controlled educational programs and institutions. As well, programs specifically oriented to aboriginal people achieved some success, such as the Employment Support Program and the Community Schools Program which supported community involvement and student retention in urban primary and secondary schools.

While income support, social services and illness treatment programs were useful for dealing with existing problems, preventive health and social programs offered a means to preclude them. The new universal services introduced were expensive, but focused on high-risk groups in need; namely, the sick, the elderly, children, youth, and the disabled. Where they were under the control of the province, strategies for cost control were often successful, but other strategies which were not introduced could also have been helpful, such as country-wide purchasing of drugs instead of provincial-level only and even greater use of paraprofessionals.

Overall the social justice innovations had beneficial impacts, but none of the social problems they were meant to address were eliminated. Some were much improved, however, such as poverty among seniors, families with children, and disabled workers. A start was made in addressing aboriginal disadvantage, but limited progress was felt at the individual level by those who benefitted from employment and educational programs and funding of aboriginal organizations.[8]

Opportunities for Innovation not Realized

An assessment of the innovations of the Blakeney government is not complete without an examination of the innovations that did not happen and those that did not succeed (Tables 3, 4). The economic radicalism and social conservatism of the government played a key role here. In the interests of social justice the government gained control over its resource industries. With the same objective it introduced a universal drug plan, children's dental plan and new income security programs. But distributive justice did not play itself out so clearly with regard to specific disadvantaged groups, such as Indians and Metis, women and children.

Indian and Metis people were, and continue to be, the most disadvantaged in Saskatchewan. During its first years the government established the Human Resource Development Agency to address this issue, including a mandate for employment of aboriginal people within the government. During the early years of the government a volatile and hostile relationship developed between Metis people and the government, leading to road blockades and sit-ins. The HRDA leadership was openly critical of the government, and the agency was abolished. As the former Premier says in his Afterward, the government came to believe that support for groups in opposition to the government could not be provided and the issues fought out within the government, it had to be done outside the government structure. In a government which relied so heavily on its public service to deal with issues, this outsider position represented a real power disadvantage for these groups.

Some other efforts to increase the power of aboriginal people met similar fates. By the end of the Blakeney government, the ESP program no longer had the government's full support. Likewise, the initial efforts to change the power structure in the north failed, only to be reborn in 1980.

The institutions of the Blakeney government serving women, the Women's Bureau and the Advisory Council, faced a similar problem to that of HRDA, but they tolerated the (implied) constraints on public criticism of the government.

---

[8] For a critical view of these issues, see Harding, 1995.

TABLE 3

Innovations Not Introduced

Innovation backlog (innovations ready to go)	Why Rejected	Fate
Nurse practitioner program pilot	Decision to implement provincially was withdrawn at last minute due to opposition from medical profession	Not introduced
Provincial pension plan	Lack of funding, government mandate ended	Not adopted by next government
Provincial accident and sickness plan	Lack of funding, government mandate ended	Not adopted by next government
Provincial pre-natal nutrition program pilot	Pilot unsuccessful — objective to increase birth weights of high risk of babies of high risk mothers not achieved	Not adopted
Provincial child and youth safety sunsetting[1] program	Change of government	Not extended by next government
Provincial community-based seniors prevention program pilot	Change of government	Pilot abolished by next government
Provincial pre and post-natal program for urban aboriginal women pilot	Change of government	Pilot abolished by next government
School-based reproductive health program pilot	Lack of public support	Pilot abolished by NDP government
Proposal to expand worker participation in regulating work organization and environment: expand the concept of "risk" subject to attention of workplace health and safety committees, to other matters which concern workers: monotony, pace of work, the job cycle, planning, new machinery, sexual harassment, scheduling of work.	Change of government	Proposals not adopted by next government
Work Environment Board pilot	Change of government; difficulties with pilot	Pilot abolished by next government
Guaranteed annual income	Required federal-provincial program	Federal/Provincial Agreement not reached
Close child and youth corrections facilities, replace with community-based group homes	Staff (policy and planning) branch could not get support of line (operational) branches	Did not get past department: not approved

[1] Sunsetting programs are approved for fixed terms, in this case four years.

TABLE 4
Innovation Failures

Innovations Rejected	Reason	Outcome
Promotion of community activism, including criticism of the government, by government agency (HRDA, DNS)	Government could not tolerate fire within its own belly	Program abolished, groups outside government funded
Land Bank Program permitted farmers to sell land at market prices to the provincial government, then farmers to buy it at a later date, with preference given to the former owner's family members.	Land prices were increasing and family members remained unable to purchase the land, creating a situation with many losers and only one winner (the purchaser), an unenviable position for any government.	The opposition made an issue of it. The program remained in place, but was left to languish.
Saskatchewan Science Council	Not as productive or relevant as expected	Abolished 1979
Crown corporation advertising campaign	Large Crown corporation sector in disfavour because the government had described commercial objectives for it, and was accumulating capital and assets, but was paying few dividends for the people of the province.	Opposition made an issue of it, and it may have been a factor in defeat of the government in 1982.

The benefits to be derived from using paraprofessional staff who were more like the recipients were not realised to any large extent, but could have included employing people from the target groups, thus helping to alleviate their financial problems and empowering them in relation to their other problems. This issue was a factor in many of the innovations implemented and proposed, including the children's dental plan (abolished by the Conservatives), the employment support program (refocused by the Conservatives), the practical nurse program (arrested at the point of implementation), the aboriginal-run educational programs, the pre-natal nutrition program (never implemented) and the proposed community health worker program (never implemented). The changes in power relationships involved were important in the resistance to these programs.

The opportunity to support children in a substantial way through publicly-supported day care was also lost. Blakeney believed that pre-school care of children was a private, not a public responsibility, and so day care subsidies were only provided to low income people (although the upper income limit before the subsidy was completely eliminated was quite generous, in the order of $30,000 familly income per year in 1980).

While these opportunities were denied in part because of fiscal constraint, they were also not adopted or eliminated because of social conservatism. Some opportunities to address fundamental social disadvantages and discrepancies were not achieved. Although more could have been done, I do not believe that their loss discredits our assertion that the government was innovative. It does point out that this government functioned in a social and political context and that it too faced constraints and restraints. It also highlights the fact that the government was innovative but not revolutionary.

Significance of the Innovations

While the policy changes described in this book were innovative, **distinctions should be made about the significance of the changes and their comparative innovativeness.** A small program for improving the employability of persons on welfare does not have the breadth of impact that universal programs have, such as the children's dental health plan, the drug plan or the provincial library system. In the same way, while acknowledging that these are difficult to make, distinctions can be made about how innovative programs were. Nationalizing potash mines or introducing a hog marketing system, while they have major effects, are not as innovative as using paraprofessionals to do dental work, having factory floor workers do occupational health and safety inspections, or creating aboriginally-run training programs for Status Indians and Metis people. In every case, however, the resistance to them came from those who would lose financially or who had a stake in the existing system.

A broader issue arising from these distinctions and from our book is the question of **whether government policy innovation amounts to social change**, what we might describe as innovation on a societal scale. It does not appear to me that this was the case in Saskatchewan. Power relationships in the province did change to some extent, for example Status Indians achieved greater political power, working people gained power in relation to their employers, and disadvantaged people gained higher incomes and greater purchasing power. Economic power relationships changed somewhat too, due to the control which the province achieved over the economy, especially in potash and uranium. However, none of the economic changes survived the subsequent Conservative government, so they could hardly have been societal changes, or they could not have been abolished so quickly. The Saskatchewan culture had not changed to the point where the innovations had become the normal, natural, institutionalized way of doing things.

Was This an Innovative Government?

The concept of an innovative government has not been examined in the literature, before, but when a government introduces as many innovations as the Saskatchewan government of 1971–82 did, the question is begged: was this an innovative government?

No government is the first to do everything, but an innovative government can be recognized as an innovator and an early adopter of many innovations, in an attempt to bring about significant reform. We have identified a total of 147 innovations which the Saskatchewan government introduced as an innovator (first) or early adopter (second or third) among Canadian governments in the course of an eleven year government. These are divided between 126 policy (Introduction, Table 1) and 21 process innovations. Other studies have looked at innovations across governments, but even the studies which reviewed the most innovations have only identified the same magnitude of innovations (Walker, 1969; Borins, 1994) as our study. Using our operationalized definition, we therefore conclude that **this was an innovative government**. There have not been many.

The government was also successful in introducing its innovations. Very few innovations were initiated as programs (not pilots) without being successfully implemented, although some were nevertheless failures (Table 4). Two innovations, however, the Human Resource Development Agency and the Saskatchewan Science Council were created and then abolished within a few years.

While this has been difficult to measure in hindsight, **these innovations had some success in accomplishing their objectives**, as outlined in the chapters of this book. Overall, some economic and social success was achieved (Table 2).

A **backlog of piloted innovations** (Table 3) was created, ready to be implemented in a next wave of innovation. This as much as anything was indicative of institutionalized innovation, but the next wave never came — the government was defeated instead.

This innovative government was nevertheless also successful politically. The typical unsuccessful government lasts one term (usually four years) in Canada, the typical successful government two or more terms (about eight years or more). The Blakeney government was reelected three times, and was in office for eleven years. Political consistency allowed sufficient time to introduce, fully implement and evaluate innovations. This can be possible across governments, as we have seen with the current adoption of balanced budgets among Canadian governments, but innovations only rarely experience the same ongoing, widespread support in one jurisdiction.

So, the Blakeney government was an innovative government. This conclusion leaves me with a nagging question, however, concerning whether an innovative government is also a creative one. Most of the ideas for the

246

innovations came from the party and the political platform, not from the elected or appointed officials. Thus it was not the model of an innovative government that I had imagined, namely a vital agent, actively reassessing and recreating itself. New innovations were conceived during the Blakeney government; a few were implemented, such as home care; some were piloted, such as Work Environment Boards and preventive health initiatives; but most of these were not implemented in an (imagined) new wave of innovation (Table 3).

IMPLICATIONS FOR PUBLIC SECTOR INNOVATION

What does this example of an innovative government say about the positions taken by Thompson and others, that **bureaucracies are not open to nor able to effectively implement innovation?** Their description of innovation is certainly true — bureaucracies do resist innovation. While this book has demonstrated that a government and a public sector can be innovative if the right factors come together, it has also demonstrated that this bureaucracy, in which the government ultimately looked to its bureaucrats rather than its own political staff for policy advice, **was able to be innovative**, but was **not able to sustain it**. Political direction was required for the Blakeney government to be innovative, and when that waned, so did the level of innovation in the government. Both politicians and bureaucrats became involved in public administration, the government shifted its focus to the constitution and reelection, and away from generating new ideas. Nevertheless, the bureaucracy had been able to respond appropriately to a government which wanted changes, creating a senior civil service which was thoroughly involved with them, new bureaucratic structures to support them, and effective implementation of innovations when that was what was wanted.

We have also shown how the innovative government's own bureaucracy became less innovative over time and may indeed have come to resist change. James Wilson described the Blakeney bureaucrats too when he outlined the conditions that made innovation possible in the American military:

> A few intellectual leaders within the corps made the argument for change. They found support from a key executive.... The executive in turn created two important assets for the advocates of the new mission — a degree of organizational autonomy ... and a set of incentives (in the form of new opportunities for promotions.... (Wilson, 1989, p. 221)

He likewise described them later when he indicated:

> Resistance to innovation is all the stronger when the members of the organization are endowed with a strong sense of mission that enjoys substantial support from political superiors who supply money and authority to the agency. (Wilson, 1989, pp. 221–22)

Writings on the STEP program in Minnesota indicate a similar pattern (Hale, 1991; Hale and Williams, 1989).

It is one thing to make changes to someone else's program. It is quite another to consider and welcome changes to programs you yourself have implemented. This is true for both politicians and civil servants, and supports the notion of moving both ministers and civil servants around in the interests of favouring innovation in a bureaucracy.

Was the Innovation Thrust Sustained?

While it is clear that the Saskatchewan government was highly innovative in its early years, this major change focus was not sustained: **the government was not as innovative in its later years as in its earlier ones.**

The fact that the later years of the government's term did not see the introduction of nearly so many innovations as its early years would seem to have several causes. The government and civil service were **preoccupied with the constitution** and absorbed with the consequences of some of its earlier actions, which had lead to two **court cases** over potash. It was also immersed in the consolidation and management of the innovations it had already introduced, and its deteriorating financial situation. Because of the worsening economy, much attention was directed to finances and new management ideas were being encouraged and executed through the Budget Bureau. The **focus moved to public administration and accountability, and particularly to balancing the budget.** With high interest rates and inflation, real revenues levelled off, meaning every program had to cut back in order to balance the budget. The budget was consistently balanced, but it became increasingly difficult to do, and there was a political cost to success.

Many of the ideas the government and the civil service had developed **had already been realized.** Once most of its initial platform had been implemented, the government **lacked a major agenda for change**. The innovations it still wanted to implement, for example, a Saskatchewan pension plan and a sickness and accident program, were both **costly programs** which the people of Saskatchewan could not afford at that time and were no longer interested in, due in part to the next reason.

Many farmers, business people and "baby boomer" home buyers had assumed **large debt loads**, so the high interest rates of the late 1970s and early 1980s put severe pressure on them. The public mood therefore turned toward a **search for individual benefits** rather than publicly shared benefits from the provincial wealth.

Finally, the province **no longer had incremental funds** with which to implement innovations. New or different programs could only be implemented through reallocation if a balanced budget was to be retained. This was just as hard for the Blakeney government as any other. Few people who have a benefit wish to give it up so that someone else or they themselves at another time of need can have it instead. The government did do a certain amount of reallocation — the reduction of all non-salary budgets by 2%

each year starting in 1977 is one example. However, this approach did not create sufficient flexibility both to fund maturing programs and to introduce new programs. Still, **two new major programs**, Indian and Metis initiative and the home care program were funded at this time. In parallel, the government was drawing down from the Heritage Fund to **pay for new and expanding Crown Corporations**.

Another conclusion which can be drawn about the government as a whole is that **an innovative government has unique needs** compared to a government which is only introducing a few innovative programs. Key among those needs is political will, excellent management, and adequate resources. Without them, so much innovation could not occur.

In addition, **the Blakeney government made no particular effort to communicate to others in Canada about the innovations it was introducing**. Its focus was provincial, and it was not even especially good at communicating the value of its innovations to the public or publics of Saskatchewan, let alone those of Canada. When Blakeney was active in the national arena it was in support of better federal or national programs and specific issues in the Constitution rather than to publicize Saskatchewan policies.

The inertia that seems the inevitable result of declining resources, absorption with the economy, and an administrative rather than a policy focus, was damaging to the New Democratic party and government, based as it was on a social movement, not just a political party. Members of the party and many individual sectors of the public became dissatisfied with the government. At the same time, the NDP had pulled out all the stops for the 1978 election, which it managed to win handily, increasing its majority from 39 to 44 out of 61 seats. As a result, it did not feel as fearful of the 1982 election, especially since its only (premature) poll indicated it was in a safe position. To its astonishment, the NDP lost the 1982 election, managing to win only 9 (later downgraded to 8) of 64 seats.

So why, if the government's inventive and effective programs were meeting the population's needs, did the government suffer such overwhelming defeat? Both the initial success and the eventual electoral failure of the government, after three terms in office, turn in good measure on its record, and an essential part of that record is its policy and program innovations that are the subject of this book. The government may have lost its support because of many factors: distracting constitution-making (from the perspective of some Saskatchewan client and interest groups); too much emphasis on economic development, too little on social issues; decelerating increases in revenues and an unwillingness to promise costly new programs; a perception of aloofness; high inflation and interest rates; a two-party instead of a three-party fight (a key factor); and the blossoming of neo-conservative politics. One thing is certain: this principled, well-managed, but no longer innovative government fell victim to a populist swell of demands for change and more personal rather than economic and social benefits.

Perhaps, like the CCF government before it:

> The limitations placed on provincial action ... have meant that with some important exceptions ... the party exhausted most of the innovations within its power within a few years after taking office. From then on, it would seem, its main claim to electoral backing was the ability to administer the province better than its opponents. (Lipset, 1968, p. xxi)

Without excellent management, these CCF and NDP governments could not innovate successfully, but without innovation the government did not survive.

Can/Should an Innovative Thrust be Sustained?

We must also ask **whether an innovative government**, as opposed to the introduction of individual innovative programs as needed, **is sustainable or** whether it is **even desirable** to sustain it. From the experience of the Blakeney government one would conclude it is not sustainable. As to whether this would be desirable, I am inclined to say "no." Innovation is not something that is agreeable in and of itself. It is good only when the changes it brings about improve the situation of the government, agency, employees or public involved. Ongoing change is very difficult to deal with both for individuals and agencies. In our current society of enormous and ongoing change, governments must change as well, but it must be done in a thoughtful way and with appreciation that a government's capacity to change moves through patterns and winds down. Thus, while introduction of innovative programs is often worthwhile, the opportunity to create an innovative government presents itself only rarely.

One author in this book speaks about actions the Blakeney government and civil servants could have taken to **avoid subsequent changes to innovative programs by the next government**. Heartbreaking as many of these changes were to the people involved with the programs, I believe that the choices of the electorate must be respected. If the public no longer supports government programs, they should be abolished. We had no other mechanism for measuring this than elections at the time of the Blakeney government. Today's consultation mechanisms provide some further information, which should be used, judiciously: public services should be more permanent than the next poll.

While a pessimist about the possibility of sustaining programs in the face of political opposition, I also believe that a democrat must accept the changes of the next government. Bureaucrats who are open and creative must, and will, remain open to change. Locking in programs makes changes difficult for every government, not just the next one, and will come back to haunt the perpetrator.

250

And so the innovative Blakeney government came to an end in the changed economic and political environment of the early 1980s. High inflation and interest rates developed, agricultural and resource prices dropped, and neo-conservatism gained credibility and came to power in Great Britain, New Zealand, the USA, Canada and Saskatchewan.

REFERENCES

Blakeney, A. and S. Borins. 1992. *Political Management in Canada.* Toronto and Montreal: McGraw-Hill Ryerson Limited.

Borins, S. 1994. *Public Sector Innovation: Its Contribution to Canadian Competitiveness.* Kingston: School of Policy Studies, Queen's University.

Hale, S. 1991. "Reinventing Government the Minnesota Way." *Public Productivity and Management Review.* 15:2 (Winter): 123–131.

Hale, S. and M. Williams, eds. 1989. *Managing Change: A Guide to Producing Innovation from Within.* Washington, D.C.: The Urban Institute Press.

Harding, J., ed. 1995. *Social Policy and Social Justice: The NDP Government in Saskatchewan during the Blakeney Years.* Waterloo, ON: Wilfrid Laurier University Press.

Lipset, S.M. 1968. (Copyright 1950) *Agrarian Socialism: The Cooperative Commonwealth Federation in Saskatchewan.* Garden City, New York: Doubleday and Co.

McLeod, T. and I. McLeod. 1987. *Tommy Douglas The Road to Jerusalem.* Edmonton: Hurtig Publishers.

Statistics Canada. 1992. *Public Finance, Historical Data, 1965–66 to 1991–92.* Catalogue no. 68-512, April 1.

———. 1993. *The Canadian Global Almanac.* Ottawa: Statistics Canada.

Walker, Jack L. 1969. "The Diffusion of Innovations Among the American States." *American Political Science Review* LXIII (September): 880–99.

Wilson, J. Q. 1989. *Bureaucracy: What Government Agencies Do and Why They Do It.* New York: Basic Books, Inc.

Reflections on Innovations I Hoped to See
by Allan E. Blakeney

The last words of Cecil Rhodes were reputed to be "So little done, so much to do." I sometimes feel that these words were written for reform-minded politicians as they leave office. That is certainly the feeling I have as I recall the years in office between 1971 and 1982.

The Broad Vision

The New Democratic Party of Saskatchewan prepared for the 1971 Provincial election by working out a detailed election program, "New Deal for People." This 21-page booklet contained more than 100 specific proposals for action by a new government.

Many of these proposals represented improvements on what had been done previously in Saskatchewan or by other provincial governments in Canada. A number of the proposals, however, were clearly new, fresh and out of the mainstream of prevailing ideas.

As with anyone else assuming a new position, I was influenced by my background and my perception of the job at hand. I did not grow up in Saskatchewan. I did not move to Saskatchewan until 1950 when I was nearly 25 years of age. As I looked at what I saw in Saskatchewan and tried to understand it, it struck me that Saskatchewan society and Saskatchewan life was characterized by two or three broad themes. One theme was that of economic insecurity. To an extent that I had never experienced elsewhere, Saskatchewan people felt that their economic future was influenced by factors beyond their control and that as surely as there would be good times there would be bad times. Cycles would be sharp and would be largely unpredictable. Nature was sometimes a friend, sometimes an enemy but always to be taken into account. International market conditions created effects which were difficult to predict and almost impossible for Saskatchewan people to influence. Memories of the depression — "The Dirty Thirties" — were still to be found in the recesses of the Saskatchewan psyche.

Another theme that distinguished Saskatchewan from other places where I had lived was the sense of community. In rural Saskatchewan and to a lesser extent in urban Saskatchewan, the ability of people to diagnose a social need, organize, and together work to fill that social need was truly astounding. The number of people who had the social skills to organize a meeting, conduct it, arrive at a decision, and prod the group into laying out a plan of action, was prodigious. I often said that if I were driving down a country road and had the misfortune to strike two pedestrians, the chances of my having struck a president or a secretary of a voluntary organization was at least fifty-fifty. Because of the harshness and uncertainty of life, prairie people had learned the skills of working together and had preserved them. When a people live with economic uncertainties, a harsh climate, and physical isolation much greater than that faced by most other Canadians, they recognize that they may some day need a friend. In such a world Saskatchewan people have learned to cherish and nurture the neighbourly virtues.

With this background I felt that it was the role of any government of Saskatchewan to reduce the sense of isolation and of economic insecurity which permeated Saskatchewan life and to encourage and strengthen the sense of neighbourliness and community which had helped to make Saskatchewan such a unique social laboratory. Many of the proposals set out in New Deal for People, 1971, and most of what the government did during the 1970s, were designed to respond to those characteristics of Saskatchewan life.

I will try to illustrate these broad themes by referring to some of the major areas of government activity.

Agriculture and Rural Life

The major industry in Saskatchewan was, and is, farming. The chief products of the farms — wheat, barley, oil seeds, beef and pork — are sold largely outside the province and often outside Canada. Since these products are sold under international market conditions over which neither the people of Saskatchewan nor their government have any control and at prices which are notoriously volatile, economic stability for farmers is always sought after and rarely achieved. The uncertainty is added to by the unreliability of moisture and other weather conditions.

A number of possible approaches to these issues were open to the government. Most of these were tried. They included:

1. steps to deal with commodity price fluctuations;
2. steps to deal with adverse weather conditions for field crops;
3. steps to make farms and small towns more satisfying places to live and bring up children;
4. steps to help retiring farmers sell their farms for cash so that they would have a secure retirement, and to allow people to enter farming who did not have the cash to buy a farm.

Here we see the interweaving of the objectives of improving economic security and of strengthening the sense of community.

With respect to achieving some price stability we worked with the Federal government to get price support and supply management programs in place for dairy, poultry and egg producers. We provided financial assistance for farmers to get into these areas of agricultural production so that Saskatchewan's quotas under national programs would be fully used and these relatively stable areas of agriculture would provide secure incomes for an increased number of farmers.

We encouraged farmers to broaden their production base from field crops to include livestock production. Livestock products are sold primarily in North America where price fluctuations are not as dramatic as they are with grains which are sold on world-wide markets. We provided a measure of price support for producers of beef and hogs through beef and hog price stabilization programs. The price supports sheltered farmers from the worst drops in prices, at the sacrifice of not being able to take advantage of some of the peaks, and provided a significant level of stability for both farmers and their bankers. One of the many adverse consequences of the boom and bust cycles in agriculture is that it can sometimes be very difficult for farmers to obtain credit from ordinary financial institutions. Credit is a necessity in highly capitalized industries like modern agriculture, especially for younger farmers, and price support programs greatly improve access to credit.

Turning to field crops, strenuous efforts were made to create new markets for crops other than wheat, barley and oats. Rapeseed, and a particular variety of rapeseed named canola, became a major oilseed crop. Production of a wide range of other crops was pursued, with modest success.

The major steps to improve economic security for farmers were the reshaping of a federal-provincial-farmer-financed crop insurance program to guarantee against loss of yields because of weather conditions. The greatly improved crop insurance plan proved to be an absolute godsend to farmers in the 1980s. The other major effort was a federal program to provide broad general support for the western farm economy in times of depressed prices through the Western Grain Stabilization program. With these programs, one year of drought or even two was not a financial catastrophe for most farmers, nor was a year or two of depressed prices a disaster.

There was a further ground for unease among rural people. Since World War II, they watched and conditionally welcomed the technological changes which transformed the way they lived and worked. No longer was farming an activity carried on by a nearly self-sufficient family supplying many of their own necessities and using for their farm operations locally bred horses fed by crops they grew. It was now an activity carried out with massive and expensive machines produced outside the prairies and often outside Canada, fuelled by expensive petroleum products and using methods requiring costly chemical fertilizers, insecticides and herbicides. The technology allowed a farmer to farm huge areas of land, and economics forced the farmer to do so.

As the number of farm families declined, there was a gnawing and well-founded fear that the small town that served them would disappear and with it the opportunities for education, health, recreation and cultural services for themselves and their children close at hand. Farmers had had to expand to survive and their life savings were invested in land and machinery. When retirement time came, they had no ready cash and their children could not afford to buy the now valuable farm operation. This was the situation in rural Saskatchewan, as it appeared in 1971.

The government considered what it could do to preserve a good number of the towns which were the service centres for farm people. If some of their business functions were declining, perhaps we could preserve and add to their educational, health, social and recreational functions, and thereby make life in the smaller towns and on the farms which they served a little more satisfying that it otherwise might have been.

We did our best to retain schools. We instituted province-wide collective bargaining for teachers' salaries, so that the salaries in the small towns were the same as they were in Regina and Saskatoon, making them very attractive salaries in the smaller centres. We improved the system of provincial grants to school boards so that, up to a defined provincial standard, every school had approximately the same amount per student to spend on its schools.

With respect to hospitals and nursing homes, we retained some small hospitals in rural areas when strict medical cost control criteria may have dictated otherwise. These hospitals helped to keep doctors in smaller centres and to provide some sense of security to families living on the isolated farms and in the villages of Saskatchewan. Changing medical and surgical standards forced a change in role so that the smallest hospitals came to do most of their work in the areas of long-term care, convalescent care and emergency care, but a sense of security was still provided. The road ambulance service was vastly improved, to add to the existing air ambulance service, and highways were improved, particularly those serving small-town Saskatchewan.

Nursing homes were constructed with a population base far below what federal authorities regard as minimum. In the case of both small hospitals and small nursing homes, unionization of staff was encouraged and province-wide bargaining for wages and general working conditions were instituted so that, in general terms, working conditions were similar throughout the entire province. This made employment in hospitals and nursing homes in smaller centres financially attractive, with the result that competent staff were recruited and retained.

Grant programs were mounted. One lasting five years, the Community Capital Fund, was directed to improving the social infrastructure of cities, towns and villages. This was followed by another five-year program directed specifically to cultural and recreational facilities in these centres. The two programs produced a flowering of new hockey rinks, curling rinks, swimming pools, community halls and smaller parks.

One could not help but be impressed by what some small communities could do with grant money. One community in southern Saskatchewan had constructed a rather fine outdoor swimming pool. I questioned the mayor as to where they got the money for that pool. He quoted me a figure for its cost. I scoffed at him and said that the bare cost of the materials would be quite a bit more than the figure he quoted, assuming that all labour was free. He advised me that all labour was indeed free, including that provided by the skilled tradesmen, and that while the community had paid for the pumps and filters associated with the pool, cement and some other components had been donated. It appeared that the hardware and cement merchant also kept cattle. Surrounding farmers delivered barley to his cattle operation at no cost, in exchange for which the hardware merchant donated cement to the project which, along with gravel produced from somewhere by farmers in farm trucks, provided the concrete from which the pool was constructed by volunteer labour. In another community, farmers and towns-people acquired some cutting rights over Crown land, went into the forest in the winter, cut the trees, pulled them out of the bush with their farm tractors, found a local person to saw the wood, and in due course used the wood to construct the huge rafters which were key components to their new skating rink. A skating rink organization was formed which hired people who were temporarily unemployed in the town and who (perhaps) qualified to earn grants under federal and provincial "winter works" programs. Money earned and grants received were given back to the rink association, and so a first class skating rink resulted.

Many, many communities found ingenious ways to turn the rules of provincial and federal grants into fine recreational facilities. Some of these projects seemed to be latter day examples of the five loaves and two fishes biblical story. In the course of projects like these the sense of common purpose of the communities was further strengthened. In these towns there was no grumbling to the effect that the town had to provide facilities for farm families who lived outside the community and did not pay town taxes. The facilities were community facilities in the full sense of the word.

Another initiative related to community colleges. When the government assumed office in 1971 there was no community college system of any kind. The government did not feel it could afford a conventional community college system with buildings at different locations throughout the province and faculties teaching at those locations. We devised a community college system which had virtually no buildings and virtually no permanent academic staff. The province was divided into regions and colleges were organized for each region. The college consisted of an organization with an office and a handful of administrative staff to organize the program. Classes were offered in churches, schools, halls and other public buildings throughout the province. Instructors were obtained on a contract basis from the university centres of Regina and Saskatoon, and from technical institutes at Moose Jaw and Saskatoon. As well, high school teachers and other people with particular skills were contracted to give courses. In many areas the public response was overwhelming, with well over 10% of the adult population enroled for one or more courses. In this way post-secondary and continuing education courses were offered in many hundreds of communities across Saskatchewan. The community college program achieved a great deal with limited resources and was a clear success.

To deal with the problem of assisting older farmers to retire with dignity and young people to get into farming without a massive amount of capital, we introduced the Land Bank plan. It was a plan whereby the provincial government would buy farm land from retiring farmers and lease it to young farmers on attractive lease terms, with an option to purchase the land. My thought was that as young farmers got established they would buy their land from the Land Bank plan. This, in turn, would provide money for new purchases and leases to new young farmers. We failed to consider the strength of the forces of farm consolidation. Young farmers did get started. They did prosper and buy land. Unfortunately for the program, they bought land from private owners and retained their Land Bank leases, because they too felt the need for a larger and larger land base. As the Land Bank Commission bought more land and sold little, unease about government ownership of farm land grew. And, as farming prospered, there were more and more applicants for each parcel of land that the Land Bank had available. It proved impossible to convince the disappointed applicants that the selection process was completely fair, as we felt it was.

Land Bank was, therefore, only a partial success. It achieved some of its purposes but many people were not convinced that the Land Bank was the best approach to the acknowledged problem. It is not that the idea was superseded by a better one. Rather it was that no approach to the intractable problem of getting farm land into the hands of the next generation was both effective and generally acceptable to the public.

Considering agriculture and rural life, we tried a number of new approaches. We had a few major successes, and more that succeeded only in part.

Economic Diversification

Aside from bringing some stability to farming and farm communities, we hoped to spur the development of the non-farm sectors of the economy. We were disappointed that while Saskatchewan produced oil and gas, potash and uranium, very little of the head office activity associated with these industries took place in Saskatchewan. Not only were senior management located elsewhere, but many of the lawyers, engineers, architects, advertising and accounting firms and suppliers that served these industries were located outside the province. We contrasted this with co-operative and Crown-owned enterprises which procured much of their goods and almost all their services locally.

During the 1970s when rising international prices made Saskatchewan resources much more valuable, and when federal government taxation policies threatened to take from Saskatchewan much of the increase in value, it became clear that the best way to shield these assets from heavy federal taxation was to take them into provincial government ownership.

After considering these circumstances, the government decided to take a much greater role in the ownership and operation of the major resource industries. Saskatchewan Oil and Gas Corporation, Saskatchewan Mining Development Corporation and the Potash Corporation of Saskatchewan were organized to increase the government presence in the oil, uranium and potash industries.

For these resources, we devised new royalty schedules which were very different from previous schedules or from those used elsewhere. They were highly sensitive to the profitability of the companies. The broad rationale was simple. If fixed royalties were set and they proved to be too high, the resource companies forced governments to reduce them by the threat to discontinue operations. If the royalties were too low and the companies were seen to be enjoying too good a deal, pressure would mount on governments to act to break the royalty agreements or subvert their spirit by other taxes. Both results produced tension and animosity between governments and resource companies. Variable royalty schedules avoid many of those problems.

Our ownership and royalty policies produced a large increase in provincial revenues and gave Saskatchewan a larger percentage of the gross value of these resources than accrued to any other province where they were produced.

There is no doubt that these Crown enterprises (Potash Corporation of Saskatchewan, SaskOil and Sask Mining Development Corporation) spent a far higher percentage of their head office and procurement dollars in Saskatchewan than did private resource companies. The Potash Corporation carried on a vigorous research program in Saskatchewan. Top management of these firms was in Saskatchewan, producing ideas for possible new developments, as top managers frequently do. A nucleus of enterprising entrepreneurs was developed. New relationships with working people in these enterprises were beginning to develop.

I was excited by what was accomplished in resource management. I was disappointed that we were unable to convince Saskatchewan people more fully of the direct and indirect benefits that flowed from the public ownership of these major enterprises in Saskatchewan. As we saw it, increasing the spinoff benefits from resource extraction and processing was one of the more solid forms of diversification of an economy.

The conventional vehicle for diversification, manufacturing, increased five-fold in ten years, particularly in metal fabrication and farm machinery production. The increase was based on the availability of steel from our local steel mill, Ipsco, and on rising farm prosperity. A growing high technology sector developed in Saskatoon, based largely on an enterprise which sprung from the University of Saskatchewan, SED Systems. An industrial park, Innovation Place, was developed on the campus of the University of Saskatchewan in association with the University.

These efforts were in accord with what I felt was our best hope of diversification. To me, the most promising fields were processing resources that we produced, manufacturing products which we imported and for which there was a market in Saskatchewan and the prairie basin, and developing a few high tech products for broader markets.

Proposals for mega-projects such as major aircraft industries and the like to be developed with massive government support were rejected as economically unsound.

We had a reasonable measure of success. But I continued to be surprised at the extent to which the local business community appeared to support mega-projects which involved heavy financial involvement by governments as the best answer to the need for diversification.

Finance

I regarded it as fundamental that a province like Saskatchewan, with a volatile economy, act very prudently in financial terms. Budgets were to be balanced if reasonably possible. In the event, our government had eleven successive budget surpluses and no deficits. We felt that hidden deficits in the form of unfunded liabilities in pension and workers compensation funds should be tackled. Unfunded liabilities were effectively eliminated in the pension funds of Sask Power, Sask Tel and the Workers Compensation Board. For the public service and teachers' pension funds, steps were taken so that, for new employees coming into the system, pensions were fully funded. So far as I am aware, that was a first for Canada. As a result, pension fund liabilities, of the kind that threatened bankruptcy for the City of New York, are unlikely to threaten Saskatchewan if prudent policies are continued.

The province's credit rating with the United States rating agencies rose from A to A+ to AA to AA+. This meant that when Saskatchewan needed to borrow money, it was available at a reasonable rate of interest. And we had put aside money for a rainy day, or in Saskatchewan terms, a non-rainy day, in a provincial Heritage Fund.

I regarded our innovations in dealing with pension plans and our general financial policies as a success.

Social Issues

Not all Saskatchewan was part of a close-knit rural society based on farming and the informal social safety net that it provided, both rurally and in urban centres. There were people in the towns and cities and in the countryside who needed the help of governments. There were people of aboriginal origin who were outside the social mainstream.

Some of these people needed only more money. Some needed additional tools to help them control their own destiny more fully. For the first group, we pursued a policy directed towards the idea of a guaranteed annual income. For the second group, further approaches were needed. Clearly there was overlap.

Guaranteed Annual Income

Our government was attracted to the idea of a guaranteed annual income whereby everybody in society would be guaranteed a minimum income. The idea is frequently put forward by those who deplore the amount of administration involved in our many income support programs, federal and provincial. And it must be conceded that the complexities of programs such as Old Age Security, Guaranteed Annual Income, Canada Pension Plan, Canada Assistance Plan, Unemployment Insurance, and many other programs at the federal and provincial level, can be daunting. The advocates of the guaranteed annual income idea urge us to sweep away the superstructure of programs and put in one program for everybody, guaranteeing a minimum income.

We saw two main problems. First a guaranteed annual income, if high enough to provide a decent standard of living, might be a disincentive to a small number of people who could take productive employment but might not if a reasonable income was guaranteed. Second, we suspected that many members of the public felt that how much income was guaranteed should vary from a fixed level depending upon considerations other than need, e.g. how much a person was receiving before he or she became unemployed, or whether the recipient was a war veteran, or whether the recipient had paid premiums or taxes earmarked for the program. We had not resolved our thinking with respect to some of these issues. But we felt that we could take some steps to see that incomes, not necessarily at the same level, were guaranteed for people injured in auto and industrial accidents, senior citizens, lower income people with larger families, and people who were unable to work because of illness or accidents.

The disability payments under the Automobile Accident Insurance Act which went to any person injured in such an accident, regardless of fault, were increased and were paid not for a maximum of two years but as long as the disability lasted.

261

As is mentioned elsewhere in this volume, Workers Compensation was changed to emphasize rehabilitation and to index disability payments to increases in the rates of pay earned by workers in the work category of the injured worker.

A program of supplementary payments to lower income senior citizens was introduced to add to payments received under the federal Old Age Security and Guaranteed Income Supplement programs. Late in our term, we developed a program to target payments to senior citizens who did not live in their own homes or in public housing. We had found that single senior citizens in this category seemed to be the most in need.

For people with limited potential to earn but who had larger families, we introduced a Family Income Plan which paid substantial amounts based on the number of dependent children. This frequently increased incomes by a large percentage and had the incidental effect of ensuring that the earnings and the Plan payments together always clearly exceeded the amount payable under the general welfare payment program, the Saskatchewan Assistance Plan.

Later in the term, we took steps to introduce a universal sickness and accident program modelled after that of New Zealand. Public hearings were held and ideas gathered but the plan had not been introduced by 1982.

Similarly, work was done on a Saskatchewan pension plan. The idea was to top up the Canada Pension Plan for those people who did not have other pension plans. First steps to ensure that other pension plans would, in fact, deliver pensions — steps to require early vesting and the like — were taken but work was not completed on the overall plan by 1982.

Other Social Issues

For people outside the economic and social mainstream, other methods of help were attempted. The general approach was to assist people to organize to press their cause. Some of the attempts to help disadvantaged people get a greater control over their own destiny were reasonably successful. Programs to assist people of aboriginal origin to get higher education were successful — some spectacularly so. The number of aboriginal people at Saskatchewan universities in 1971 numbered a few dozen at most. By 1982, this number would have been many hundreds, perhaps as many as a thousand.

There was a lively network of non-governmental social service agencies supported by government funds and by a central coordinating body, the Saskatchewan Association of Non-Governmental Social Service Agencies, also non-government — which gave support, encouragement, and advocacy skills to the front-line agencies. I saw great promise in this approach.

Some efforts at this type of social animation were spectacular failures. A Human Resources Development Agency was established as a government agency to assist groups of disadvantaged people. This assistance consisted of relatively shrill advocacy against existing conditions and therefore, against existing government programs and administrators. Relations with the line departments understandably deteriorated. Public servants cannot easily be persuaded to accept strong criticism in public from other public servants and then continue to work with their critics. We learned a lesson. If there is to be criticism of the inadequacy of government programs for the disadvantaged, and there should be, this criticism comes best from a non-government agency, even though it may be financed by government. Public servants accept the strange ways of politicians who finance government critics; they understand less well the actions of fellow public servants who level public and often unfair criticism against public servants and the programs they administer and to which they are loyal.

Labour Legislation

Others have dealt with some innovative labour legislation. I will deal with only one aspect, the right to strike.

When our government assumed office in 1971, we promptly repealed the legislation permitting the Cabinet to terminate strikes in essential services. Our philosophy was that the right to strike was a civil right that all employees should be able to exercise without any general restriction or prohibition. We took the position that if a particular strike was causing very serious social consequences, then the Legislature should be convened and legislation passed to terminate the strike and provide for a resolution of the dispute. In this case the government would have to justify before the Legislature and the public why this interference with ordinary civil rights was justified. The highly public nature of these proceedings, we felt, was likely to restrict interferences with workers' rights to a minimum number of cases of genuine social upheaval.

The trade unions took the public position that any interference with the right to strike was unjustified and generally opposed all back-to-work legislation. In political terms, the result was that the government was attacked by trade unions when back-to-work legislation was passed. The attacks were much more vigorous, because of the public nature of the proceedings, than were the attacks mounted by trade unions in neighbouring provinces where legislation frequently prevented classes of workers, e.g. hospital workers or electric power workers from striking at all, and in some cases gave the Cabinet, as opposed to the Legislature, a right to terminate strikes and require compulsory arbitration.

Under such circumstances we were sorely tempted to abandon our commitment to unrestricted free collective bargaining and enact restrictions of the kind in force in all other provinces. We did not do so. We continued to believe that forcing a legislature to pass specific legislation before depriving working people of their right to strike was a salutary restraint on governments. The only restriction was one which applied when there was no legislature, i.e. during the course of an election campaign when no legislature legally exists.

263

My Own Agenda

One of the disappointments which I incorrectly thought I might suffer in government was the difficulty in getting some of my personal agenda built into a government program and getting it accomplished. If it was a simple thing, I could frequently get it done by asking someone to take hold of the idea and see that it was followed through. But a more complex idea could not be handled this way. My staff frequently did not understand fully what I was talking about, and I could not explain it clearly. I knew what I wanted to achieve, but not always the steps which would bring it about. All the difficulties were raised with me and it became very hard to insist that the idea must be tried unless I myself had analyzed it and assessed the possible adverse consequences. In the event, when the process began to consume quite a bit of time, I laid some of the projects aside for a more suitable opportunity, which never arrived.

One such failure was an idea I had with respect to farm land on the periphery of a city. It seems to me entirely possible that, in principle, such farm land could stay in the hands of farmers and continue to be farmed, but that the developmental value of the land, i.e. any increase in value it may have over and above its value as farm land because of its future potential for urban development, could be purchased well in advance of urban expansion. This would allow the land to be farmed until urban growth required its use. It would allow the farmer to be paid early for the developmental value of the land. It would allow sensible planning of later urban expansion knowing that the additional cost of the land was limited to its value as farmland. This is a good deal easier to estimate than its value for urban development purposes. It seemed to me that such an arrangement would benefit both farmers and urban planners. I tried to get some research done on the idea but was not able to refer anyone to any place in the world where this idea is used. I was met with recitals of problems, rather than options for achieving the objectives and I eventually gave up the concept.

One item on my personal agenda which I did see move forward, although not quite as far as I would have liked, was the promotion of urban parks which would be established by statute and have a statutory land and financial base. I hoped this would mean that it would be hard for a provincial government or a city council, by one move, to destroy the work of decades. Early in the 1960s, I had had the opportunity to be part of a formation of such a park authority in Regina, the Wascana Centre Authority. The Authority was organized to develop and maintain as a unified park, the grounds of the Legislative Building in Regina, a series of parks operated by the City of Regina along the shore of Wascana Lake opposite the Saskatchewan Legislative Building, and the grounds of the new University of Regina campus being developed east of the Legislative Building. The idea was that we would have a statutory body, the Wascana Centre Authority, with a board of directors composed partly of Government nominees, partly of City nominees and partly of University nominees. There would be a minimum base budget set by statute and based upon the property tax base of the City of Regina, a base with a modest escalation factor built in. Thus the yield from two mills times the City's assessment base was Regina's contribution with the Government and the University contributing percentages of the City share. Architectural and landscape controls were developed for the whole area of close to 1,000 acres.

I regarded the experiment and the model as outstanding successes. When elected in 1971, I hoped to use the model to create parks in other major Saskatchewan cities. We were successful in getting a park established in Saskatoon, the Meewasin Valley Authority, which was organized to protect and develop the banks of the South Saskatchewan River as it flowed through the city of Saskatoon. The City of Saskatoon, the University of Saskatchewan and an adjoining municipal authority were involved. Similarly, a park authority, the Wakamow Valley Authority in Moose Jaw, was organized to develop the banks of the Moose Jaw Creek. Each of these has been operating successfully. If any partner wishes to cut its financial contribution or to dispose of any of the park land, it is necessary to bring a bill before the Legislature. Even though the province has passed through times of acute restraint, budgets have been cut by statute on only one occasion. I feel that there would have been further cuts in the park projects had they not been established on a statutory basis.

For people who do not live on the prairies, it is hard to explain the affinity with the land which prairie people have. They have a great sense of the bare elements of a landscape — earth and sky. But in the same way that they cherish the broad horizon and big sky, they put great store on the little oases of green which surround the few bodies of fresh water that dot or snake through the prairie. The parks at Regina, Saskatoon and Moose Jaw are an effort to see that the bodies of water and the grass and trees which surround them are havens of contrast with the seemingly endless brown, green, gold or white of the sequentially monochromatic prairie.

The park authorities which were organized provided a little extra by way of development and maintenance, some security of funding to permit some longer term planning and a way to rally and focus the very considerable public support for parks and the beautification of communities. I was sorry that we did not get a park organized in Prince Albert along the same lines. There are many natural beauty spots close to Prince Albert so the need was not as great. Nonetheless, the river running through Prince Albert is an aesthetic resource which I would have liked to see protected by statute.

Another idea I hoped would come to fruition, was the development of the cores of Saskatchewan cities. I had seen many United States cities, large and small, where business had moved to perimeters of the city, where a good deal of the housing had moved to the suburbs, and where the inner city was decaying. Not only do these developments destroy the tax base of the civic government, but more important, they destroy the sense of common purpose and pride in their community which the residents of a city must have if it is to thrive socially and economically. Saskatchewan cities were vulnerable. Saskatchewan is very much an automobile province where people expect to use their own private automobile and not public transit for most of their activities. The cities and larger towns serve a wide surrounding area of farmers and village residents which makes suburban malls commercially attractive. If the decay of the downtown areas of major centres was to be avoided, there had to be new and attractive shopping facilities created downtown. The principal problem facing either a city or a private developer in accomplishing this was the assembling of land. It was doubtful whether municipal authorities had the right to expropriate land for such a purpose and it was certain that the municipal councils did not wish to take the financial risks that might be involved. It was my thought that the government of Saskatchewan could get involved in the assembling of the land upon which shopping facilities could be constructed by the private sector on the basis of long-term leases of the land. The residual ownership of the land could be turned over to the municipal authorities. I had hoped that the leases would be, in part, leases giving to the landowner a share of the gross receipts so that, at some future time, the shopping centres would begin to be a significant source of revenue for the municipal authorities, as the gross sales (in nominal dollars) increased with the increase in economic activity and particularly with the increase in inflation.

We were successful in assembling land and promoting the construction of downtown shopping centres in Regina, and in two small cities, Prince Albert and Weyburn. We were unsuccessful at getting any enthusiasm for the idea in Moose Jaw, Swift Current and some other centres. I believe that this partnership between the provincial government and municipal government and some other parties will serve to anchor the downtown core of the cities involved. At least in the city of Regina, I felt that this type of development was important for other reasons. Much of the lower and middle income housing in Regina is close to the downtown core. Retail shopping centres provide many jobs and I count it important that these jobs be as close as possible to where the likely employees might live. In cities which can afford only indifferent public transit, it adds a great deal to the quality of life for a lower income employee to live close to his or her place of employment. I was disappointed that the civic officials in Regina did not appreciate the long-term possibilities of the arrangements made with them and that they readily acquiesced in the later sale of the whole project to an out-of-province developer.

Native Issues

In the back of my mind I had another reason for wanting to get quality retail establishments and up-scale or at least mid-scale housing in the cores of the cities. Saskatchewan was seeing major social changes in the 1970s. A very large number of people of native Indian origin were moving from reserves and other rural areas to the major cities. They were encountering a sharp culture clash. In general, they had not had the opportunity for quality education and were not able to bid for better paying jobs. Native birth rates were high. While strenuous efforts were being made to offer opportunities to people of native origin, there was a real possibility that if the cores of the cities decayed, the areas might become ghettos for the poor with the additional factor that many of these poor would be people of native origin. This required action, including not only revitalization of the commercial core of the cities, but construction of a substantial number of units of reasonable quality public housing and the acquisition and upgrading of private housing in the cores. I saw this as a holding action to protect city core areas while greater efforts were made to see that being in the city and being native was not almost synonymous with being poor.

Perhaps my greatest disappointment was the amount left undone after eleven years in the field of relations between native and non-native people in Saskatchewan. Undoubtedly the greatest ongoing social problem in Saskatchewan is the relationship between native and non-native people. The number of people of native origin in Saskatchewan is of the order of 12%. Demographic trends indicate that this could be 20% in a relatively small number of years. Since many areas of the province have very few people of native origin, this means that in some areas, notably the major urban centres and the northern portions of the province, the people of native origin will be a very substantial percentage of the entire community.

I early reached the conclusion that white society was not going to solve the problems of native people. The good will, often uninformed and intermittently displayed, of non-native people is not enough to bring about solutions to the many problems encountered by people of native origin in Saskatchewan. Native people would have to solve their problems themselves. Our job, as a government, was to give them the tools and let them finish the job.

As I viewed it, the problems of people of native origin required two sharply different approaches. In northern Saskatchewan, being the north half of the geographic area of Saskatchewan beyond the range of agricultural land, people of native origin were a substantial majority of the entire population. Here, I feel that the government's course of action should be to set up organizations based upon popular election and provide these elected bodies with the authority and the financial resources to deal with many of the problems which have affected the lives of northern people. In 1971, there were elected councils in only three northern communities, La Ronge, Creighton and Uranium City, in each of which many people of non-native origin resided. We moved quickly to set up elected local government councils and school boards in most of the communities in northern Saskatchewan. In a very short time, the local government and school administration in the north was in the hands of local people. This effort had to be combined with a great increase in economic opportunities in northern Saskatchewan. Here the strategy involved using the largest possible number of native people to build the roads, sewer systems, schools and other public works which the north so desperately needed. There were many success stories involving building major school projects where virtually all the employees were local people of native origin. The next step was to see that people who operated these public facilities were people of native origin. We had a good deal of success in training people to operate highway maintenance equipment. Appropriate curricula were devised for northern schools. A northern teachers education program (NORTEP) was organized with the cooperation of the universities to train northern teachers partly on the job and partly through academic programs offered by the universities in northern communities. This had considerable success, but I was disappointed that we were not able to move faster. I was disappointed also that we were not able to get a similar program mounted for training the great majority of people who worked as conservation officers, social workers, police, and provincial and local government public servants so that most of these jobs could be filled by people of native origin. The progress in these directions was substantial but proved to be much slower than I had hoped.

When mining came to northern Saskatchewan, our government required that 50% of the people who worked for the mining companies be northern residents, essentially people of native origin. If the mining companies could not get people of native origin who were trained, they could train them. We negotiated a fly-in arrangement with the mining companies where people would work long hours for one week and then have one week off, that they could live in their local community and be picked up by plane to be taken to the mine for their week-on stint and then home again. This had the advantage of not requiring that towns be built at the mine sites, towns whose life depended upon the uncertain geology and economics of hardrock mining. I felt that this approach was an outstanding success. I have been disappointed that in the 1980s, the drive to see that the largest possible number of employees of northern mines were native northerners slowed and that more and more of the employees of the mines were non-native people living in Prince Albert or Saskatoon.

The situation with native people in southern Saskatchewan, where they are the minority, is a very different one. Here they could not use the ordinary institutions of democratic government to forward their aspirations since natives were a minority who were visible and discriminated against by the general public. The approach here had to be to strengthen native-controlled organizations. Money was provided in substantial sums to the Federation of Saskatchewan Indians and to the Association of Metis and Non-Status Indians (as the organizations were then named). In many cases, particularly with the Metis organizations, the money was used to organize

268

protests against the provincial government. We had to be tolerant of this. If native people were to solve their own problems, they had to organize to do it. The first steps in organization almost certainly had to be to organize against something. A target had to be selected. Governments, federal and provincial, were the obvious ones. In due time, the organizations would not only organize against identified opponents and proclaim broad objectives, but also identify narrow and attainable objectives which could be worked for.

And that did happen. We spent a great deal of time with the Federation of Saskatchewan Indians sorting out unfulfilled treaty land entitlements and arrived at a formula for calculating the amount of land involved in each entitlement where the treaties were unclear. We felt that, except for brief periods, we got indifferent cooperation from the Government of Canada. I was frankly very disappointed that we were not able to complete more settlements of unfulfilled treaty land entitlements.

With respect to natives in Southern Saskatchewan, a major thrust was in education. We organized and established a Gabriel Dumont Institute with the cooperation of the Metis organization, and the Universities. So far as I am aware, this is the only Metis-controlled post-secondary institution in Canada. Its impact on Metis society is becoming significant. An Indian community college to offer services to Indians on reserves was organized as was an Indian cultural college in Saskatoon. At the University of Saskatchewan, a native law institute was developed. It is the most successful and perhaps the only institute in Canada specifically designed to prepare native people to enter law schools and, in due course, to graduate as members of the legal community. The biggest single effort was the Indian Federated College at the University of Regina. We worked with the Federation of Saskatchewan Indians and the University to launch this. The President of the University, Dr. Lloyd Barber was one of the driving forces. I was disappointed that we could not induce the federal government to make this a major federal-provincial initiative. From a small beginning, the Indian Federated College had, by 1991, more than one thousand full and part-time students of native origin at any one time. The number of graduates in education, social work and, recently, in business administration disciplines is becoming impressive. It is beginning to have a very marked effect on the Indian and native community.

I remember an occasion when I was donating an Indian Chief's headdress to a high school in Regina where there was a very large number of students of native origin. The drop-out rate for these students was high. The teachers at the school arranged a ceremony involving Indian cultural activities. Virtually every one of the people involved in the ceremony was a graduate of that high school who had gone on to the Indian Federated College in Regina and were pursuing post-secondary education careers. The message was unarticulated but powerful.

The Future

The 1970s were a time of lively social ferment in Saskatchewan. I felt that the people of Saskatchewan viewed their government with more possessiveness and less cynicism than is the case in the 1990s. To the extent that today's cynicism is a result of things not done in the 1970s, I am disappointed. I believe that the genius of Saskatchewan people has been their ability to use their social institutions including their provincial and local governments to shape many of the decisions which affect their lives. If Saskatchewan people lose confidence in these institutions and allow the key decisions which affect them to be shaped by the forces of the marketplace, I feel that Saskatchewan people will be poorer in all respects and the things that have made Saskatchewan a special and fascinating place to live and work will quickly fade away. The future of social innovation in Saskatchewan is unclear.

Indices   Subject Index

272

Indices

Name Index

Contributors

HONOURABLE ALLAN BLAKENEY, served in the Saskatchewan public service for 8 years; member of the Saskatchewan Legislature for 28 years; Premier of Saskatchewan for 11 years. Currently Visiting Scholar, College of Law, University of Saskatchewan.

JOHN BURTON, Director of External Relations, Potash Secretariat and member of the Board, Potash Corporation, 1975–82; former M.P. Currently a private consultant.

JOHN BURY, M.D., former Director, Community Health Services, Director of Health Promotion, and former member, Formulary Committee of Saskatchewan Drug Plan, Saskatchewan Health. Physician, Saskatoon Community Health Clinic, now retired.

LARRY FLYNN, regional director and acting director, Employment Support Program, Saskatchewan Social Services, 1974–84. Currently Program Consultant, Health Canada, Winnipeg.

GERRY GARTNER, former Deputy Minister of Saskatchewan Agriculture, Chief Planning Officer, Deputy Minister of Industry and Commerce, and Executive Director of Transportation Agency; former head of the Canadian Egg Marketing Board, now private consultant, recently project manager, Agricultural Diversification Program, Bangladesh.

ELEANOR D. GLOR, former Senior Analyst, Budget Bureau, Department of Finance; Senior Analyst, Planning Bureau, Department of Executive Council; Director, Program Development, Saskatchewan Health. Currently an Executive with Health Canada, President of the Innovation Salon, a discussion group about public sector innovation, and Editor, the Innovation Journal, an electronic journal about innovation in the public sector.

279

JERRY HAMMERSMITH, Director of Community Development (1972–73) and Minister (1979–82), Department of Northern Saskatchewan. Currently Supervisor, Corporate Development, SaskEnergy.

ROBERT HAUK, Economic Planner (1977–81), Department of Northern Saskatchewan. Now Human Resources Consultant, Saskatchewan Wheat Pool.

HUGO MALIEPAARD, former Executive Director, Policy, Planning, Research and Environmental Assessment Branch, Saskatchewan Environment. Now retired.

ROBERT SASS, former Associate Deputy Minister, Saskatchewan Labour. Now professor, Department of Industrial Relations and Organizational Behaviour and Director, Labour Studies Program, University of Saskatchewan.

GORDON SNYDER, member of the Saskatchewan Legislature for 22 years, former Minister of Labour, Government of Saskatchewan, 1971–82. Now retired.

TOBY STEWART, former Director, Employment Support Program; former Executive Director, Office of the Treaty Commissioner for Saskatchewan, now Special Programs Manager, Audit and Evaluation Branch, Indian and Northern Affairs Canada.

KEITH TURNBULL, former Director and Executive Director, Saskatchewan Provincial Library. Now Deputy Director, Public Services, Edmonton Public Library.

STEVE WOLFSON, former Assistant Executive Director, Saskatchewan Children's Dental Program. Now Dean, National School of Dental Therapy, Saskatchewan Indian Federated College.

TOM WALLER, Acting General Counsel, Crown Investments Corporation, 1977–82. Currently partner and solicitor with Olive, Waller, Zinkhan and Waller.

ALLAN WALKER, former Research Officer and Field Representative with two community colleges, Saskatchewan Department of Continuing Education. Currently Dean of General Studies, Wascana Campus, the Saskatchewan Institute of Applied Science and Technology.